1718

THE LABOR-MANAGED ECONOMY Essays

THE LABOR-MANAGED ECONOMY Essays by

JAROSLAV VANEK

CORNELL UNIVERSITY PRESS

ITHACA AND LONDON

First published 1977 by Cornell University Press.
Published in the United Kingdom by Cornell University Press Ltd., 2–4 Brook Street, London W1Y 1AA.

International Standard Book Number 0–8014–0955–1
Library of Congress Catalog Card Number 76–16682
Printed in the United States of America
Librarians: Library of Congress cataloging information appears on the last page of the book.

Preface

In 1970 and 1971 I published two books on worker and employee self-management, *The General Theory of Labor-Managed Market Economies* and *The Participatory Economy*. Both books dealt with a rather novel subject, and in many respects I found myself covering entirely new ground. Even though I tried to produce a general theory of an economic system, I realized subsequently that I had left many empty spaces and had not adequately covered other matters. This realization served as a moving force for writing these fifteen additional studies. Neither these essays nor the studies by my fellow economists complete what needs to be done in the area of labor management. An enormous additional task remains, yet I hope that this volume will be useful to others interested in self-management.

In preparing several of these essays, I received help from others—my colleagues and students—help which I greatly appreciate. Some of the papers have not been published previously; others were published in an abridged version, or in non-English journals which normally are not accessible to the American reader; and some are reprints from English-language periodicals.

The material is classified under six headings that define the six parts of the collection. Part I, a summary paper, also serves as an integrating piece for the entire volume. Part II is devoted to empirical work, and the papers deal with self-management in the real world. The two papers of Part III discuss the very important problem of income distribution. Part IV, probably the most significant in terms of its subject matter, is devoted to the problem of funding and investment in a labor-managed economy. In Part V the reader will find four essays in formal microeconomics and macroeconomics. An essay dealing with broader historical and evolutionary questions concludes the volume.

The first paper is very broad in scope: as such it indicates to the reader the extent of the subject dealt with in the collection. While it does not present any significant new findings, it brings together from other and far more extensive material the principal conclusions regarding the self-managed economy. Particularly it compares the efficiency of labor management with that of other forms of economic organization and attempts to clarify and in some instances to correct previously accepted notions of the comparative efficiency and social desirability of labor management.

Part II contains four papers inspired by, or dealing with, actual experiences of self-management in the world today. Chapter 2 is devoted to the theoretical interpretation of the Peruvian law of social property, promulgated in 1974, which defines a self-management sector in that country. On the whole my conclusions as to its overall design are favorable, the provisions of the law being consistent with basically efficient functioning of that sector of the economy, but, of course, much will depend on how certain parameters of the law are implemented, parameters which the law leaves undefined and subject to discretionary action on the part of the authorities and institutions of the social property sector.

The remaining three papers of Part II focus on the most significant example of self-management, that is, on the economy of Yugoslavia. Chapter 3 is an outgrowth of a colloquium by the author with the Association of Yugoslav Economists in the spring of 1972 in Belgrade. I prepared a comprehensive set of notes for the one-day meeting, but it was quite impossible to cover all the material. Thereafter, at the suggestion of two Yugoslav economic institutes, I transformed the notes into a manuscript of considerable size and then abridged it for publication in *World Development*. The abridged version is reproduced in this volume. Basically it evaluates the performance of the Yugoslav economy in the light of each aspect of the formal economic theory of self-management. In this way it is possible to study separately problems of the Yugoslav firm, the Yugoslav industry, or the economy as a whole, and to suggest solutions to microeconomic and macroeconomic problems including monetary and foreign-trade variables. Generally, the study concludes that the Yugoslav economy could perform well above its present, already quite satisfactory, level if certain fundamental changes and adaptations are accepted.

Chapter 4, prepared in cooperation with a Yugoslav economist, Milena Jovicic, is, in a sense, the principal empirical piece supporting the evaluation contained in the preceding chapter. It shows that a good deal of variation in income per worker—a serious distributional as well as allocational problem of Yugoslavia—can be explained by a variation in capital intensity among industries. Not only does this indicate that alternative solutions might be commendable with respect to pricing or taxing of capital in Yugoslavia, but also the results strongly suggest efficient planning procedures. The study also provides a rough estimate (in fact, an estimate of a lower limit) of the efficiency of capital in Yugoslavia. Some such estimate, it is argued, should serve as a base for the real capital price or rental that seems to be necessary in that country to achieve both distributive and allocational effectiveness.

Chapter 5 is of a more theoretical nature. Only the premises regarding the behavior of a Yugoslav labor-managed firm were drawn from Yugoslav experience; the rest of the paper is a theoretical elaboration of the various patterns of behavior to which such premises could lead, and permits the identification of those which could enable the firm to function most efficiently.

Part III of the volume, devoted to questions of income distribution, contains two papers that are quite different in size and probably also in importance. Chapter 6 is a modest generalization of the theory of labor participation and labor income distribution in a self-managed firm in situations where different skill and job categories are present. In my *General Theory of Labor-Managed Market Economies* the solution was worked out on the assumption that the distributive shares for members of alternative job and skill categories are shown by fixed coefficients emerging from the democratic self-determining process within the firm. Having studied the existing practice in a number of self-managed productive organizations, I thought it desirable to examine also the more general situation where the distributive shares can become variable, themselves functions of one kind or another of the performance of the enterprise. For example, for reasons of incentive or otherwise, the higher-income groups in the firm can be assigned, through the democratic process, a remuneration schedule more sensitive to the overall performance of the enterprise than that of lower-income working groups who may prefer a greater income stability.

An abridged version of Chapter 7 appeared in the *Economic Journal*. The entire piece is reproduced here in the belief that the original version contains a good deal of useful analysis. The paper goes quite beyond my *General Theory* in that it considers the allocation of and workers' choices among income, effort, and other variables of the labor-managed firm in situations of underdevelopment where the actual or potential members of the working collectives live, so to speak, in the vicinity of their subsistence limits. This then permits attention to be focused on the solutions offered under such conditions by self-managed firms on the one hand and by capitalist firms on the other. A long-range dynamic analysis of decision-making power, stressing the distribution of rents, leads to the conclusion that the democratic organization of the firm can yield far superior results—results which can make the difference between a long-range takeoff from underdevelopment and a continued state of inactivity and economic paralysis.

The three papers of Part IV deal with the investment decision and capital accumulation and are probably the most important addition to work previously done in the area of labor management. They seek solutions to the most significant stumbling blocks and impediments to a massive development of democratic productive organizations. Chapter 8 considers a large number of specific problems that may arise in funding and accumulating capital in self-managed organizations, and thus points the way toward what should be the most effective solutions in that general area. It also proposes a concrete approach fulfilling the conditions of economic efficiency. The approach consists in a legal redefinition of property rights of productive capital comprising two categories and assigning a distinct individual or group of individuals to each category. This leads to a notion of two types of ownership of one and the same piece of capital, one referred to as basic ownership and the other as usufruct ownership, the latter being fundamentally and inalienably assigned to the working community. Of course, this is only one possible efficient solution; another is of a more institutional kind and has been discussed in my *General Theory*, Chapter 15.

Whereas Chapter 8 was written primarily for the practical policy maker, Chapter 9 is devoted to the problem of optimal funding of labor-managed firms in a more formal theoretical manner. It shows as a *sine qua non* of successful labor management that capital assets should not be provided, as in capitalist corporations, through collective retained earnings, and without remuneration. By contrast, the efficient labor-managed firm—which promises to outperform capitalist productive organization, whether state-owned or privately owned—calls for funding at an appropriate scarcity-reflecting price or rental of capital assets, preferably from sources external to the firm. If some of the capital must come from the firm's own savings, it should come in a manner separate from the rest of the activities of the firm; especially, the claims on principal and income should be traceable to individual members of the working collective.

Since in some situations, especially in developing countries, it may be difficult to secure external funding on a continuing basis, an efficient hybrid solution is proposed in Chapter 10. It consists in providing self-managed firms with an initial endowment on which income is charged, but the income can be retained by the paying organization. This then guarantees a certain kind of mandatory growth of the productive organization while preserving the condition of a scarcity-reflecting cost of capital which is necessary for an efficient allocation of capital resources.

The first study of Part V focuses on the investment decision and its overall efficiency implications. Compared to my earlier work (*General Theory*, Chapter 14), it provides extensions and generalizations in several directions. First, the fact that quality of work can vary from occupation to occupation is recognized and introduced into the investment decision. Second, the conventional techniques developed for project evaluation in capitalist firms can be adapted to labor-managed firms by introducing the concept of an accounting wage—even if labor incomes under self-management are not wages in the usual sense of the term. The third and probably most significant extension is the recognition of uncertainty in the real process of investment decision making, and the corollary introduction into the analysis of uncertain and variable incomes for both the members of working collectives and the investors. Fourth, the social efficiency of the various investment procedures is appraised.

Chapter 12, written with Alfred Steinherr, completes a proof originally proposed earlier (in *General Theory*, Chapter 6) to the effect that under self-management, *ceteris paribus*, we can expect less and less aggressive advertising and promotional activity than in capitalist differentiated oligopolies. The proposition was questioned by James Meade ("The Theory of Labor-Managed Firms and of Profit Sharing," *Economic Journal*, March 1972); in Chapter 12 we attempt to provide answers to Meade's query.

In Part II of my *General Theory,* I developed the macroeconomic theory of the labor-managed economy; but that analysis is fairly cumbersome, abstract, and theoretical. Moreover, it deals with a closed economy and leaves unanswered the questions raised by the existence of international trade and the balance of payments. Chapter 13 is an attempt to produce a macroeconomic model sufficiently simple and at the same time sufficiently general to overcome these shortcomings. Relying entirely on simple geometric analysis, the model determines all the major macroeconomic variables, including those concerning foreign trade, in a simultaneous general equilibrium solution. The analysis not only enables the reader to understand the interdependency and simultaneous determination of variables such as prices, labor incomes, interest rates, exports, imports, and investments, but also makes it possible without difficulty to answer questions in the area of macroeconomic policy. Chapter 14 is a response to another piece by James Meade. It was called for by the necessity both to rectify certain flaws in Meade's analysis and to arrive at new results.

In the last paper I attempt to generalize and make mathematically more exact a theory of socioeconomic evolution of systems and societies through time, a theory first suggested in my *Participatory Economy.* The basic idea is that systems are subject to certain laws of motion emanating from (disequilibrium) nonfulfillment of certain equilibrium conditions and from the processes of invention, education, and implementation in a number of key areas or dimensions. By its very nature the theory is sketchy and incomplete, but in some respects it seems able to overcome some fundamental flaws of the materialist dialectics of history.

JAROSLAV VANEK

Ithaca, New York

Contents

PART I

AN OVERVIEW

1 | Decentralization under Workers' Management: A Theoretical Appraisal*

The purpose of this paper is to carry out a theoretical appraisal of a labor-managed economy of the Yugoslav type. In my opinion, it is this type of economy that represents, by and large, the true aspirations of reformers in eastern Europe.

There is full justification for such an endeavor. On the one hand, the empirical studies which we have on the subject are not fully conclusive; on the other, even if quantitative results fulfilled some accepted criteria of statistical significance, we still might want to verify them through a theoretical evaluation. Moreover, it ought not to be forgotten that the Yugoslav experiment is unique and comparatively young. To compare its real performance with that of systems which have been tried in a large number of instances over long periods is not quite fair. At least to supplement the empirical studies, it is thus necessary to compare the corresponding theoretical models.

Besides the direct and practical objective, related to the economies of eastern Europe, there is also the more academic question of the theoretical literature on the subject at hand. The latter, although of excellent quality, is extremely limited. In fact, there are only two important articles on what I would call economics of labor participation—those by Benjamin Ward [7] and Evsey Domar [3].[1] These authors do not make anything near a full evaluation of an entire economic system. And yet, the findings emerging from such a limited coverage often are taken as characteristic of the efficiency of the system. For example, Ward's perverse supply elasticity in the short run is taken by many as proof of the absurdity of labor

* This paper was presented to the session on "Participation and Eastern Europe" at the December 1969 meeting of the American Economic Association. It appeared in the December 1969 issue of the *American Economic Review*.
1. At the time of this writing.

management. Perhaps the best and most authoritative illustration of the overall pessimism regarding the labor-managed economy is contained in Abram Bergson's more recent evaluation of market socialism [2].

At this stage of the argument, I do not want to dispute any specific points regarding the labor-managed economy; that will be done explicitly or by implication later in our discussion. I only want to contend that to appraise an economic system it is necessary to consider all of its major aspects. And this is what I propose to do.

The task would be an impossible one if each point were to be fully explained or proven. Fortunately, I have produced a more complete analysis elsewhere [5], [6], and thus I can restrict myself here to the presentation of the main conclusions, supplementing these with brief indications of the underlying reasoning. I will further limit my analysis by concentrating on questions of global economic efficiency, leaving out, as much as this is possible, the mechanics of the system.

I will first consider what may be referred to as a dehumanized model where, as in conventional capitalist theory, labor is considered merely a factor of production, of constant quality, exogenous to the system. This is done in Sections I and II. In Section III, by contrast, I discuss some of the most important special dimensions which emerge from the participatory nature of labor management. The principal objective of the remaining section is an overall evaluation of the labor-managed system in comparison with other major world systems.

I. The Pure Model

In what I call the pure model, I make basically the same assumptions as those underlying the contributions of Ward and Domar noted above. They can be summed up as implying a perfect, competitive, and smooth neoclassical world in which the moving force, contrary to the capitalist situation, is maximization of income per laborer. There is only one type of labor, perfectly homogeneous, and active only as a factor of production. The only characteristic emanating from labor management is income sharing and the behavioral principle of maximization just noted. It should be clear from the outset that an economy thus defined is far from the complex reality of Yugoslavia or any other economy adopting labor management; however, in my opinion the assumptions capture the ideal form of the economy, and thus their implications should be studied as a first step in any comprehensive evaluation.

To de-emphasize the single-firm approach used by Ward and Domar, it may be desirable to reverse the process and start with the discussion of a complete full employment general equilibrium solution of the labor-managed economy (situations involving unemployment will be taken up in the next section).

Let our starting point be the ideal conditions of perfect competition and full employment. We may make the observation that when all firms of an industry use the same technology and free entry is guaranteed, the labor-managed economy will be Pareto optimal. In other words, just like its ideal capitalistic counterpart, the labor-managed economy will be producing the maximum producible output from given resources, and the maximum social satisfaction for a prescribed distribution of income.[2] These conclusions follow from the fact that competitive labor-managed firms equalize factor marginal products to factor returns for all factors including labor, from competition in nonlabor factor markets, free entry of firms and identical technologies.

By contrast, as has been pointed out by Ward [7], if technologies of different firms within an industry are different, the optimum solution will not be reached by the labor-managed economy because the equilibrium behavior will not lead to equalization of marginal value products of labor among firms. In this context the capitalist alternative appears as superior, on the assumptions made. Of course, if imperfections in the labor market are permitted, the differences in marginal productivities of labor among firms and industries may be just as important. In any case, the comparative inefficiency of the labor-managed case here discussed should not be too pronounced. In fact, the labor-managed firms are all bound to operate at a point of maximum factor productivities (i.e., where their technologies are linear-homogeneous), the comparative shortcoming being merely imputable to the fact that the more efficient ones do not produce enough. Moreover, as we argue later in Section III, labor-managed economies will normally be in a much better position to proliferate the best technology throughout the industry. Finally, even if in the case studied the labor-managed economy will produce less than the

2. We will speak of the distributional effects of labor management in Section III.

capitalist economy with identical factor endowments, it can be shown that it will generate a stronger demand for, and correspondingly higher returns to, capital. Thus accumulation and growth may proceed at a higher rate, leading to more output and more consumption over time.

While recognizing the abstraction and lack of realism of all of the pure theory presented in this section, we may say that the perfectly competitive model just discussed is the least realistic. Indeed, the requirements of product homogeneity and a very large number of sellers (producers) are satisfied only in a few industries. Much more frequent is some degree of monopoly power coupled with product differentiation and, in many instances, active sales promotion. It is in this context, I believe, that Ward's earlier conclusion of greater restrictiveness of labor managed monopolies, while formally correct, is misleading when we want to evaluate the theoretical performance of the system.

It is true that if the government or some other external agent were to set the number of firms for each industry at one, such a monopoly would be, *ceteris paribus*, more restrictive and thus socially more harmful than a capitalist monopoly. But in the real world monopolistic tendencies and market power are hardly ever of this type. Rather they derive from the fact that efficient production is consistent with only a limited number of firms given the size of the market, the desire of firms to accumulate and grow, the artificial creation of barriers to entry, and so on.

If labor management is viewed in this more realistic context of the entire industry, one can make a case for it which is strong indeed. On grounds of several arguments, labor management can be expected not only to yield market structures more competitive than any other free economy, but also to prevent a good deal of wasteful and harmful sales promotion. The first and perhaps simplest argument is that with an increasing scale of operation, the benefits from participation—incentives, identification, and involvement—will tend to diminish.

Thus it can be expected that, all other things being equal, the point of maximum efficiency, which also is the point of long-run equilibrium for a labor-managed firm, will be reached for a lower level of output than for a firm operating with a hired labor factor. And thus, figuratively speaking, there will be room for more firms in a given industry.

The next point also hinges on the most efficient scale of operation. The labor-managed firm will never grow beyond that scale, whereas a capitalist firm often will, its growth being governed, even after greatest technical efficiency is reached, by the desire for profit maximization. Two extreme situations may further clarify the essence of this argument. Consider an ideal firm operating under constant returns to scale and facing a constant price yielding positive unit profits under capitalism. The equilibrium level of operation of that firm, if capitalist, is (at least in theory) infinite, while if labor-managed, it is finite and indeterminate at any level of operation. The simple crux of this deduction is that while the first firm must grow indefinitely to maximize profits, the second maximizes income per laborer at any level of operation. The other extreme situation is similar to that just described except that the firms in question face a less than infinitely elastic demand function. In that situation the capitalist monopoly, as is well known, will find its equilibrium where the marginal (and average) cost reaches the marginal revenue; whereas the labor-managed firm must operate at zero output, or, more realistically, with only one employee; indeed, as the reader will easily verify, under the assumed conditions income per laborer will be maximized with only one member of the labor-managed firm. Clearly, under the assumed conditions it would take a very large number of firms to fill the industry (with a reasonable return to labor), but by the time such a large number would enter, the market power of each firm would become very low or disappear altogether.

Probably the most significant comparative advantage of the labor-managed oligopoly arises in connection with product differentiation and sales promotion. It can be shown that the labor-managed firm will in equilibrium produce less and engage in a less intensive advertising campaign than an equivalent capitalist firm as long as the latter makes positive profits, a condition which obtains virtually without exception. Especially if we realize that it is precisely the more extreme doses of exhortational advertising that constitute the heaviest social costs, the advantage of the labor-managed alternative is considerable. Not only can we expect a significantly less concentrated industry, but the external diseconomies, mind pollution, and the like should be significantly reduced or completely eliminated.

The last point deserving mention is based on the simple notion that there is a far greater desire to decentralize within democratic structures than in nondemocratic ones. For example, even with very small or no economies of scale, a capitalist, or for that matter a Soviet-type, firm will tend to retain its centralized organization, whereas the labor-managed one will attempt to subdivide itself into autonomous decision-making and production units based on location or other functional characteristics. I am quite convinced that this tendency is present with the labor-managed alternative for other reasons than the stronger production incentive of small groups.

Finally, before concluding this section, we ought to reconsider Ward's negative supply elasticity and discuss that and related issues in the context of general equilibrium efficiency. It is true that if short-run reactions of competitive firms were as posited by Ward, the resulting inefficiency could be quite considerable, and what is equally important, at least some markets could become unstable. The contention which I want to argue below is that matters are far from being so bad.

First of all, we have the two arguments made by Domar: One, with more than one product by the firm, even short-run elasticities can be positive and quite high for an individual product; two, even with only one product the supply elasticity in the short run must be positive if the firm operates with an (active) external labor supply constraint, reflected by a labor supply function of finite elasticity [3]. In addition, there is the problem raised by Joan Robinson [4] in her critique of Domar. Using my own words to push the argument a step further, how can one reasonably expect that a working collective will mutilate itself (discharging, say, one-tenth of the membership), if it has already realized a significant gain from a price increase, say 10 per cent of income, for the sake of gaining an extra, say, one per cent? Indeed, this sounds like an extract from a book of rules of capitalist conduct. While what underlies the above rhetorical question certainly is true, I would further like to point out that the elimination of the negative elasticity argument does not even call for any higher morals. In the short run, a single-product producer operating under perfect competition will have very little possibility of capital-labor substitution; in terms of Ward's diagrams, the relevant stretch of the marginal productivity of labor will generally be very near a vertical line. And, consequently, the normal short-run supply elasticity of a competitive labor-managed firm producing a single output can for all practical purposes be considered zero, even if group solidarity were absent.

Before leaving the short-run, two observations are in order. First, let it be noted that the zero elasticity eliminates possibilities of instability and reduces a good deal the loss of general equilibrium efficiency (note that in a world with only single-product firms a change in relative prices would now keep, in the short run, the point on the production possibility locus unchanged). Second, in the context of aggregate national income analysis, the zero short-run elasticity is by no means something to frown on; but this we will discuss in the next section.

Finally, a few words on long-run adjustments within the general equilibrium framework. Again, the introduction of an additional piece of information from the real world helps a good deal. It is reasonable to expect that with most firms the point of constant returns to scale (the point corresponding to the minimum of the long-run average cost curve) in reality is not a point, but a whole range (of "efficient outputs")—a range the end of which is hard to establish empirically. But within such a range, as we have noted already, the long-run equilibrium of the labor-managed firms becomes indeterminate. The firms now can arbitrarily determine their scale of operation, and the most logical is that given by the size of the working collective, more or less exogenously determined. But as the reader will find easy to verify, under these conditions the long-run supply elasticities will be positive and can be quite high even with single-product firms, and the general equilibrium adjustment to changing demand conditions will be quite efficient indeed. Of course, the most efficient and full (Pareto) optimal adjustment will occur once labor incomes are equalized through entry and exit—or, with firms operating under constant returns to scale, through expansion or contraction of existing firms.

II. Macroeconomics

We now turn to the determination of aggregate variables such as income, employment, the price level, and so on. I feel that it will be most expedient first to summarize the principal results that can be obtained for the labor-managed economy and then, to the extent that space permits, to elaborate on some of them.

The first observation is that unemployment is conceivable in a labor-managed economy, but if it occurs it will be of an entirely differ ent nature—because of different causes and different duration—than unemployment of the Keynesian type in a capitalist economy. A second important point is that variations in effective demand can be expected in the labor-managed economy to lead primarily to variations in prices and not much or not at all to adjustments in income and employment. A third and related point is that on the whole there will be little natural cause for secular inflation, although variations in prices may be wide if markets are entirely free. Fourth, even if unemployment arises there will always be natural forces to restore full employment after a while, provided that capital markets are competitive. Fifth, the macroeconomic general equilibrium that simultaneously determines the aggregate variables must be stable provided that real cost of capital varies with the general price level, and almost certainly it will be stable even if the money cost of capital is constant.

The key to points one and two is the low or zero short-run supply elasticity of firms. If for one reason or another the existing number of firms at given product and factor prices is incapable of employing (in equilibrium) all the labor force, then unemployment will prevail, and the supply elasticity being low, short-run changes in demand will be translated into price-level variations. Note that this has nothing to do with wage rigidity. Such rigidity in fact is highly unlikely if not impossible in the labor-managed economy because of the residual nature of labor income and the direct managerial ability of labor to make choices between price reductions on the one hand and idleness and sales reductions on the other. Thus, contrary to a capitalistic situation, a symmetrical flexibility of prices, up and down, and no systematic inflationary tendency should be expected.

Point four is a logical consequence of the fact that if there is unemployment, the unemployed will be in a considerably favored position in completing with existing firms for capital funds for development of new projects. Indeed, with very low unemployment incomes those currently unemployed will be able to offer considerably better terms to the lender. And thus any significant degree of unemployment carries with itself strong, even if perhaps not overly speedy, self-correcting forces. The prime vehicle of the latter is entry, and perhaps also expansion of existing firms (often into new lines of production) operating under constant returns to scale, whose scale of operation is arbitrary. It should be noted here that no parallel remedy exists for Keynesian unemployment; here either entry or expansion of existing firms implies opening of a deflationary gap and the ensuing return to a less than full employment equilibrium.

Point five asserting stability of the macroeconomic system involves some slightly involved mathematics, and consequently I omit its demonstration. Full proof is contained, however, in my *General Theory of Labor-Managed Market Economies* [5].

We may sum up by taking the position of the policy maker in the labor-managed economy: He need not fear autonomous variations in demand as a cause of cyclical unemployment. Rather he may look out for such variations in order to prevent fluctuations in prices. In this endeavor he will be greatly assisted by an open and competitive foreign trade sector. Full employment does not entirely disappear, however, as the policy maker's problem. But he must be concerned with it as a matter of long-range strategy, primarily ensuring perfect functioning of the capital market with proper interest structures. More actively, he may want to take discretionary steps—market research and consulting, indicative planning, forecasting, and so on—to enhance the speed and efficiency of new entry and expansion. In the final analysis, however, he has a considerable advantage compared to his capitalist colleague in that matters are bound to improve even if perchance he falls asleep on the job.

III. Special Dimensions of Labor Management

Even if the labor-managed economy can pass with flying colors the scrutiny of conventional micro- and macroeconomic theory, as presented in the preceding two sections, its greatest strength lies in what we may identify as its *special dimensions*—dimensions largely absent in other economic systems. They are all related to, contained in, or emergent from the managerial function of labor, that is, of all participants of the enterprise. The field of analysis opened by these special dimensions is so vast that it cannot be treated in a single section; consequently we will restrict ourselves here to the outline of a few of the most important arguments. In my larger study referred to earlier, I devote to the subject several chapters [5, Part III], and I certainly cannot pretend that even my analysis there is exhaustive.

The first and simplest consideration is that, contrary to the models studied in the two preceding sections, labor is not unique and homogeneous, but rather that in every enterprise a large number of individuals of different skills and qualifications cooperate in a common endeavor. One necessary task of labor management is thus to decide on the distributive shares among the different labor categories. The specific form of the distribution schedule—indicating, for example, whether the director gets four times the pay of the janitor—will be the outcome of two sets of forces: Conditions of the labor market, or, more precisely, of the quasi-labor market, because there is no conventional labor market in a labor-managed economy; and the collective will of the working community as it emerges from the democratic decision-making process of labor management.

Since the labor-managed firm in equilibrium (i.e., when maximizing income for each laborer) will equalize the income of each labor category to the corresponding marginal value product, the first set of forces will guarantee that the allocation of labor throughout the economy will be at least approximately consistent with maximum aggregate output.[3] The second set of forces, on the other hand, will guarantee a reasonable distribution of income, consistent with the generally accepted notion of justice for a particular segment of society, a particular community, or a particular period of time. This "dual" optimization of social welfare, striking a balance between the mechanistic rules of efficient resource allocation and a collective expression of distributional justice, seems to be a solution superior to that offered by either set of criteria in isolation. The cardinally important thing is that the "dual" system guarantees that major mistakes will not be committed in either the allocational or the distributional sphere.

The labor force in a labor-managed economy is not only diverse but also of variable quality. And this brings us to the second important *special dimension* of labor management. Without any doubt, labor-management is among all the existing forms of enterprise organization the optimal arrangement when it comes to finding the utility-maximizing effort—that is, the proper quality, duration, and intensity of work—by the working collective. Not only is there no

---

3. In pure theory a frictionless system should generate perfect income equalization through entry and/or exit of firms. However, considering that in the real world there is never enough time to bring such an equalization process to completion, given imperfect information, attachments and loyalties of individuals to the working collective, and the like, the competitive forces can be expected to produce only approximate results.

situation of conflict between management and the workers that might hinder the finding of the optimum, but the process of self-management itself can be viewed as a highly efficient device for communication, control of collusion, and enforcement among the participants.

This should be contrasted with the situation of most other enterprises where the worker normally will be furnishing a minimum effort consistent with the retention of his job. It is true that expectation of promotion or a raise may stimulate effort over the acceptable minimum, but recall that this factor should be equally operative in all firms, and thus it does not establish a comparative disadvantage of the labor-managed firm.

Our second special dimension may conveniently be summarized in a diagram. In Figure 1.1 we measure effort (E) to the left of 0 along the horizontal axis, whereas on the vertical axis we find a (average) laborer's income Y. A typical transformation function for the labor-managed alternative between effort and income is indicated by the contour ab (note that with some fixed costs it takes some effort to generate zero income). By contrast, a typical transformation function in capitalist enterprise is indicated by the rectangular broken contour defined by point k. Its comparative deficiency is of two kinds: (1) Point k is below ab, because of some residual profit normally not distributed among the members, and (2) and much more important, ab is continuous. As a result of both (as the reader may verify by drawing a set of convex indifference lines), losses in individual and collective utility, that is, in real income, will occur in one type of undertaking as compared with the other.

Third, as shown by the diagram, there is another special dimension, Z—in fact, it should be understood as a summary index standing for a very large number of special dimensions—also entering the utility function of the members of the working collective, together with income and effort. As indicated by the three-dimensional transformation locus in Figure 1.1, attainment of higher levels of Z involves an opportunity cost in terms of income and/or effort. Nevertheless, this new dimension further augments the number of choices of the working community and thus unambiguously (as shown by the equal-utility contours u, u', u'' and the maximum-utility point e) its real income. It is the comparison between point e and point k that should, in the context of our present analysis, be

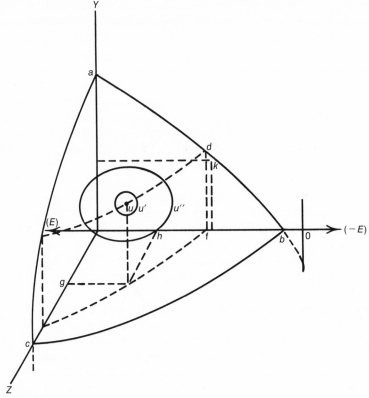

Figure 1.1

included in any comparison between a labor-managed and a capitalist, or, for that matter, a Soviet-type firm.

It would hardly be possible to be exhaustive in explaining all the variables for which Z actually stands. However, some illustrations should be helpful: For example, the working collective, or a subgroup of it, may prefer a conveyor belt to a traditional way of intraplant transportation, even if this should involve a reduction in money income. By contrast, a capitalist would perform such a substitution only if profit could be increased. Another example is training and education of some members of the community at the expense of the enterprise. Again, the corresponding motivation and decision making is entirely different from what it would be in other firms.

still another example is collective consumption using part of the global income of the enterprise, including housing, recreation, and so on. Moreover, the enterprise as a whole may undertake at its own expense social action directed toward the outside, the local community or the broader one, and thus derive intangible real income— we may call it peace of mind—for itself.[4]

The last example brings us to a fourth category of special dimensions, related to Z but not exactly the same, referred to as Z'. It resembles Z in all respects, including that it enters the utility index, except that it does not affect money income or effort of the working community. The transformation locus with Z' substituted for Z would thus appear as a cylindrical surface generated by lines parallel to the Z' axis. Normally, such a surface will be truncated at some finite level of Z' and, obviously, an equilibrium will be found (with indifference loci convex everywhere) at the corresponding ridge, at a level of collective utility again unambiguously higher than at a point such as d with two dimensions only. To give substance to this rather technical exposition, let us give at least one example, a significant one. We have noted in Section I that the long-run equilibrium of a competitive labor-managed firm operating under constant returns to scale—a condition encountered in many real situations—is indeterminate with respect to scale of operation. Under such conditions, total employment and output of the firm may become our Z' variable. The working community considers it a positive utility to maximize employment in the community; the external constraint, and the ridge line of our above discussion, now are given by the full employment in the community.

In my opinion, the argument just made has a good deal of relevance and when further generalized can become even more significant, especially in the context of less developed countries. The generalization is based on the recognition that in most situations— especially in manufacturing—we cannot postulate perfect competittion; some market power will always be present. In such situations, however, all it takes is to reclassify Z', a zero opportunity cost variable, into Z, a positive opportunity cost variable. But the absorption

4. Some will object that all this can be done by individuals or through nonbusiness-based groupings. This is true, but it holds even for the labor-managed system and thus the potential of action by firms, the primary generators of resources, still constitutes a comparative advantage.

of unemployment in the community remains a positive good from the point of view of the working collective. Thus a solution involving higher employment than that dictated by strict income-per-laborer maximization still may be expected.

IV. Concluding Observations

Before attempting a summary evaluation of the labor-managed economy, two more matters ought to be taken up which normally enter the appraisal of an economic system. The first is the question of ability to mobilize national savings for accumulation. The second is the question of the capacity of generating technical progress and innovation.

Regarding the capacity to mobilize investment funds, the labor-managed economy, especially its socialist version, is in a very strong position. Since labor-managed firms must pay for the use of capital the corresponding value of marginal product, and taking a reasonable set of estimates of national capital stock and marginal capital productivity, the economy can generate net savings of between 20 and 30 per cent of national income just by retaining capital income for reinvestment. These percentages, already among the highest currently encountered in the real world, can further be augmented through private savings, government surpluses, or, as in Yugoslavia, through an obligation of firms to repay investment loans from current income.

With respect to the second question, the case for the labor-managed economy is somewhat less clear cut; but in the final analysis, it would be difficult to conclude that the system in question is at a comparative disadvantage. When it comes to "small" inventive and innovative activity emerging as a side effect of the productive process itself, the incentives, unity of purpose, and ease of communication offered by labor-management (and by income sharing, which is an integral part of labor management) are conditions unequalled by any other system. On the other side of the spectrum, with respect to basic research and major scientific developments, the firms only rarely play a decisive role; thus in the present context the difference between alternative systems cannot be very important.

It is the middle of the spectrum, for "medium size" incentive and innovative activity, that would seem the most important. Here the modern capitalist corporation almost certainly has a comparative advantage with its own low-cost—and often quite abundant—funds that it can employ in research and development. On the other hand, a socialist economy, labor-managed or other, is likely to have a distinct advantage in proliferating innovations throughout the whole economy.

Let us now try to make a summary evaluation of the labor-managed system. I realize that such an endeavor must always contain a certain element of subjective judgment. This is so because summary evaluation really means constructing an aggregate ordinal index based on a combination of several evaluations, not all of the same sign; clearly, some weights must be employed and these, to a degree at least, will be subjective.

With this in mind, and basing myself on ten years of intensive study more than on the present exposition, I cannot forego a set of strongly favorable conclusions; I cannot avoid them, even though I realize that I am contradicting the majority of our profession who have thought about the problem, and even though I may risk earning the displeasure of some.

In brief, the labor-managed system appears to me to be superior by far, judged on strictly economic criteria, to any other economic system in existence. In the sphere of allocation efficiency (concerning how well it utilizes its resources in national production), it is at worst equal to the Western-type capitalist system in the context of a full-employment model (as discussed in Section I), while it is definitely superior in the context of the macroeconomic model (as discussed in Section II) and in the context of its special dimensions (as discussed in Section III). On the side of the system's capability to grind out an efficient pattern of income distribution, there are also strong reasons to believe that a socialist labor-managed economy will do a better job than other market systems. This conclusion is based not only on the argument of collective decision making within the firm (as argued in Section III), but also on the fact that in the socialist economy the income share of capital, whether reinvested or not, will accrue to the society as a whole and not to a select group of individuals.

Compared to the Soviet-type command economy, the question of distributional efficiency really is empty of meaning because income distribution is decided by decree and not by some mechanism inherent in the economic system. As for allocational efficiency, which is far more important for our comparison because inherent in the system, we only have to recognize with Bergson [1] that the Soviet-type command economy is less efficient than market capitalism, and recall the above evaluation of the two market alternatives. In fact, even the weaker postulate of approximate equality between the two major world systems would suffice here to establish a preference for the labor-managed alternative over that of a command economy.

Two remarks, less strictly economic and stemming much more from intuition than from careful analysis, may be in order before closing this discussion. First, it seems to me that the comparative advantage of labor-managed systems becomes even stronger once we leave the strictly economic frame of reference and replace it with one that takes account of broader human values. Second, taking a very long view of world events, it seems to me that if there is a meeting ground for the presently conflicting major world systems and ideologies, it is one not too far from the system discussed here.

References

1. A. Bergson, *The Economics of Soviet Planning* (New Haven: Yale University Press, 1964), p. 341.

2. ____, "Market Socialism Revisited," *Journal of Political Economy*, 75 (Oct. 1967), 432–442.

3. E. Domar, "The Soviet Collective Farm as a Producer Cooperative," *American Economic Review*, 56 (Sept. 1966), 734–757.

4. J. Robinson, "The Soviet Cooperative Farm as a Producer Cooperative: Comment," *American Economic Review*, 57 (March 1967), 222–223.

5. J. Vanek, *The General Theory of Labor-Managed Market Economies* (Ithaca, N.Y.: Cornell University Press, 1970).

6. ____, *The Participatory Economy: An Evolutionary Hypothesis and a Strategy for Development* (Ithaca, N.Y.: Cornell University Press, 1971).

7. B. Ward, "The Firm in Illyria: Market Syndicalism," *American Economic Review*, 48 (Sept. 1958), 566–589.

PART II

REAL CONDITIONS

2 | The Economics of the Peruvian Law Defining the Self-Managed Sector of Social Property*

With an Appendix by FERNANDO COLLAZO

This paper is designed to familiarize the English-speaking reader with the economic contents of the Peruvian law of social property and then to interpret the implications of the law in terms of formal economic analysis. Accordingly, Section I summarizes the economic essentials of the law, primarily those relevant for our analysis of economic behavior. Section II analyzes the short-run behavior of a self-managed firm under the provisions of the Peruvian law. Section III considers the long-range characteristics of the firm, especially its growth. Section IV deals with the implications of the law for the structural efficiency of resource allocation in the Peruvian economy. An exact and detailed interpretation of the law, including accounting definitions, is presented in the Appendix by Fernando Collazo.

I. The Economic Essentials of the Law

According to the law, the social property sector in Peru rests on a dual structure consisting, on the one hand, of a supporting national fund of social property assisted by various national and regional executive bodies and, on the other, of the self-managing firms themselves.

The supporting system performs various functions for the firms of social property. Of these by far the most important is providing the initial funding of the self-managed firms, thus making it possible for groups of working men to start productive organizations without initial funds of their own. Any self-managed firm thus started is

* This paper originally appeared in "Self-Management in Peru," Series of Unpublished Studies no. 10 (Ithaca, N.Y.: Program on Participation and Labor-Managed Systems, Cornell University, June 1975). I express my sincere appreciation to Tom Davis, Tom Bayard, Fernando Collazo, Santiago Roca, and José Tong, of the Cornell Department of Economics, who have extended to me their helping hands in preparing this paper.

required to repay to the national fund the full amount of the initial loan over a contractually stipulated number of years, normally (but not necessarily) with an additional interest charge on the loan.

Turning now to the productive organization, let us recall first that it is labor-managed: that is, all rights to control, manage and exploit the productive resources are vested collectively in the regular workers of the enterprise. Its supreme democratic body is the general assembly, which can elect the necessary representative bodies and select its manager, the head of the executive structure. The firm operates in various product and factor markets and is free to make decisions without interference from the outside.

The remuneration of labor, that is, the membership of the firm, assumes two distinct forms. The first is the wage bill, W, whose level and structure must be agreed on by the National Commission of Social Property. The second is a portion of operating surplus assignable to the membership of the firms and will be defined presently with greater precision.

The total operating surplus of the firm is obtained as a difference between the total value of sales and other income of any kind on the one hand and all costs and the wage bill on the other hand. Out of this surplus, as noted already, the initial loan is repaid, after which the law stipulates that the firm must continue to make payments to itself, again from its surplus, at least as large as the installments of the repayment. These amounts are added in the balance sheet of the enterprise as part of its patrimony or net worth, and can be either invested by the firm in its own real assets or deposited with the national fund of social ownership through acquisition of convertible debentures.

At its inception or during its operation, the firm can also raise capital by selling debentures with variable income (*accio-bonos*). This income must be in the same proportion to the distributable surplus (defined presently) as the capital contributed by sales of debentures is to the rest of the firm's total capital. Thus, if debentures constitute one-fifth of the firm's total capital, one-fifth of the distributable surplus must be paid to the holders of these debentures. The total capital of the self-managed enterprise is composed of the value of these debentures, if any, the initial endowment from the national fund of social property, and the subsequent contributions from surplus.

The variable income debentures can be acquired under the Peruvian law only by financial institutions. For purposes of our subsequent formal analysis we will assume that there is no such investment. The results would not be altered substantially without the assumption.

In addition to the deductions from total economic surplus, the self-managed firm also is required to pay an amount, a taxlike contribution to the national fund of social property, equal to 10 per cent of the total amount of the surplus and the remuneration actually paid during the current period of operation, W, minus twice the legal minimum wage income, W^*. For purposes of analysis, and not to make the analysis overly cumbersome, we will assume that W and W^* are equal.

The total surplus after these deductions (and after other deductions of lesser importance)[1] yields what the Peruvian law calls the taxable income of the enterprise. From it, after tax is deducted, we obtain the distributable surplus by adding the amount of repayment or mandatory accumulation already noted. The proportion of the tax is not further stipulated in the law. For the purpose of our subsequent theoretical analysis, we will assume that t is some given percentage of the taxable surplus.

II. The Short Run of the Peruvian Labor-Managed Firm

To analyze the behavior of the Peruvian self-managed firm let us first consider the short run, that is, the situation where the physical capital stock available to the firm is constant at the level K_o and only the labor membership of the firm, L, is a variable. We will further assume that the firm is perfectly competitive, selling its product x in a market at a price p and hiring capital at a constant price r. Because we will not be concerned with intermediate inputs and costs, we can think of x as real value added by capital and labor or as total product in a process using no intermediate inputs.

Figure 2.1 shows the total revenue curve of the firm, px, plotted against the only variable input, labor. The first essential element of analysis, represented by the horizontal line rK_o, is the firm's fixed capital cost. We recall that it may be charged by the social property lending agency on the initial loan establishing the firm.

1. One of them, amounting to 5 per cent of the economic surplus, is for purposes of reserves formation; we will return to this in Section II.

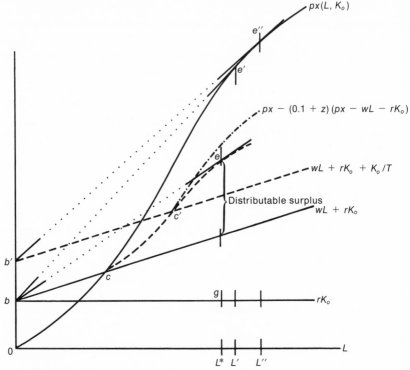

Figure 2.1

Also originating at b in Figure 2.1 is an upward-sloping line bc reflecting the fixed capital plus variable labor cost of the firm. Of course, the wage is not a market wage but rather determined by the working collective and agreed on by the social property sector. Not to make the diagram overly cumbersome, as we have noted already, we postulate that the wage rate w equals twice the legal minimum wage.

The distances between the costs line (bc) and the total revenue curve represents total surplus, or as referred to in the law and in the Appendix to this paper, the economic surplus.

Out of this surplus first must be paid several fixed amounts independent of the level of employment and of the level of surplus, in particular and especially the repayment of the initial loan or mandatory further accumulation, amount to K_o/T, where T is the repayment period. For simplicity, as indicated by the description of the line $b'c'$ in Figure 2.1, we take this fixed obligation to consist only of this capital charge. But, as indicated in the Appendix, there are some other amounts to be paid. To obtain the so-called taxable surplus, the Peruvian firm must also deduct, in addition to the capital charge, certain amounts proportional to the economic surplus. In Figure 2.1 these deductions are reflected by the dashed-and-dotted contour cc', and the charges are reflected by the term $(0.1 + z)$. The first number represents a 10 per cent contribution to the funding of the social property sector at large, and z stands for several other small proportional charges, including those for a special reserve fund to be used during workers' retirement.

The taxable income for various levels of employment now becomes reflected in the diagram by the wedgelike area with its point at c' and defined by the dashed-and-dotted and straight-dashed lines respectively. As is again shown more carefully in the Appendix, a proportional tax at the rate t is levied on that income (that wedge), and the amount of the tax is measured by the vertical difference between the dashed-and-dotted line and the dashed line passing through e.

As shown in the diagram, following the definitions given in the Appendix, the distributable income is finally obtained by adding to the taxable income after tax the amount K_o/T, i.e., the initial capital repayment or mandatory accumulation.

Thus the total net income received on a current basis by the working collective is represented by the addition of the labor cost and distributable income such as the distance ge in Figure 2.1. It is this quantity per worker, that is, divided by the corresponding level of employment L, that the working collective is expected to maximize in the short run by selecting the appropriate level of employment. Since income per worker is represented by the slope of a line connecting point b with alternative points on the line ce, this slope—that is, the total distributed income per worker—will be maximized when the two lines become tangential to each other. This happens at point e in the diagram. Point e, then, represents the short-run equilibrium of the Peruvian self-managed firm and to it correspond all of the other equilibria of other variables. In particular we note the equilibrium level of employment L^*. The mathematical equilibrium condition, which is shown in Section III, is simply that the income per worker must equal the marginal or incremental distributed income consisting of both the wage and the distributable surplus.

It can be fairly easily seen that the various taxes and contributions and accounting and repayment rules generally lead to employment restriction, that is, less employment than would prevail without these factors. Recalling that many things are not exactly fixed in the Peruvian law of social property, and that even if they were fixed they could be changed, we may state the same thing in more positive terms: several useful propositions can be made upon careful examination of Figure 2.1. First, and perhaps simplest to observe, is that the higher the rate of return r on capital, the higher the point b will be on the vertical axis and the higher, other things being equal, the employment. Second, it can be noted, again *ceteris paribus*, the lower the tax rate t, the higher the dashed line $c'e$ will be, and given the proportionality by which that line is obtained, also the higher will be the equilibrium employment point. Third, and using the same type of argument, with reference to the dashed-and-dotted contour passing through point c', it will immediately be seen that if z or the 10 per cent contribution to the social property sector were reduced, the dashed-and-dotted line would shift proportionately upward, all the way to the original total revenue curve px for zero contributions, and during that process employment would also be increasing. Because, of course, the social property sector needs resources for investment and further development, a positive proposition can be made to the effect that employment will increase in any particular self-managed firm if a levy on capital (or on land, in the case of mines or farm cooperatives) is substituted for the proportional levy on the economic surplus.

The fourth proposition is related to the determination and definition of the distributable surplus which, under the Peruvian law, also contains the capital K_o/T. If that capital charge were to be taken out of the surplus and not distributed to the working collectives, then, at least in the short run, we would have a situation where instead of a fixed capital charge Ob we would have a fixed capital charge Ob' in the diagram. And this, other things being equal, would have a strong positive employment effect. In particular, if no other charges or taxes were levied and the total revenue contour were relevant, the employment would increase from L' to L''. A fifth proposition can be made similar to proposition 4 and based more or less on the same rationale. If all funding of new firms were performed through loans of indefinite maturity—that is, with T approaching infinity—and the interest rate r were augmented so as to move b to b' in Figure 2.1, employment would be significantly affected without any change in the amounts of capital invested.

Recall our simplified assumption that fixed charges on the economic surplus consist only of the capital charge. In reality there are other such charges which do not enter the distributable surplus. The effect of such charges, other things being equal, is comparable to moving point b in the diagram upward; the effect on employment will then be positive.

All these results could have been obtained using algebra, as could the equilibrium solution for the self-managed firm in the short run. In the following section a simple set of such results will be obtained for both short- and long-run situations.

III. The Long-Run Equilibrium of the Peruvian Self-Managed Firm

Let us now turn briefly to the equilibrium conditions in the long run. We are now assuming that the capital stock, K, becomes a variable. For the moment we will not consider problems of accumulation as stipulated in the Peruvian law (see Section IV). We postulate only that the firm can hire services of capital at a price r in a perfectly competitive capital market, in any amounts it may desire. We shall also disregard for the moment the related question of repayment and augmentation by that amount of the distributable surplus. We can do so most conveniently by assuming the period of repayment T to be infinity.

Using these assumptions we find the definitions of total labor income and labor income per worker, Y and y respectively, in relation 2.1, where G and a are given by relations 2.2 and 2.3:

$$Y = yL = px(1 - G) - (wL + rK)G - rK \qquad (2.1)$$

$$G = a + t(1 - a) \qquad (2.2)$$

$$a = 0.1 + z. \qquad (2.3)$$

The other notations are known to us from Section II.

Using subscripts to indicate partial differentials and differentiating relation 2.1 with respect to L and K respectively, we obtain the two key equilibrium conditions for the two factors of production:

$$y = px_L(1 - G) - wG \qquad (2.4)$$

$$r = px_K(1 - G) - rG. \qquad (2.5)$$

Relation 2.4 actually is the algebraic expression for the equilibrium condition derived in Section II.

To study the nature of this equilibrium of the Peruvian self-managed firm in the long run, let us first state

$$px = yL + rK + pxG + wLG + rKG, \qquad (2.6)$$

the fact that total value of product px is distributed between the incomes actually disbursed to labor and capital respectively, plus the various tax charges, as found in relation 2.1. If we now substitute into relation 2.6 the two factor income shares, yL and rK respectively, from the equilibrium conditions stated in relations 2.4 and 2.5, after some simplification we obtain:

$$px = x_L L + x_K K. \qquad (2.7)$$

Relation 2.7 is nothing but the well-known Euler theorem; thus the Peruvian self-managed firm fulfills in the long run the all-important optimality characteristic of self-managed firms.[2]

Namely, the firm will maximize average factor productivities for any prescribed ratio of capital to labor. Using the terminology of my *General Theory of Labor Managed Economies*, the firm will operate at the locus of maximum physical efficiency.

What about the position on that locus? Let us divide relation 2.5 into relation 2.4. After some simplification we obtain

$$\frac{s/(1 - G) + w}{r} = \frac{x_L}{x_K} \qquad (s = y - w) \qquad (2.8)$$

where s (also defined in 2.8) represents surplus, that is, the excess of income per worker over the statutory wage w. It is immediately apparent that with G equal to zero—that is, with zero levies a and t—we obtain the *efficient* equilibrium condition to the effect that the

2. See my *General Theory of Labor-Managed Market Economies* (Ithaca, N.Y.: Cornell University Press, 1970), chap. 2.

marginal rate of substitution between capital and labor equals the ratio of the factor incomes. However, it is also clear from relation 2.8 that with positive levies—that is, with G positive—the numerator of the left-hand expression will be increased. As a consequence the firm will behave as if labor earned relatively more or capital earned relatively less. That is, a substitution of capital for labor, *ceteris paribus*, will occur as a result of either or both positive levies a and t. This only confirms two of our employment-restricting effects identified in Section II. But, of course, a full evaluation of the structural and efficiency effects of the rules inherent in the Peruvian law can not be obtained without an overall study of general equilibrium.

IV. General Analysis and Conclusions

In this section, I will take up several subjects in a less systematic manner than in the preceding sections, subjects more related to practical problems of implementing the self-managed sector in Peru. In this way also we will arrive at our principal conclusions.

First I would like to turn to some characteristics of the social property law which may cause problems. The first and probably most significant is the fact that the amount of repayment of a firm's initial debt, equivalent to bb' in Figure 2.1 or to A in the Appendix, actually is paid out twice, once as a repayment to the social property sector and once to the distributable surplus. But it is raised only once, as is implied by the construction bb' in Figure 2.1. Where are the resources for the second payment to be found if, for example, the workers decide to distribute the totality of distributable surplus? In the early period of operation of the firm, of course, capital amortization funds can be used, but this would leave the firm at the end of amortization without any assets whatsoever, and the entire operation would have to be re-funded from social property funds. Of course, there are the reserve funds raised under z in Figure 2.1; but these may be insufficient or nonexistent if the surpluses are too low.

A second point concerns the distribution of the distributable surplus. It will be recalled (see relations 4a and 4b in the Appendix) that the totality of the distributable surplus is to be allocated between workers and the owners of *accio-bonos*. But is this correct, since the totality of the repayment (A in relation 4a of the Appendix) is to constitute a debt of the workers to the enterprise? Of course this debt is to be amortized out of reserve funds at the time of the workers' retirement, but this does not dispose of the problem as a matter of principle.

These and several other problems, especially the comparative arbitrariness of wage rates and correspondingly of the economic surplus, suggest that it might be better to charge substantially higher interest (*Ob* in Figure 2.1) on the initial loan without necessarily expecting repayment. Moreover, the role of the *accio-bonos* could be taken over by variable income debentures of finite or indefinite maturity, yielding on the average a somewhat higher rate of return than the social property funds and variable with the performance of the enterprise as measured by income or income per worker. I have discussed elsewhere the merits and more technical aspects of such a solution.[3] Of course this solution would also have the great advantage of producing, other things being equal, higher levels of employment.

Let us now turn to the key aspects of structural efficiency of resource allocation implicit in the social property law. We already know the favorable result that the social property firms in the long run will operate at a point of maximum physical efficiency. In other words, the resource allocation within the firm will be optimal. But how will resources be allocated among firms? Suppose, first, that the economy is totally self-managed, with no other economic sectors, and that the various fiscal parameters such as a, t, and so on are the same for all firms, as is the rate of interest at which capital is obtained. Then interfirm efficiency of resource allocation could be guaranteed provided that through free entry or policy-induced creation of new firms, actual incomes per worker are equalized. In this situation of total self-management, with no links to international or other capital markets, the problem of insufficient employment noted in Sections II and III would disappear, provided of course that capital costs and interest rates are set competitively (presumably at a high level) and provided that such rates are charged on the capital of social property firms. It will be recalled here that such interest levies are not mandatory according to the law. If, on the other hand such levies are not charged, or if there is another capitalist segment in the economy, all interest rates are determined by international competition; then there will be inefficient allocation of resources.

3. See Chapter 11, below.

Specifically, the self-managed sector will provide less employment in the economy than it ought to.

In fact, since there is a good deal of unemployment or underemployment of labor in Peru today, irrespective of the more refined structural considerations just advanced, there is every reason to charge a price on capital in the social property sector and to charge it at the highest possible levels consistent with decent incomes and living conditions for those employed in the social property sector.

With a good deal of wisdom the authors of the social property law were concerned with imparting to the self-managed firms a considerable growth potential which would be to a high degree autonomous. Justification for this rests not only in the accumulation motive but also in the desire to create relatively large firms and thereby economize on managerial and technical cadres so scarce in any developing economy. But there may be some difficulties related to the specific methods of attaining these objectives. Some of them we have pointed out. In concluding I would like to advance a solution which may fulfill the same requirements of growth and accumulation and at the same time satisfy, at least approximately, some of the other objectives of the internal, structural, and employment efficiencies of the system. I have discussed the method in greater detail elsewhere and I believe that it is being considered, perhaps in a somewhat modified form, by policy makers in Yugoslavia.[4] I can thus state the essence only very briefly. Suppose that a policy of a high capital cost is adopted with funding based on indefinite repayment ($T = $ infinity). The self-managed firms then are given the option to use the interest payments on initial capital themselves for further expansion provided that on such new accumulation, as much as on the old, they continue paying the same high return. If the firms do not want such funds because they do not have investment projects yielding as much return as r, then of course they can effectively pay the amount rK to the social property sector, thereby not accumulating any further social assets or liabilities.

It can be shown that, besides all the advantages noted already, this solution, like a servomechanism, will keep the economy on course at all times at or near a dynamically efficient solution. At the

4. See Chapter 10, below. The information on Yugoslavia was given to me by Professor Cecez of the University of Sarajevo.

same time the social property sector will be bound to grow at a rate approximately equal to the rate of interest r without any further injections of capital. With such injections the rate of growth can be even higher.

In addition to the various efficiency properties there is also inherent in the complex of solutions advanced here a quality of simplicity. I believe that in a truly well-functioning self-managed economy where working people effectively control their economic destinies, simplicity and ease of understanding are of paramount importance. What is equally important, most or all of the forms suggested here really are consistent with the existing law of social property. It is only necessary to give specific, sometimes extreme, values to some of the parameters already built into the law.

Appendix: The Accounting Identities and Institutional Structure Defining the Peruvian Self-Management Sector

By FERNANDO COLLAZO

In what follows are presented the main economic magnitudes and and relationships concerning the Peruvian self-managed firm in the form of accounting identities. The numbers in the column on the right refer to the article or articles in the social property law where the corresponding item is to be found. A diagram is also included in which the organizational structure of the social property sector is shown.

Disposition of Income in the Peruvian Social Property Firm

No. of Article
of the Law

(1) $\quad E_{ex} = pQ - (C^{nl} + W)$ $\hfill$ 100

(2) $\quad E_{ec} = E_{ex} + X$ $\hfill$ 101

(3) $\quad E_t = E_{ec} - (F + I^* + R + H_1 + A + V + P + U)$
$\hfill$ 102, 103

$\quad\quad\quad = (1 - a)E_{ec} - [f \cdot (W - W^*) + A + Z - f \cdot p^*]$ $\hfill$ 75

$$\text{where } F = f \cdot E_{ec} + f[(W - W^*) - p^*] \qquad 108$$

$$I^* = i \cdot E_{ec} \qquad 92b$$

$$R = y \cdot E_{ec} \qquad 92e$$

$$H_1 = h_1 \cdot E_{ec} \qquad 162a$$

$$Z = V + P + U$$

$$a = (f + i + r + h_1)$$

(4a) $\quad E_d = (1 - t)E_t + A \qquad\qquad 105$

(4b) $\quad E_d = Y_B + Y_i \qquad\qquad 106$

$$= b \cdot E_d + (1 - b)E_d \qquad 86$$

where $\quad Y_B = b \cdot E_d$

$$Y_L = (1 - b)E_d$$

$$b = Accio\text{-}bonos/Patrimonio\ neto$$

(5) $\quad Y_L{}^n = Y_L - (H_2 + C) \qquad\qquad 106$

$$= (1 - d)Y_L$$

where $\quad H_2 = h_2 \cdot Y_L$

$$C = c \cdot Y_L$$

$$d = h_2 + C$$

(6) $\quad y_L{}^n = Y_L{}^n/L \qquad\qquad 107$

(7) $\quad W = \displaystyle\sum_{j}^{s} w_i L_i$

(8) $\quad W^* = w^* N \qquad\qquad 108$

(9) $\quad y_{ij} = (w_j + y_L{}^n)L_{ij} + c_i C$

(10) $\quad Y_L^* = W + Y_L{}^n + C$

Symbols

E_{ex} = Exploitation surplus (*Excedente de explotación*)
E_{ec} = Economic surplus (*Excedente económico*)
E_t = Taxable surplus (*Excedente imponible*)
E_d = Disposable surplus (*Excedente distributable*)
Y_L = Workers' surplus

Y_L^n = Workers' net surplus

Y_L^* = Total workers' income

P = Price of output

Q = Output

C^{nl} = Non-labor costs

W = Advanced "wages"

X = Net income (including capital gains) from sources other than the operation of the firm

F = Mandatory contributions to the National Social Property fund (Fondo Nacional de Propiedad Social)

I^* = Funds voluntarily allocated to investment

R = Legal reserves (not necessarily linked to the Economic Surplus)

H_1 = Mandatory contribution to the Housing Fund

A = Amortization payments on the *aporte transitorio* if the latter has not been entirely repaid; otherwise, mandatory deductions for investment

V = Capital gains from revaluation of fixed assets ($=$ value adjustment $-$ depreciation adjustment)

P = Accumulated losses

U = Donations

W^* = Minimum "wage bill"

w^* = Accounting wage equal to twice the minimum wage or *salario vital*

w_j = Daily wage for workers in classification j

L_{ij} = Number of days worked by worker i belonging to classification j

L_j = Number of days worked by workers in classification j

N = Number of workers

Y_B = Disposable surplus allocated as return on the outstanding *accio-bonos*

H_2 = Discretionary contributions to the Housing Fund

C = Collective consumption

y_L^n = Workers' net surplus per day worked

y_{ij} = Total income of worker i belonging to classification j

p^* = Accumulated losses currently being compensated

t = Average tax rate

c_i = Percentage of total collective consumption accruing to worker i

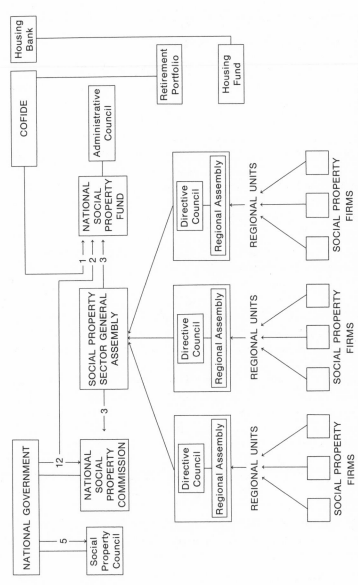

Organization of the Peruvian social property sector; arrows indicate delegation of power and numerals indicate number of persons delegated as representatives.

3 | The Yugoslav Economy Viewed through the Theory of Labor Management*

In the days of Marx, the major problem was the liberation of the working man from the capitalist. The contribution of Yugoslavia to socialism is the liberation of the working man from the state. But socialist labor-management cannot assume the position of the leading world system, which belongs to it, until it liberates the working man from himself as a collective capitalist.

Preliminary Considerations

This study is the outgrowth of a set of notes which I prepared for a meeting with the Association of Yugoslav Economists in March 1972 in Belgrade. The meeting's primary purpose was to use the theory of labor-managed market economies in analyzing economic problems in Yugoslavia. As usually happens, the meeting did not cover as much ground as one would hope and my notes remained largely unexploited. I felt that this was a pity, assuming that both the theoretical analysis and my observations bearing on Yugoslavia could be of use to the economic profession, and therefore I most willingly responded to a request from the Zagreb and Slovenian Economic Institutes to put my observations into writing.

The final result contained eleven sections, each dealing with a specific problem or aspect of the Yugoslav economy. Three sections have been omitted here as less directly relevant to an English-speaking audience.

All eight divisions follow the same pattern. Starting with theoretical conditions for various types of efficiency, we proceed to the

* This paper appeared in *World Development*, vol. 1, no. 9 (September 1973). I should like to acknowledge the invaluable contribution of Tom Bayard of the Cornell Department of Economics, who helped with the final editing of this study.

theoretical significance of these conditions, the degree to which these ideal conditions are fulfilled in Yugoslavia, and finally to suggestions for alternative or remedial policies.

The entire analysis is founded on the basic behavioral postulate that each labor-managed firm attempts to maximize the social utility or satisfaction of its working collective by acting on a number of variables or objectives. However, the firm's key objective is to maximize total net income after taxes for *each* member of the collective, given a predetermined income distribution schedule, its resources and market conditions.

There is nothing extraordinary about the assumption. It has been made by many others, and it resembles similar assumptions of still other economists. For example, Professor Korac [5] postulates as an objective the maximization of income per unit of labor, as we do, but he takes labor as directly used as well as embodied in capital goods. We feel it is more natural for a working collective to extract from its resources as much current net income as possible for each member, regardless of how much embodied labor in capital it actually uses. The effect of capital on the production decision will be felt only to the extent that the working collective must fulfill some cost- or debt-service obligations connected with the use of its capital.

We depart from Professors Ward [14] and Domar [1], who also assume the maximization of income per worker, in one important respect. We assume that maximization applies to *all* in the collective, not only for those who, in a dynamic situation, would be remaining members, having thrown out of work others whose incomes might be minimized, but this will not have great significance for the present study.

Yugoslav readers may find my report too critical. I simply want to note here that my attitude toward Yugoslav self-management is as positive as can be. Not only would I want self-management, as the most humane form of economic organization, to become the rule everywhere in the world, but I am also convinced and I feel that I can demonstrate [8] that it will happen one day, even if most of us will not live to see it.

If I am critical, it is because I am convinced that the contemporary form of self-management in Yugoslavia is not optimal, either economically or humanly, and I believe that precise economic analysis can contribute to its improvement.

If this study can be at all useful, it must first serve as a basis for a wide, critical discussion by both policy makers and economists. If I am wrong on any points, they can be argued. By contrast, if at least some of my arguments cannot be refuted, then they should be given serious consideration. The Yugoslav economy would benefit from it a great deal. More important, so would the dozens of less developed countries who look upon Yugoslavia as a model for developing a viable and humane system, superior to the two major world systems which they so distrust.

I. Efficient Resource Allocation within the Labor-Managed Firm

I.1. *The conditions of efficiency and other postulates*

In addition to the general behavioral postulates in the introduction, we postulate here that a labor-managed firm in its typical realistic form produces under conditions of increasing returns to scale up to a certain scale of operation, and thereafter its returns are constant or diminishing. In addition, at least in the long run, some degree of substitutability among factors of production (i.e., labor, capital, land, raw materials, fuels and semifinished products) is possible.

Given these conditions and also those presented in the introduction, the labor-managed firm will—or in a realistic context will over time tend to—allocate resources efficiently provided that the following conditions are satisfied (the precise meaning of efficient allocation is presented in Section I.2.).

The firm must be a price-taker in all markets in which it operates, that is, in all markets in which it sells its products and in markets in which it buys *all* its nonlabor factors of production, including capital. By price-taking, we understand that the firm cannot affect such prices, being too small a seller or buyer with respect to the size of the market as a whole.

It is not difficult to understand the meaning of these conditions. They postulate perfectly competitive markets, or artificial generation of such conditions through price controls, or price ceilings as practiced in Yugoslavia. Some difficulty of interpretation arises with respect to capital, and also some additional postulates must be made with respect to that factor in order to obtain efficient allocation of all resources within the labor-managed firm.

First, it will be noted that capital, in the broad sense of the expression, includes both the physical assets (plant, equipment, and so on), and their financial counterpart—whether a debt to an external lender, or an "ownership" collective, social, or other. One way to avoid this duality in stipulating our optimal conditions would be to assume that the labor-managed firm could lease its productive assets at a constant price as any other current input. That price would then 'contain' both a certain interest cost and amortization (or use-up) cost of the asset.

Since in the overwhelming majority of cases capital assets are not leased by firms on a current basis, we must contend with this fact and state our optimal conditions for capital accordingly. The first requirement is that the labor-managed firm have access to a financial capital market in which it can borrow and in which it or its individual members can lend (save) at a constant single rate of interest (except perhaps for a small margin between lending and borrowing rates to cover risk and operating costs). In addition, to prevent the lender from exercising any control upon the borrowing firm, the firm must have the unalienable right to refinance a loan upon maturity at conditions then prevailing in the market *as long as* it has fulfilled all its debt-service obligations, whatever they may be.

The debt-service obligations in the case of financing of inventories or working capital[1] would normally be payment of interest on an outstanding debt, adjustable from period to period (e.g., ninety days) according to conditions of the short-term capital market. In the case of fixed assets, plant and equipment, the debt service should contain debt retirement (repayment) over a period as truthfully as possible reflecting the useful life of the assets, and interest on debt. The total payment of interest and repayment should as much as possible constitute a constant charge for the labor-managed firm. In some cases a constant annuity (e.g., ten annual installments of 142 dinars on a total loan of 1,000 dinars repayable over ten years) would be desirable. In other situations, with obsolescence, and increasing

1. It is imperative to establish legal upper limits on working capital and inventories which can be financed through external credit in order to prevent unconstrained distribution of income based on goods produced and not sold.

repair and maintenance costs, heavier debt-service charges in early years may be preferable with, for example, repayment in equal installments, and interest payment only on debt outstanding.

A very important requirement in connection with debt repayment is that such repayment be made from depreciation funds of the firm, so that no collective ownership of the working community would accumulate over time. Such accumulation will always occur if repayment of debt is performed (mandatorily or because this is required by the working of the capital market) out of current income of the firm, and depreciation allowances are used to finance new expansions of plant and equipment. Of course, the stipulation of obligatory refinancing of debt on the part of the lender is of cardinal importance here, because without it the firms would always tend to seek the "security" of collective ownership.[2]

In fact, the security of the labor-managed firm must be even greater than that. It must have access to new capital at the prevailing market rate of interest (which in Yugoslavia might be quite high) provided only that its project evaluation shows a sufficient return and provided that it is found correctly prepared by an impartial committee of experts.

Also of great importance here is product-price stability, because without it *real* interest costs become widely different from *nominal* costs and many difficulties can arise. Some of these can be corrected by "escalation coefficients" attached to debt-service contracts, but price stability is always preferable. As we will note later, this is one of the many *serious* reasons for seeking price stability in Yugoslavia, even at the cost of temporary price ceilings.

I.2. *Significance of efficiency conditions for the operation of the labor-managed firm*

Given the general conditions presented in the introduction and those of the preceding section, the labormanaged firm will over time tend to produce most efficiently in the sense that (*a*) it will use such amounts of all factors (including labor) as to equalize the remuneration of the factor per unit to the productive contribution of the last unit of that factor employed; and (*b*) it will maximize the average

---

2. Note here that insurance against adverse market conditions and declines in incomes can be sought through reserve funds (voluntary or mandatory), or through economy-wide insurance schemes.

factor productivities of all productive factors (including labor) *for* the factor proportions it effectively selects, i.e., it will reach the most efficient scale of operation.

While the desirability or efficacy of result (*b*) is easy to understand, result (*a*) deserves additional elaboration. Realizing that productivity of any single factor (labor or nonlabor) is diminishing as the amount of that factor used is increased, with all other factor inputs held constant, result (*a*) guarantees a maximum contribution of the particular factor, given the specific productive process of the specific labor-managed firm, and given its scale of operation, to the total national product of the economy. Note that if result (*a*) were not attained, the national product could always be augmented by using an additional unit of input (say, a ton of fuel worth 1,000 dinars) to produce additional output worth more than the corresponding cost (e.g., 1,200 dinars worth of output), thereby increasing the net product of the firm and that of the economy by the difference (in our example, $1,200 - 1,000 = 200$ dinars).

Now it remains to be explained *why* the conditions set out in the introduction combined with those given in Section I.1. lead to results (*a*) and (*b*). The rigorous proofs of the deductions are given elsewhere. Here we will restrict ourselves only to an intuitive exposition.

Result (*a*) is obtained from the motivating principle of maximization of income per worker, given the income-distribution rules (or income-distribution schedule) agreed on democratically by the working collective. If (*a*) were not to hold, using more or less of a factor (including any kind of labor) would increase the income of each and every member of the collective. For example, suppose that the productivity of an additional bus operator, measured in dinars, in a transportation firm is 100,000 dinars while, given the income-distribution schedule (between ticket collectors, maintenance men, director, and so on) and the market conditions faced by the collective, the current income of the bus operator is only 50,000 dinars.[3] Then bringing one new bus operator into the collective will generate a net surplus of 50,000 dinars. That amount can be distributed—according to the income-distribution schedule—to all the old members of the collective, while paying an increased income to the new members.

---

3. This figure is assumed to contain both take-home pay and collective consumption, and possibly tax obligations per man.

And thus the nonfulfillment of result (*a*) contradicts the maximization objective, and its fulfillment, by implication, is consistent with the objective of maximization of income per worker.

Let us now turn to result (*b*), that is, the efficient scale of operation of the labor-managed firm. Two independent conditions stated in Section I.1 are necessary for this result. First is the condition of a constant selling price, independent (at least approximately in the real world) of the volume of sales.[4] Second is the condition of obtaining capital *externally*, also at a constant price (i.e., interest and repayment conditions largely unrelated to the size of the investment). We will consider the two in turn, again restricting ourselves to common-sense arguments.

The necessity of a constant selling price for an efficient scale of operation is easy to comprehend. We only have to note that if prices were declining with the volume of sales (i.e., if there is a downward-sloping demand curve), the labor-managed firm, producing at the most efficient scale (where its total factor productivity is maximized), could always increase the value of its output per unit of inputs (i.e., per unit of all inputs combined in constant proportions) by restricting output somewhat. Indeed, such a restriction would increase price, i.e., revenue per unit of sales, and this, with unchanged inputs per unit of sales, would increase income per worker. Consequently, the equilibrium level of operation of a labor-managed firm possessing monopoly power must fall below the efficient scale of operation. By implication, if prices cannot be affected by restricting output and sales, the efficient scale of operation will necessarily be reached. It is of great importance to realize that by imposing price ceilings this salutary condition is produced artificially and, as we will argue in the subsequent two sections, can also have positive effects on the level of output and growth of industrial production.

The second condition is perhaps more difficult to explain, and for a truly complete explanation the reader should refer to the References, especially my paper "The Basic Theory of Financing of Participatory Firms" [11]. But to give the essence of the argument, consider a labor-managed firm which must entirely rely on its own collective funding of investments from its income. That firm, at any

---

4. Of course, the condition can be obtained by perfect competition or price controls or ceilings.

level of capital accumulation, will try to maximize labor productivity (i.e., the average value-added product of labor). And it is known that on any production function subject to increasing and then constant returns to scale, the point of maximum labor productivity for any given level of capital stock is well below the point of efficient scale of operation. At the point of maximum the marginal and average productivities of labor are equal, and thus, with a positive marginal productivity of capital, output per unit of both inputs can be increased by increasing employment of both capital and labor in constant proportions. What follows is that the point of maximum labor productivity is found in the zone of increasing returns to scale, below the efficient level of operation.

If the workers are perfectly free to decide on accumulation from income, this inefficiency of self-financing will generally be further compounded by the fact that for a given workers' income time preference (say 20 per cent) the necessary productivity of investment that would induce them to save and accumulate must be well above that figure (say, 50 per cent). This is because the worker, saving collectively, can basically hope only for returns in the form of increased current income, and not in the form of recuperating his savings at a later date, as he would, for example, by saving at a local savings bank.[5] Thus, the collectively self-financed labor-managed firm will tend to be not only too small with respect to an efficient scale, but also, if workers are truly free to decide on investment, undercapitalized. Of course, in some realistic situations, where for example firms are called on to accumulate 25 per cent of income (e.g., see [4], the Social Agreement of Serbia, signed December 31, 1971) just the opposite can happen, and the firms may turn out to be overcapitalized. But we will return to these questions in Section I.3.

I.3. *The degree of fulfillment of efficiency conditions in Yugoslavia*

While the propositions and deductions of the preceding two sections are solidly based on exact economic theory, we are now moving onto softer ground, where observation and judgment also play an important role. Also, the writer could observe Yugoslavia's economy—even if over many years—only from the outside, and had a

---

5. The recent Amendments to the Constitution of Yugoslavia attempt to tackle this problem in a partial and, in the mind of this writer, most unsatisfactory manner.

direct exposure to Yugoslavia's economic problems only in the past four months.

We may begin our discussion with what I consider the brighter picture of the internal resource allocation of Yugoslav firms: It is the conditions in markets for goods whether those of finished products sold to consumers or investors, or of intermediate goods sold for further processing. Given market structures, given competition from international markets, and given the practice of price controls and price ceilings as we know them in Yugoslavia, our condition of price-taking—i.e., at least approximate independence of volume of transaction from price—is fairly well satisfied, and the imperfections on this level, in the view of this writer, are not serious.

Partial (not logically and statistically fully conclusive) evidence is offered in our analysis [9] where no statistically significant impact of market structures in Yugoslav industries was found on the formation of incomes per worker. Moreover, the practice of registering price changes and the practice of price freezes go a long way to produce artificially the constancy of prices needed for internal efficiency of the firm.

As a highly tentative—yet very significant—hypothesis, I would argue that price controls such as the price freeze of 1972 have a most salutary effect on industrial production and consequently on the development of the country. The very satisfactory (and perhaps unexpected) advance of industrial production in the first quarter of 1972 was perhaps attributable to these forces. The argument is simple: An effective[6] price ceiling conduces firms to expand output from production points below an efficient scale to ones closer to or at such an efficient scale. In that context, the fact that the period 1958–63/4 in Yugoslavia was one of considerable price stability coupled with a high rate of industrial expansion should not be overlooked. As far as the present writer can ascertain, that price stability was heavily conditioned by price controls of various forms.

The theoretical argument for moving from an inefficient to an optimal production scale through price control (or price ceilings or price freeze) has a simple common-sense counterpart. A labor-managed firm with some degree of monopoly power can increase

6. By "effective," we mean a ceiling that sellers would like to break through if they could, but they are compelled not to do so.

incomes over time through both increases of prices and increases of sales. By contrast, with a price ceiling, it can do so only by increasing output in the long run and moving to a more efficient scale of operation.

Thus we have two significant cases in Yugoslavia for price stability, through price controls if necessary. First, such stability brings order to the structure of real and nominal interest rates. Second, it "makes the monopolies and oligopolies behave."

We shall now turn to the second major aspect, efficient *internal* resource allocation within Yugoslav labor-managed firms, which, in my view, is far less satisfactory. In fact, it constitutes one of the two weakest aspects of the Yugoslav economy.

We recall that an optimal (or ideal) situation would require that the use of the totality of the current value (*sadasna vrednost*)[7] of the assets of productive organizations in Yugoslavia be effectively paid for by these organizations at some rate reflecting the scarcity of capital in Yugoslavia, perhaps as much as 15 per cent. This figure is consistent with a study by Jovicic and Vanek [9] and with other empirical results for Yugoslavia. The interest payments actually made by Yugoslav industries are only a very small fraction of that amount, and the situation is rendered even more acute in view of the continuously depreciating value of money through inflation, on which account the nominal payments should be far in excess of the 15 per cent real return.

The situation is primarily the result of collective self-financing, partly voluntary, partly induced by moral suasion, and the Social Agreements [4]. With self-financing, of course, the product and income of capital (i.e., of embodied labor, in Marxist terminology) is transformed, in major part, into rents accruing to those currently employed in the Yugoslav labor-managed industries.

Not only does this lead to unequal distribution of incomes, because the rents can vary a good deal from industry to industry (see [9]) and from firm to firm, but also the subjectively low cost of capital is bound to produce, for those who have capital (i.e., existing firms), unnaturally high capital-labor ratios. This implies low employment capacity of existing firms, and scant hope of creating new firms to

7. Henceforth we will use the term "current value" for *sadasna vrednost*, which is defined as the real value of productive assets after depreciation.

employ those unemployed at home or those migrating *en masse* to West Germany and elsewhere.[8]

The unfortunate effect of incorrect capital intensities is often further accentuated in "second" and "further rounds" by policies which are designed to prevent inequality of personal incomes among firms. For example, in the Social Agreement of Serbia (see Korac [5]) those with high incomes must accumulate more, there being no economic force to control the capital intensity of such accumulations; rich firms can thus acquire the most labor-saving (automated) equipment which will greatly increase the productivity and incomes of those employed without giving much employment to others. In turn, the higher incomes, through such arrangments as the Social Agreement of Serbia, will lead to even higher and more capital-intensive accumulations,[9] and thus in a never-ending cumulative process the rich enterprises will grow richer, the poor ones and the unemployed will be left behind. In addition, for the reasons explained in the preceding section, heavy reliance on self-financing will tend to leave existing firms at a comparatively inefficient *scale* of operation, falling short of the most efficient scale.

The movement toward mergers which we have observed in Yugoslavia in the last five years or so is also symptomatic of this problem. Two, three, or more firms in the same or related fields may be operating at a less than efficient scale for the reasons given earlier (self-financing and perhaps monopolistic tendencies). To overcome such inefficiency they merge, hoping to grow thereby to an efficient scale, which they may reach or approach, but because most or all of their capital is collectively financed, important capital rents accrue to those employed. And with such rents, there will definitely be resistance to the employment of new workers, with whom such rents would then be shared; on the contrary, there may be a tendency to further increase capital intensity either by accumulation with the same membership, or through reductions of membership. Again, under such conditions, to recall òne or two million workers from western Europe or to employ the domestic unemployed may not be a simple task.

8. We will return to this again in Section III.

9. In the process the maximum permissible income—some 200 per cent of the industry average—may be reached, and this will not only accentuate the cumulative process but can also have disastrous effects on labor incentives and the very spirit of self-management.

In the opinion of this writer, self-financing and the overall treatment of the problem of enlarged reproduction may also generate certain almost schizophrenic frictions within the self-management process. Suppose that a firm finds itself at a significantly less than efficient level of operation. The technical director and the general manager will see this and try to expand through significant allocations to funds (*fondove*) and reductions (or insufficient increases) of personal incomes. (This author was told that such situations are frequent in many firms deemed successful—e.g., the television and electronics firm in Nis.) But the workers, more interested in their personal and immediate incomes,[10] may oppose such expansion. If, however, the directors, supported by policy makers and public opinion, prevail, the expansion may cause a good deal of resentment and loss of faith in self-management. It is important to note that were all investment funds obtainable from sources external to the firm, even at a high cost, the movement to the most efficient scale of operation would be a natural result of economic forces, desired by the entire collective, workers and directors alike, and no schizophrenic tendencies or loss of faith in self-managment could arise.

I.4. *Policy recommendations to improve internal resource allocation in Yugoslavia*

First, a few introductory remarks. The remedial action suggested in this section is directly linked to the problem of internal resource allocation of labor-managed firms, which is the subject of Section I. However, the policies recommended should always be viewed as part of a global revision and improvement of the entire system and, if undertaken, should be implemented after careful preparation (perhaps of several years), critical discussion among policy makers and scientists, and formation of a general consensus. It is also this global character that will not allow us here to enunciate in detail all the aspects of remedial policy belonging to Section I, because some of these aspects derive from and are also an integral part of questions and conditions discussed elsewhere.

10. These interests were quite clearly demonstrated by a highly qualified worker from Sarajevo (a member of the Party Central Committee who attended the Second Party Congress in Belgrade in early 1972) in an interview on Belgrade television on March 9, 1972; he noted that workers, especially those who still make 60,000 old dinars and less, are after all primarily interested in increasing their current incomes.

Price stability and price-taking (as explained in Section I.1) are of enormous value to the economy, for the two reasons given here and for a number of other reasons. Therefore such stability and such reproduction of competitive conditions should be brought about, in the short and intermediate run (perhaps up to 5 to 10 years), through price controls, ceilings, and freezes. But this must be done in a very careful and scientific manner. The price freeze of 1972 was only an initial step in that direction.

In what I call here a "scientific manner" two major problems must be contended with. First, there is a global, or aggregative problem, related to problems of overall monetary policy and conditions of foreign trade relations. Second, there is the structural problem, in the sense that relative prices and values must change over time; this belongs more to the sphere of overall indicative planning and steering of the economy in a structurally efficient manner. To the first problem we will turn more carefully in Section VII, and to the second in Sections II and VIII.

I am not advocating here perpetual price controls. Eventually Yugoslavia should be able to have a perfectly free market mechanism, with competitive price-taking and very little monopoly power—both of which are required for the internal efficiency of resource allocation. But this will require time and a good deal of learning about the precise functioning of the economic system before we can get there. The price elasticities in the labor-managed economy on the whole are low and this implies that minor disturbances (whether autonomous or policy-induced) can generate wide price fluctuations under free market conditions; but these must be avoided if a secure and well-functioning economy is to be achieved in which firms, households, and society as a whole can plan their future with calm and security.

The question of correct structural price formation is also linked to, and cannot be resolved without also resolving, the other graver problem of correct pricing of capital and external financing. We will now turn to that problem, and to its relation to the price problem.

If we could start *de novo* without worrying about history—i.e., about policies and actions taken in the past—the ideal situation would require that the totality of the real capital assets (fixed assets and inventories of all kinds) of productive organizations be financed from external sources at some scarcity-reflecting real rate of interest, perhaps 12 or 15 per cent, and that funding of assets be repaid from depreciation allowances and not from income. It is toward such a situation that Yugoslavia ought to move over a long period of time, if it wants to attain a truly efficient and economically democratic state.

The ideal situation by no means implies coercion of labor-managed collectives to finance externally—they would always re-remain free to finance collectively through their own savings. But it is obvious that with approximately equal borrowing and lending rates in the capital market (say, our 12 or 15 per cent) and assurance that at these rates funds could always be obtained[11] and that any loan upon repayment (and upon scrapping of the depreciating asset) could be refinanced, no working collectives would ever want to finance collectively from their own income. If they wanted to save, they could and would do so individually at the high returns noted above—and such savings would then only further increase national capital formation over and above the accumulation based on depreciation and interest on the socially-owned national capital stock (we will turn to problems of global accumulation in Section VI).[12]

Under ideal conditions, the effective price structure should be consistent with a price for capital which accurately reflects its scarcity value. We will return to this structural problem in Sections II and VIII.

But it is time to turn from the "ideal" world to the historically conditioned state in which the economy of Yugoslavia must operate today. It would be possible, even if very difficult, to levy a capital-scarcity-reflecting tax of some 12 to 15 per cent on all current value of capital, and to make all interest payments to banks on loans for financing these assets deductible from the total tax liability. The

---

11. The lending agency or bank, at such high rates, could only question the correctness of the project evaluation, but could never refuse a loan at the (market-clearing) rate.

12. Some Yugoslavs argue that this might lead to a new rentier class living on such high interest returns. My reply is that once we are sure about the honesty and integrity of a man's income, he should be perfectly free to sonsume it or save it. It is another matter that very high (perhaps confiscatory) inheritance taxes should be introduced—without which the rentier class could develop over time even in present-day Yugoslavia. Also, it should not be forgotten that many incomes in today's enterprises are rents derived from accumulation, often accumulation performed by others than those earning these rents.

total amount of such taxes would be earmarked for further lending at 12 to 15 per cent to productive organizations for investment and subsequent repayment under the "ideal regime." All depreciation allowances on existing capital should also be tapped for the national (or regional or republican) investment fund. Over time the importance of the tax would be diminishing in total accumulation, and that of the new ideal regime increasing—and thus, eventually one would disappear and the other take over.

Of course, the productive organizations would have to be instructed that they are no longer expected to accumulate from their own income.[13] The entire net income after taxes would be at their current disposal for personal and collective consumption. For many—perhaps most—labor-managed organizations this would represent an improvement in current income, and the adoption of the new system would be easy. In other instances immediate adoption might cause a net loss to workers. In such instances a gradual transition could be envisaged, reaching full implementation only after a few years. The gradual transition might imply more favorable price setting, or temporarily reduced tax rates on capital.

II. The Structural Efficiency of Resource Allocation among Existing Labor-Managed Firms

II.1. *The efficient conditions*

So far we have examined the conditions for the optimum utilization of productive resources within a single labor-managed firm. We now take the logical further step and examine the problem of the efficient allocation of resources among labor-managed firms and industries. We shall leave aside and reserve for Section III the problem of the full utilization of resources—especially the full employment of labor resources—and shall consider here only the conditions for existing firms and industries to produce the maximum output from the resources which they actually have at their disposal.

To allocate existing resources efficiently among existing firms and industries two conditions must hold. First, it is necessary that the same prices be charged to all producers (users) for the same nonlabor

---

13. All worthwhile investments being fundable through borrowing from a social fund.

productive factors, be they capital, fuels, raw materials, semifinished products or any other, and also that the remuneration of labor (i.e., of the free producers) be identical for work of identical type, intensity, and qualification. The second condition is the absence of monopolistic or monopsonistic tendencies, that is, as in Section I, price-taking by all labor-managed firms.

It is interesting to note here that the first condition, in respect to the human factor, necessary for the efficient allocation of all resources also guarantees—because of its requirement of equality—distributional efficiency, which has been so much on the minds of Yugoslav policy makers in recent years.

II.2. *Significance of the structural efficiency conditions*

It was not difficult to state the structural efficiency conditions and to explain their efficiency implications. The second condition, as we saw in Section I, guarantees that each individual labor-managed firm, in the microeconomic sense, will (or will tend to) produce most efficiently. The first condition, in turn, assuming that the second holds, guarantees that all the firms and industries taken together will maximize national product.

To see this we have only to recall that, if each firm exhibits a rational maximizing behavior, the remuneration of any factor, including labor, per unit of that factor must equal the productivity of the last unit of that factor employed. And thus, if all firms pay the same price for a given productive factor, their respective productivities of the last unit employed in various firms and industries must also be the same. It is this equality that guarantees the most efficient structural allocation of resources. Note that, if productivities of the last units of factors employed were different in different labor-managed firms, the reallocation of one unit of a factor from a low- to a high-productivity firm (or sector) could always increase the total national product.

For example, if a ton of fuel contributed 100 new dinars to output in one firm and 200 in another, reallocation of that ton of fuel from the first to the second firm would add 100 new dinars to national product (i.e., 200 − 100 new dinars).

By implication, it is only when the productivities of last units of factors employed are identical (in our example, say 150 new dinars for a ton of fuel) that reallocation of factors can no longer increase national product from existing resources at the disposal of labor-managed firms. Consequently, when such an equalization—guaranteed by competitive markets and equal factor prices for all—occurs, the national product from resources available to firms will be at a maximum.

II.3. *The degree of realization of structural efficiency in Yugoslavia*

We now turn again to the real world, specifically, to the economy of Yugoslavia. We can again begin with the brighter side of the picture. It concerns raw materials and intermediate products, semi-finished goods, fuels, and the like. In this area—whose consideration may have been one of the dominant historical motives for Yugoslavia's adopting a market economy—conditions may be considered satisfactory, even if perhaps not perfect. Monopolistic tendencies are not strong and price controls and price ceilings and freezes, if anything, tend to induce both price-taking and equalization of prices among users. We do not have to detain ourselves here, as more analysis and comment is called for in the other, far less satisfactory, area.

That area involves what we usually refer to as primary factors of production—labor (the free producers themselves), capital or embodied labor, and in a sense also natural resources, whether renewable (such as farm land) or nonrenewable (such as mines).

In connection with the labor factor, the structural allocative inefficiency has been in the newspaper headlines for some time in Yugoslavia, but in a distributive rather than allocative context. Incomes, often for identical skills and qualifications, were found to differ widely among firms, professions, and industries. To this writer, by and large, this is not surprising, but is rather a natural consequence of the overall legal and institutional environment, investment practices, and a comparative lack of overall economic planning and orientation. The unhappy thing appears to be that measures taken to remedy the problems of income distribution will not improve the allocative problem, and sometimes may even worsen it.

This writer and Jovicic [9] have found wide differences in incomes for unskilled workers among Yugoslav industries. And there is no doubt that such differences, or even larger ones, exist among individual firms. These differences imply an inefficient allocation of those employed in the economy. As in our example with a ton of fuel, the reallocation of labor from low- to high-productivity and high-income sections would certainly increase national product.

Of course, some of these income differentials are the result of imputed rents of capital and natural resources contained in labor incomes,[14] but this does not alter our basic proposition: Wide inequalities, whatever their reason, always imply structural inefficiency. In fact, the greater the rent, *ceteris paribus*, the more restrictive its effect on unemployment, and the higher will be the productivity of the last unit of labor employed.

The condition with respect to capital is no more satisfactory in Yugoslavia than that with respect to labor. The form of actual financing of productive investments in Yugoslavia, the comparative slimness of the capital market, the rather arbitrary limits on interest rates, and, more recently, some of the Social Agreements, all combine into a complicated situation, which, if it may resolve some other problems (especially those of income distribution), certainly does not contribute to structural efficiency, i.e., to the equalization of capital costs and capital productivities of the last units of capital employed among firms and industries.

The first important element of our analysis is that under self-financing (i.e., the funding of investments by firms out of their own incomes) the equilibrium productivity of capital to which the collective will want to go will heavily depend on the time preferences of the members of the working collective. These may be quite different among firms. Moreover, the average age of the members of the working collective will also play an important role. Considering that by and large the greater part of collective savings cannot be recovered by the individuals who have contributed to those savings, the willingness to invest by collectives will depend on the number of years that they can benefit from a given investment; and this in turn will depend on the age of the workers. Of course, such conditions will vary from firm to firm, and thus the equality of productivities is not guaranteed. Also, the capital productivity that the workers will want to accept, for the same reasons of nonrecuperability of principal, will have to be far in excess of their time preference. This in itself is inefficient—but especially so in the context of the allocation of resources through time, between the present and the future.

14. We have found this quite conclusively in our study (see Vanek and Jovicic [9]).

Let us now turn to the second problem. For several reasons the allocation of net income in Yugoslav enterprises is not truly autonomous, but is influenced by moral suasion, Social Agreements, and so on. But even if we accepted these arrangements as a perfect expression of the free will of the working collective, the stipulation of a specific percentage allocated to accumulation and funds (e.g., see [4], p. 179)—however correct and meritorious its distributive intent—must lead to very bad allocative results.

If a collective is required by the formula to accumulate, say, 35 per cent of its income, the most normal reaction will be to do so in the most capital-intensive manner, if possible without employing any new members, by automating some existing processes and reallocating existing members. The inefficiency here, primarily, involves not employing those who are unemployed or in Germany or just entering the labor force. This will be our subject in Section III. But there is also a structural effect. The formula noted above in no way guarantees the equalization of productivities of capital on the margin. The formula homogenizes current personal incomes somewhat but has nothing to do with the productivity of capital among different firms.

Thirdly, there is the state of the capital market in Yugoslavia. For statutory and other reasons, effective real rates of interest (i.e., nominal rates minus inflation rates) are extraordinarily low, at times even negative. Under such conditions, and because the actual real marginal productivity of capital in the country is perhaps 15 per cent, there is an enormous excess demand for loanable funds, both short and long. The first (short-term demand) leads to the well-known problem of illiquidity, to which we will turn in Section VII. The second (long-term demand) is of interest to us here.

With tremendous excess demand, long-term credit must be rationed in a quantitative (nonprice) manner. It is here that favoritism, political "factories," and so forth arise. There is probably no mechanism for equalizing capital productivities among firms and industries.

A further factor is the legal requirement that labor-managed firms cannot reduce the total value of their capital assets (capital consumption), most of which they have collectively financed. But they can transform their assets gradually, through depreciation and replacement, into increasingly capital-intensive ones, with various and likely declining capital productivities. Again, in this process there is no mechanism that would even approximately equalize capital productivities among users.

Finally, in our nonexhaustive list of arguments, we may note also the structural inefficiency of capital allocation between productive sectors and housing serious allocative implications. Legal real rates (legal nominal minus inflation rates) on mortage (housing) funds are for the most part zero or negative in Yugoslavia. For those who receive such funds (often quite well-off people), this then is not only an outright present from society, but it will also make for a very inefficient structural allocation of capital.

II.4. *Policy recommendations to remedy the structural inefficiencies*

First, with respect to capital, in Section I we suggested a method of approximating external funding at a constant price. To this we now have to add only the structural requirement that such a method of funding be applied indiscriminately to all firms in the country. This requirement will guarantee that no reallocation of capital among *existing* labor-managed firms could increase the national product.

As we have argued, for intermediate goods and raw materials the situation is fairly satisfactory, and thus no special additional action is required, at least not with any special urgency. This leaves us with the allocation of labor among existing firms. The perfect conditions in the capital market, combined with such conditions for intermediate products and raw materials, are unfortunately insufficient to guarantee a structurally efficient allocation of labor throughout the economy. The objective here is again, as we have noted already, the equalization of incomes and productivities of labor of equal quality, qualification, and intensity among industries.

The inequalities can arise for three different reasons, or on three different levels. First, some firms may operate at a less efficient scale than others in the same industry. That problem can be eliminated by bringing all firms to the efficient scale of operation, as indicated in Section I.

The second possible reason is that incomes are different among industries, even after payment of an adequate price for capital, because of demand and price conditions in various industries, relatively high prices and incomes prevailing where demand is relatively high. This situation actually does exist in Yugoslavia, as established in my paper with M. Jovicic [9].

The only efficient way to deal with this situation is to stimulate the entry of new firms (or, if possible, the expansion of old ones) to satisfy the strong demand and reduce prices and incomes in the high-income industries. The natural forces for entry are present, because the incomes in the corresponding industries are high. It may be necessary only to provide institutional or planning assistance, and provide information to reduce the "viscosity" of flow of resources in the right direction. We will return to this in Section VIII. Here it may be useful to note that this is the only way simultaneously to reach distributively *and* allocatively efficient solutions. Controls of various kinds on personal incomes will generally help only the first of the two objectives.

The third and last cause of differences among labor-managed firms in the same industry are differences in technology (of course, other than those imputable to different effort, working spirit, or organization, all of which should be differentially remunerated). Such differences will always exist to a degree, and should be alleviated as far as possible through the spread of information and the proliferation of the most advanced technology among all the firms of the economy.

III. The Full Utilization of Resources and Full Employment

III.1. *The conditions of full employment*

The objective of maximization of income per worker by existing firms need not lead to the absorption of all those who desire employment. There is nothing inherent in the functioning of the existing labor-managed firms that would guarantee full employment.

Two conditions must be fulfilled to ensure that the labor-managed economy will operate at full employment. First, the effective price of *all* capital (as discussed and operationally defined in the preceding parts) must be high enough to reflect the relative scarcity of capital—and, by implication, to reflect the relative abundance of labor.

Second, those who are not currently employed, such as those entering the labor force, the unemployed, and in Yugoslavia those who have migrated to the West but who would prefer to stay at home, must be able to compete effectively for available capital, i.e., current and past accumulations of capital. This second condition, in practice, hinges again on social or governmental activity, broadly defined as indicative planning, and on a certain breadth and perfection of the capital market. As such, we will return to it in Section VIII.

III.2. *The effects of full-employment conditions*

We have shown, at least indirectly, in Sections I and II that too low an effective price of capital, often produced by internal collective financing, may lead to low employment of labor in any given existing firm. By implication, a correspondingly high price, effectively paid, will tend to increase employment.

The point is rigorously proven in two papers of mine, [10, 11]. Here only two simple arguments may suffice. The first is based on a *reductio ad absurdum* but is quite powerful in making the point. Suppose that a firm has 100 million new dinars of capital which, by Yugoslav law, it cannot consume. What that firm can do is gradually to retire its old workers, and hire no new ones, and with depreciation funds buy the most modern automated equipment, maximizing productivity per worker, but at the level of only two members of the collective—the director and the janitor. In fifty years these two men will have a factory of 100 million new dinars; both will be millionaires, but the employment effect will be dismal. Note that, if the director and janitor were to pay on the automated factory some 15 per cent and depreciation, their income might not suffice, and they might better employ, as they did at the outset, some 1,000 workers and produce a good deal more output.

The second argument is somewhat more precise. As in our former example, if a collective has a given amount of capital at its disposal, and has no effective price to pay for it, it will maximize productivity per worker and operate at the corresponding level of employment. By doing this, the income of each member of the collective will be as high as possible. Now suppose that a substantial price is to be paid for the same capital, and the collective still has the same amount of capital to operate with. It will now be in everybody's interest to exploit that capital more intensively by introducing more members into the collective, because, as long as the productivity of new members is still positive, they will help the old members pay for the cost of capital used by the whole collective. These forces, thus explained, may not be too powerful in the short run, but in the long run, where there is the possibility of factor substitution, these forces which stimulate employment are bound to be quite powerful.

Let us now turn to the second condition. Given existing labor-managed firms in the economy, it may be impossible to employ everybody, at any price of capital. This may be so because the number of existing firms is insufficient, and the forces of growth and expansion of these firms may not be sufficiently strong. Or, for reasons we have already spoken of in Sections I and II, the expansion may take too capital-intensive a form, and not offer sufficient employment opportunities. Under such conditions, the labor-managed economy must create new firms with economically meaningful factor proportions. In addition to providing employment, this will also have the salutary effect of improving market structures and reducing any monopolistic tendencies. Obviously, the economic forces for entry will be present, because those unemployed or those seeking employment will be willing to work at incomes approximately comparable to those of currently employed workers.

The condition of an effective and not too narrow capital market and external funding is again of paramount importance here. If all or most of the supply of loanable funds and accumulation is in the hands of existing firms, the unemployed or those who would want to return from western Europe may never obtain access to these funds. Moreover, existing firms may be reluctant to create new autonomous labor-managed firms, because they would have to do so, for the most part, from their own funds, and then lose control over such funds. If they retain control, by contrast, undesirable monopolistic tendencies may ensue.

On the other hand, if all loanable funds are externally supplied at a scarcity-reflecting price, those seeking employment will have a definite advantage in competing for them, because they live on very low incomes (compared to those employed) and thus certain loan conditions may be acceptable to them[15] which would not be acceptable to existing working collectives. Moreover, with sufficient external funds available, creation—or procreation—of independent new firms by old ones may become much more possible, based on the

15. In the sense of considerably improving their living standards.

human factor. Promising young cadres and workers of existing firms may go out, for a variety of reasons, and solicit funds to create new firms in fields in which they have technical and other experience and qualification.

The process of creating new firms or helping old ones to grow with external financing also provides an extremely powerful tool to the planning mechanism in steering the national economy over time in the most effective direction. But we will return to this in Section VIII.

III.3. *The conditions of full employment in Yugoslavia*

The employment situation in Yugoslavia, as well as the conditions which cause it, is not satisfactory. In fact, some may consider it the darkest aspect of the economy. Domestic unemployment is very high. It is alleged that there are well over one million Yugoslav workers in West Germany. The employment index (e.g., see the Yugoslav page of the IMF *International Financial Statistics*) has barely moved from its 1963 base, stagnated for several years, and is today, some nine years later, only at about 120; it was at no more than 110 only a few years ago.

In view of the fact that there was massive investment, at a gross rate of between 25 and 30 per cent of GNP every year, the capital stock of Yugoslavia may have grown by 150 per cent since 1963. That rate, in conjunction with the observed rate of employment in the same period, indicates that precisely what we have hypothesized on theoretical grounds has occurred. The new investments and expansions in Yugoslavia have been extremely labor-saving and capital-intensive. In a period of massive migration to Germany, unemployment, and a large residual traditional sector, this is an anomalous situation indeed.

If we add the less economic effects of massive migration on the Yugoslav family, children, village life, and the like, the picture appears, at least to this writer, even more deplorable. Certainly it is not worth the hundreds of millions of dollars sent or brought back by the migrants. The same workers, with a more sensible allocation of capital resources, could produce much more for Yugoslavia while at home. But, of course, there are no institutions or policies which could induce the utilization of migrating labor resources, or recall them. As far as this writer can tell, there is not even the necessary economic analysis and understanding of the problem, which would be the precondition of any remedial policy.

To sum up, neither of the two major conditions noted in Section III.1 is satisfied. The effective cost of capital is much too low (even if some short-term rates on some small fraction of total investment may appear high). Moreover, control over that capital, by and large, is with existing producers, either directly in the form of their investment funds or indirectly through their impact on policies of banks in which they are depositors.

Second, the situation regarding entry is equally dismal. Few new firms were created in the past five years in Yugoslavia. No serious consideration has been given either to regional location or to the industrial sector in which such new firms should be established.

There is also the problem of limited long-term credit, comparable in duration to the life of the capital assets, and widespread use of short-term credit for long-term investment. Nor is such a situation conducive to the capital expansion that would give employment to those left out of the economic life (whether at home or in Germany).

Finally, it must be remembered that the capital tax, which reflected at least in part a recognition of the nationwide scarcity of capital, was first reduced and then entirely abolished. It would require more careful study, but I wonder whether a hypothesis cannot be formulated to the effect that—for the reasons explained in Section III.2—the unsatisfactory employment situation in Yugoslavia coincides with the reduction and abolition of the capital tax.

III.4. *The policies for full employment*

Very little need be said here. The policies advocated in Sections I.4 and II.4 are also in essence capable of resolving the problem of employment in Yugoslavia. An adequate cost of *all* capital to existing and potential users, external funding, and a sensible market for new investment resources are imperative. Access to the investment funds market must be guaranteed, without discrimination, for all those actually in the economy and those outside it. The interests of the latter group must be promoted by appropriate social institutions.

Preferably such social institutions should be a part, or one aspect, of an effective planning agency, with wide research and information-disseminating functions, and with the power in the last resort to create firms where and when necessary. But we will return to this subject in Section VIII.

IV. Monopoly Power and Other Aspects of an Efficient Demand Structure

IV.1. *Conditions of demand efficiency*

Thus far we have spoken about the efficient allocation of resources on the supply, or production, side. While admittedly more important in Yugoslavia and in general, the production problem is not the only one in the context of resource allocation. Resources can just as well be misallocated on the demand side. More specifically, the economy can be producing in the most efficient manner, with full employment of all resources and at the frontier of its production possibilities, and yet real national product may not be at a maximum because of a disparity between marginal social costs and prices.

For example, the marginal social cost of heating in Belgrade or Zagreb relative to the social cost of apples may be 2:1 (two to one), but in the market the two exchange (for appropriately selected units of measurement) at the rate of 1:1 because the social cost of air pollution is not reflected in the market price (it is not, being an externality, cleared by the market). In that case, it would enormously increase the real national product if the volume of heating were restricted through an appropriate tax, or if the cost of compulsory afterburn cleaning were included in the relative price, and if apple production were increased relative to that of heating services.

Besides this case of various external economies and diseconomies of the type just illustrated, an important source of disparity between social costs and prices (or marginal costs and marginal utilities) is the presence of monopolistic tendencies in the product markets. We have already referred to this condition in Section I, where we stipulated the absence of such tendencies for the attainment of an efficient scale of operation of labor-managed firms. We now have to note only that this condition has also another salutary effect, namely, the avoidance of an inefficient demand structure.

IV.2. *The efficiency of demand structure in Yugoslavia*

The question of monopolistic tendencies need not detain us, since we commented on this subject in Section I, where we concluded that such tendencies are not overly pronounced and noted the benefits of price ceilings in that connection.

Perhaps an additional word on advertising and sales promotion, especially through the television media, is in order. Besides being costly in terms of resources which could be employed elsewhere, advertising activity has the effects of (*a*) lowering the elasticity of demand for a product (increasing potential monopoly power) and (*b*) increasing that demand. Yugoslav television and other advertising techniques will in most instances have these undesirable effects on the national demand structure. The effects could be quite detrimental to national welfare, especially where incomes are low, by diverting income from necessities like food or clothing to luxuries or even things which impair health, like cigarettes. It is shameful that cigarette commercials, which were banned for health reasons in the United States, are now "dumped" on the Yugoslav public.

But the evils of advertising developed in the West are deeper than that, and should therefore be avoided at any price in Yugoslavia. It has to do with what we may call the dehumanization of life and human relations. Once one can sell anything by means of the appropriate advertising techniques—even a president, in an advertiser-organized election campaign—something quite distinct has been taken out of life.

Also, it should not be forgotten that advertising was developed in an advanced depression-bound world where demand had to be created. In Yugoslavia, where there is enormous unsatisfied demand for material things as long as people can earn corresponding incomes, the need for creating demand through advertising disappears.

We can now turn to externalities, especially external diseconomies. They do exist in Yugoslavia to a considerable degree, and while perceived as a public evil, have not for the most part entered the stage of active prevention. Air and water pollution, especially the former in the largest Yugoslav cities, are quite serious and may have extreme effects on the health of the people.

But there are others, of a more subtle nature. They include, for one thing, high-pressure advertising, of which we have just spoken. Many would also agree with this writer that the pornographic magazines which abound on Yugoslav newsstands tend to overexcite the youth and loosen their moral standards. These should be heavily taxed or prohibited, because of the grave effects—not always measurable in economic terms—that they may have on the population. We also include under this rubric excessive importation of foreign licenses, trademarks, and capitalist management techniques. All of these may be undermining the nascent forms of Yugoslav economic self-determination.

V. The Problem of "Keynesian" Unemployment and the Business Cycle

V.1. *Theoretical considerations*

In the context of the Western market economies, the problems of business cycles and Keynesian unemployment occupy an important position. We wish to inquire here whether similar problems are likely to occur in a labor-managed economy, and specifically in the Yugoslav economy.

We may start by recalling that in the most fundamental and direct sense depressions are caused in the Western market economies by the interaction of a highly elastic short-run supply of national product (i.e., price-wage inflexibility in the downward direction) and autonomous short- or long-run shifts in demand, whether for investment goods or consumption goods.

In a labor-managed market economy based on the assumptions stated in the opening section[16] the first precondition of short-run depressions is absent: the supply function of national product is highly inelastic. The reasons are quite simple. For a capitalist, with union-fixed wages, the simplest way to face slackening demand is to fire workers and reduce output. For a labor-managed working collective, by contrast, the normal short-run reaction is not to fire anyone, but rather to stick out the hard years together and, perhaps after a few months of resistance, to reduce prices and try to sell all output in that way. There are no union-given rigid wages. There may be some potential downward price stickiness in Yugoslavia, and we will return to that problem later.

On the demand side there may be autonomous shifts, up and down, or accelerations and decelerations, in demand, as in the capitalist economy, but their specific nature will depend on the particular case. We will also turn to this later.

16. But even on a broad set of others, such as those of Korac [5].

The important theoretical conclusion is that, with a highly inelastic short-run supply curve, we will have much more of a general price problem and much less of a problem of cyclical depressions of the demand-oriented (Keynesian) type. Short-run variations in demand up or down will have strong price repercussions, and little, if any, quantitative effect on physical output and employment. The unemployment that can occur, as we have noted in Section III, is of an entirely different, long-run, nature.

While the immunity to true production cycles[17] is one of the great assets of the labor-managed economy, that asset is, in a sense, paid for by a high degree of price-nervousness, only too well known (in the upward direction) to the Yugoslavs. But, of course, one need not stress that the price is a low one. Also it must be realized that even a price-nervous economy can enjoy price stability or stable price trends even without price controls, provided that it is handled with great care, precision, and understanding. In concrete terms this means two things, both related to the demand side of national product: (*a*) stability or stable growth of consumer and investment demand, and (*b*) stability and very careful management of the short-term credit and money markets. The second matter will be our subject of discussion in Section VII, while the first is considered at least through its investment component, in Section VI.

V.2. *The situation in Yugoslavia*

What we have said in Section V.1 about the short-run macroeconomic functioning of a labor-managed economy is, by and large, borne out by the facts in Yugoslavia. Effectively, we do not have true up-and-down fluctuations in real national product or industrial production. Only once did an actual stagnation occur and in general we observe fluctuations (or cycles) in the rates of growth, a phenomenon explicable by long-range supply forces, and not by (Keynesian) demand fluctuations.

At the same time, also as predicted by the theory, the price and inflation problems are considerable. Indeed, there is a significant sensitivity of prices (on account of the very low short-run price elasticities) to various autonomous or policy-induced shocks.

---

17. Not, however, immunity to cycles in growth rates, which can, as we know from Yugoslavia, be present; but to these we will turn only in Section VI.

But in my judgment, no simple theory of price variations, such as have been offered by some Yugoslav economists, can be advanced, even if econometric correlations or leads and lags can be found. These statistical dependencies represent certain regularities of behavior of pairs of variables within a broad logical structure, not the true explanation of price movements.

What we can say is that in the rough long-run sense prices in Yugoslavia, if they were fully uncontrolled, would vary with the quantity of money, corrected for real expansions in output. In the more precise, shorter-run sense the picture is very complex indeed, and we may attempt to sketch it very briefly, leaving some further clarifications and elaborations for Sections VI and VII.

The short-run supply of output is highly inelastic and shifting over time to higher and higher outputs at rates conditioned by new capacity installations and other investments of the past one, two, or even three years. The forces of supply-change themselves are complex, depending on investment decisions of many previous periods. The demand side, on the other hand, is conditioned by shorter-run phenomena, such as current incomes, current demand for investment goods, and the foreign trade situation, all of which depend heavily on monetary and/or credit policy, incomes policy, and foreign exchange policy. It is the interaction of these supply forces going some years back and the demand forces which are more current—but very complex—that would determine the Yugoslav general price level, if prices were free.

But, of course, they are not free. At various times, with various intensities, prices are controlled, the current price freeze being only one extreme form of the whole spectrum of price policy in Yugoslavia. These price policies then further complicate the picture, or blur any comprehensive logical model that could fully explain price movements in Yugoslavia. Any empirical work attempting to explain price movements would have to take into consideration all the factors outlined here.

V.3. *Suggested courses of action in regard to prices in Yugoslavia*

A complex situation does not usually allow simple solutions, but some remarks are possible. First, one earlier recommendation must be recalled. Price ceilings, temporarily, are desirable. In the context of this part, these policies are desirable to prevent the confusion of planning uncertainties and distributional effects which would be bound to result in their absence. How they should be set in relation to other economic parameters we will be in a better position to discuss in Section VII.

Here it is only necessary to note that a price ceiling has nothing to do with price rigidity of the Keynesian type, which, as we noted in Section V.1, is conducive to Keynesian depressions. A price ceiling, on the contrary, if effective, indicates excess demand and boom, rather than depression conditions.

One realistic argument should be developed before concluding. Yugoslavia has come to its present organization from a fully-planned centrally-controlled form, in which prices were fixed over long periods. In the practice of Yugoslav firms, and also built into the institutional, legal, and accounting framework, some of this rigidity seems to have survived, *in the downward direction*. For some, it is "unthinkable" to reduce prices in the face of slackening demand. Rather, an extreme effort will be made to accumulate inventories, obtain credit or external noncredit support, and so on.

In an economy with some average rate of inflation, of course, scope for price reductions in particular fields is very small; most *relative* price adjustments can be performed without any price deductions. But this would no longer be so if, one day, Yugoslavia wanted to have truly free price determination and price stability, abandoning price controls of any kind. In preparation for such a day, the institutional, legal and accounting framework as well as the actual practice of labor-managed firms would have to be altered, to permit easier price reductions when and where necessary. Some measures might include the financing of unsold inventories at a high, truly economic interest cost, limitations on such credit, and a greater reluctance to bail out those overproducing at high prices. But even more important might be the instilling, through education, of a psychological ability and willingness to reduce prices promptly when necessary.

VI. Funding the Overall National Development Effort

VI.1. *The efficient conditions*

The natural, and, to this writer, ideal way to fund the national development effort, or to secure enlarged reproduction, is to do so on a national level in a manner that fulfills or is consistent with all the efficient conditions noted in this paper. In brief and in essence, the method is to require that all users of social productive capital assets (i.e., of embodied labor) *effectively* pay an economic price for that use on *all* assets into a social (i.e., national, republican, or regional) pool of funds. This pool must be used *exclusively* for investment (simple and enlarged reproduction), never for consumption. To the extent that the real assets being financed are long-run depreciable assets (plant, equipment, buildings constructions, and the like) the corresponding depreciation allowances (calculated as closely as possible with the life of the asset and length of the loan) are also to be deposited into the general funding pool, as repayments of the loan.

The lending agency (bank or other, discussed in Section VIII) has no right ever to recall a loan before maturity, or to refuse to refinance a loan upon retirement as long as debt-service obligations are met by the borrowers. In general the agency is only an administrator of the social funds pool, and loans from it *must* be extended to any existing or accredited entering new firm at the going nondiscriminatory and capital-market-clearing rate (which might be quite high in Yugoslavia, say 15 per cent *real*), as long as a committee of experts (an expert, in the case of smaller loans) representing the social pool (i.e., society) judges the application to be honestly and correctly prepared.

The lending rate is to be nondiscriminatory and equal for all within the labor-managed sector (hopefully the whole country). Differential lower rates can be granted only by power of the government for purposes of social subsidization (e.g., to less developed regions in Yugoslavia). The fund can also sell debentures to savings institutions at comparable prices (rates) of its own, and use the proceeds for enlargement of the social investment fund. Of course, this source would always remain marginal, and household savings could preferentially be channelled into consumer credit.

VI.2. *The efficiency implications of the arrangement*

The arrangement outlined in the preceding section is highly efficient, and, indeed, optimal on many accounts. First, there is the whole set of desirable effects which was our subject in Sections I, II, and III. Their significance cannot be overemphasized, and they will all be the direct result of the arrangement discussed in Section VI. In addition, we have the fact that all income from capital in existence when the financing arrangement is instituted can *only* be used for further investment, and income from that investment again only for investment, and so on. There is never any rentier (whether capitalist or worker) who would collect the income of that capital and consume it. Only on savings that a worker or employee makes from his own income can he earn—quite legitimately—a return for the productive contribution that his savings have made to society.

In addition, social capital becomes truly social, and is allocated for the greatest benefit of the whole society, not only, or primarily, for the benefit of those groups or collectives who happen to collectively own (in the usufruct sense) a good deal of it. Everybody has, under the arrangement we have advanced, equal access to the fruits of using the social capital.

The arrangement here advanced is also an indispensable pre-condition for an effective steering (planning) mechanism for the whole labor-managed economy. With objectivized capital costs, for example, labor incomes become meaningful indicators of economic planning.[18] In this context we will return to the matter in Section VIII.

Another important advantage is the stabilizing effect of the ar-rangement on the economy. Every year investment funds and the actual volume of capital formation are obtained as the total national capital stock—a steadily and regularly growing magnitude—times some highly stable cost coefficient, all of which, except the current interest rate, are also fixed by past loan contracts. This guarantees that investment itself will become—unlike in Yugoslavia—a steadily growing magnitude over time. And thus, looking at investment as the very motor of the development and growth of a country, our arrangement will also guarantee steady progress and development of the whole economy, not only its investment component.

Perhaps even more important than steadiness and stability is the actual growth potential itself. If we took an economically reasonable interest rate of capital of 12 to 15 per cent and assumed that the value of national assets that would be priced, including national resources, would be no more than 1.5 times the gross national product (this is a conservative estimate), we obtain an annual *net* investment rate of 18 to 22.5 per cent. With a realistic national depreciation rate of

18. In this respect, see my paper with Jovicic [9].

some 12 to 15 per cent, we obtain a gross investment potential of some 30 to 37.5 per cent, unsurpassed by any economy in the world.

The important point we want to make here is simply that the arrangement suggested certainly has the potential to support, and by a wide margin at that, even the most ambitious national development program, compared even with the socialist countries whose accumulation rates have traditionally been the highest in the world.

VI.3. *The situation in Yugoslavia*

We do not have to belabor the point that it is in the context of our present subject that the ideal form of the labor-managed economy differs most from actual Yugoslav practice. We have already noted this in Sections I, II, and III. In addition, all the major[19] advantages noted in Section VI.2 are not realized in Yugoslavia because of the use of heavy internal funding and a haphazard and slim actual market for loanable funds. Workers earn rents on capital accumulated by others and wield economic power based on such alienated capital; objective planning and steering of the economy is most difficult—and for that reason virtually nonexistent in Yugoslavia; investment and accumulation are high, but not as high as they could be, and they proceed at a highly variable rate, which in turn contributes to a variety of instabilities in the economy. As noted earlier, unemployment, structural misallocation of resources, and labor migration out of Yugoslavia are also caused by the absence of the optimal accumulation method.

In the honest and reasoned judgment of this writer based on some fourteen years of study of both Yugoslavia and the theory of its system, from 1960 to 1972 the country could have grown at twice the realized rate, with a far better unemployment, regional development, and income distribution record, with substantially the same rate of accumulation (enlarged reproduction) that it actually realized.

VI.4. *The policy recommendations*

I fully realize how difficult it would be to adopt the optimal system. But on the practical plane the social benefits involved are such that in my judgment that system ought to be adopted in Yugoslavia

19. There are many other minor ones; e.g., see my papers on external financing [10, 11].

upon careful, critical, and prolonged study by all concerned policy makers and economists, through a transitional arrangement of the type already suggested in Section I and further outlined in Section VIII. Of course, the existing banking system would have to be reformed and integrated with the social pool of loanable funds.

The advantages of the arrangement would be enormous. In addition to those noted already, we should also stress that income distribution would be made more equitable throughout Yugoslavia (see Vanek and Jovicic [9]).

The fact, already noted, that the arrangement would not reduce but would rather increase the freedom of action of the productive organizations cannot be overemphasized. Nobody would forbid them to finance collectively from their own income. They would be free—and without any doubt would actually prefer—to finance from external sources, and save individually, if at all, at comparable rates of return. The working collective would still be the first to decide whether or not to undertake an investment. Under the arrangement, only social responsibility would be exercised by experts external to the firm, in examining the project to ensure that it is economically sound and well designed. But the working collective would have full responsibility to carry out the agreed-on servicing of debt.

Finally, it must also be noted that ideologically—or philosophically—the arrangement is good and honest. The capital stock of Yugoslavia, i.e., the alienated embodied labor, is hopelessly untraceable to those individuals who have created it. The only correct statement is that all Yugoslavs have created all their capital and, consequently, the interests and rents from such capital should constitute a social pool of funds. Even better, returns on "untraceable" embodied labor will never go to any one individual or group for consumption, but always for the enlarged reproduction of the economy as a whole. Only exactly traceable savings of individuals will be rewarded at an economic rate, and these individuals will always have access to the full amount of their *personal* savings. It should be recalled that today workers *earn* and *consume* rents on alienated labor other than their own, and at the same time they save collectively funds which they cannot recuperate. Also, economic power in Yugoslavia today depends to a degree on the amount of capital that productive organizations have, and not merely on their human dimension. In this, these organizations can be very unequal; under the proposed arrangement, complete equality of opportunity is restored, and the human dimension becomes dominant.

VII. The Money and Short-Term Credit Markets

VII.1. *The optimal conditions and their effects*

There are some fundamental "rules of the game" with respect to short-term credit and money that the labor-managed economy must adhere to if it is to function efficiently. First, the duration of all credit should approximately match its purpose. Thus long-term investment projects—or housing projects—should be financed through loans ranging from, say, 5 to 30 years. On the other end of the spectrum, inventories, working capital, and especially commercial transactions should be financed through credit of short duration, mostly one month to one year.

Of course, comparative price stability, about which we have already spoken several times, is imperative here, and should be secured at any price, even price controls or ceilings for a time. Without it, as in Yugoslavia today, credit terms will tend to be shortened a good deal.

Another fundamental rule is that there be, as much as possible, true price- (i.e., rate-) rationing of credit, and in particular of short-term credit, whatever the equilibrium *real* rate may be. In other words, as much as possible, credit should be available to all who want to pay its price, and no one should be turned away from the source of credit who is willing to pay the going rate.

A third rule is that the market be as "deep" and as sizable as possible, all short-term credit-worthy purposes being financed through it. A slim market, where, as in Yugoslavia, many worthy purposes may not be served, is highly inefficient and can cause serious bottlenecks in the economy.

Fourth, as for long-term financing (discussed in Section VI), all returns on short-term credit should be earmarked for investment, preferably but not necessarily in the short- and shorter-term capital markets. This will secure indefinitely an adequate growth of the short-term credit base for the economy.

It must also be realized that it is the short-term credit market through which the central bank (or other appropriate authority) injects new money into the economy. This is done through extending short-term credit unmatched by an inflow of loanable funds into the economy. That money and credit creation should be strictly linked to the overall growth and overall price requirements of the economy and not to other objectives, such as the volume of investment of all kinds. For example, if the foreseen real rate of growth of the entire economy is 10 per cent and the acceptable inflation rate 5 per cent, monetary expansion should be 15 per cent per annum, and the rule should be very strictly adhered to.[20] If short-term credit and money creation is used for other targets, e.g., a given volume of national investment, the inflationary effects may be disastrous.

Still another fundamental rule is that all transactions, both in intermediate and finished products and in services, including payment of personal incomes to members of productive organizations, be performed in cash of the parties involved, or in cash using credit (discounts, rediscounts of commercial paper, overdrafts) at the going economically meaningful rate. If this is not adhered to, many anomalies (experienced in Yugoslavia) can develop, and the whole system can get, so to speak, out of joint. For example, an expansion of the monetary mass may not have the usual expansionary effects, or with no expansion of money, inflationary pressures can set in.

VII.2. *The conditions in Yugoslavia*

Again, it is the credit-market situation, this time that of short-term credit, that appears—to this writer, at least—to be in a dismal state in Yugoslavia. With high and variable inflation rates and legal ceilings on short-term credit rates, the whole situation gets out of joint. Real rates of interest can be zero or negative at times. Under such conditions there must be enormous excess demand for credit. That excess demand can be resolved only through discretionary and often favoristically-oriented rationing of credit. The well-known state of illiquidity is only one facet of this anomaly.

But things are worse. Short-term credit is used for long-term investment, because there is virtually no long-term credit. Why is there no long-term credit? Because there is no arrangement such as the one presented in Section VI. But with short-term credit used for long-term purposes, there is little short-term credit left for true short-term purposes, especially short-term commercial credit.

---

20. It may be interesting to note that, with a realistic velocity of circulation of money of 5, this new money-cum-credit creation gives the economy an extra 3 per cent of national product of investment funds, so to speak, free.

And this not only leads to crises of illiquidity but also handicaps trade, especially exports, because Yugoslav exporters cannot offer credit terms competitive with those of foreign (especially Western) competitors.

Another anomaly of low and often negative real interest rates is the desire of virtually every Yugoslav to have his money in Western currency deposits. Considering that in fact capital is scarcer in Yugoslavia than in the Western world, economically meaningful real rates of return on savings and other deposits should be higher here than abroad. And not only would this induce Yugoslavs to leave more of their funds at home, but eventually even foreigners might want to save (deposit) in Yugoslavia, without, as at present, at the same time importing their capitalist practices along with their investments, and thus "polluting" the Yugoslav economy.

VII.3. *Policy recommendations*

It is in the spirit of this whole study and of this section that significant changes are called for. They are for the most part contained implicitly or explicitly in the two preceding sections. Here I will only emphasize some points or make new ones.

As I show in my paper on macroeconomic policy [12], the short-term credit-cum-money market and the goods and services markets are interdependent in a single general equilibrium pattern. All the major variables are interconnected, and policies and economic actions must be harmonized. In particular, monetary and credit expansions will in turn expand demand for real goods and services, and unless these goods and services expand *pari passu* the credit expansions will be inflationary.

Thus the policies for all three spheres—money, short-term credit, and real goods and services—must be harmonized. The optimal strategy for the present in Yugoslavia would appear to be to control, or at least maintain, an elastic lid on the general price level, permitting, say, the nationally agreed-on limit of 5 per cent inflation for a 5 to 10 year period. At the same time the rate of credit and money creation should be adjusted to a realistic growth target for the economy.[21] The absolute level of the mass of money would have to be such at all times as to make the price ceiling just about effective;

---

21. Perhaps as high as 10 per cent. If the reforms here suggested were adopted, such a rate would be by no means unrealistic.

that is, to preserve some degree of excess demand in the real goods (and services) market, but not to overstrain these controls.[22]

With targets of 10 per cent of real growth and a 5 per cent acceptable inflation, the warranted monetary expansion rate would be some 15 per cent per annum. In fact the 5 per cent inflation would be consistent with even a significantly lower inflation rate in other market economies without further devaluations, because traditionally the competitiveness of a young growing economy like Yugoslavia is bound to increase *vis-à-vis* old economies, even with no change in relative prices.

If foreign inflation averages 5 per cent over the next 10 years or so, the domestic 5 per cent target would, for the same reason, permit Yugoslavia, without further devaluations, to grow gradually into the family of convertible currencies over that period. A quest for immediate convertibility would appear to this writer to be highly damaging and disruptive.

VIII. Steering the Economy

VIII.1. *The theoretical case*

While a labor-managed market economy's life does not depend absolutely on a planning mechanism as do the centrally-planned economies, in the absence of some indicative planning or "steering" (to be explained presently) it will be like a drunken man, barely making it through the street, stumbling, slowing down, and moving in every direction but forward. Some degree of steering is necessary in all market economies, and especially in a labor-managed market economy.

This greater need for intelligent steering of the labor-managed economy is inherent in three of the economy's key properties. First, the short-run elasticities of supply are low for economic sectors (not so much for individual products within a sector) because labor resources are slow to move from sector to sector and capital resources are also slow, even with a perfect capital market, because it takes time to complete new projects. Second, the mechanism in the labor-managed economy (as we have seen in Section III) that guarantees full employment of resources is heavily dependent on the possi-

22. Such overstraining—not unknown in Yugoslavia—will arise in situations where, if controls and ceiling were relaxed, prices would jump up in a few weeks or months by 10 or 20 per cent or more.

bility of creating new firms, and if spontaneous entry of firms does not occur for some reason, there must be some socially responsible mechanism—our steering mechanism—to promote such entry. Third, as we have also seen earlier, an efficient structure of the labor-managed economy presupposes equalization of labor incomes (among identical types of labor) and that equalization also, among sectors of activity, can be brought about only by comparative expansions of some sectors of the economy. If such expansions are not forthcoming spontaneously, there must again be some socially responsible agent to initiate them.

The other reasons for steering or planning in the labor-managed market economy are the same as those for any market economy and have to do primarily with obtaining and spreading the maximum amount of information over time (i.e., forecasting) and in space (i.e., among sectors and firms).

In summary, the tasks of a planning (steering) agency in a labor-managed economy must be:

(*a*) Intermediate-run forecasting (up to, say, five years), especially of sectoral demand trends, and disseminating such information to members of economic sectors and potential entrants.

(*b*) Studying and publishing trends of incomes as indicators of the comparable desirability of expansion in particular sectors (of course this presupposes a correct pricing of capital). In this connection see [11].

(*c*) Closely cooperating with those administering the capital market to see that the totality of (decentralized) investment projects is at least roughly consistent with overall sectoral forecasts. Organizing or participating in sectoral conferences of producers for purposes of investment and other policy setting.

(*d*) Acting as initiator *of last resort* of entry of firms and sectoral expansion, in case there is no or insufficient spontaneous expansion forthcoming in a desired direction.

(*e*) Assisting the rapid spread of the most advanced technology to all producers, possibly acting as an intermediary in the acquisition of foreign or domestic patents for the entire economy.

The rule that the steering agency must follow at all times, and to which all the five tasks noted above must be directed, is that, with a perfect capital market and equal lending terms to all, incomes of those with equal skills be equal. This is the most efficient solution.

If in some sectors incomes are or are expected to be considerably higher (while an economically meaningful price is paid for capital, and while equilibrium prices prevail in the product markets), capital and labor resources must flow in that direction, and not in other directions. The informational function of the steering agency will be sufficient most of the time, but if it is not, the agency must have the right to stimulate entry. Similarly, if there is unemployment—and in the unemployment sector there are very low incomes indeed— then capital resources must be made to flow in that direction, even if this calls for the creation of new firms. The same holds when there is potential desire for employment, as with those in Yugoslavia who may have left the country for lack of employment opportunities.

In countries with widely divergent regions in terms of economic development, and widely different social-overhead investment (e.g., Kosovo *versus* Slovenia in Yugoslavia), of course, the objective labor-income equalization may have to be required at first on a regional level, and global equalization may only be established as a target in the very long run. But at all times it must be kept in mind that the tools of an *efficient* equalization are the proliferation of technology and the flow of labor and capital resources in the desired direction, and not straitjacketing of personal take-home incomes.

VIII.2. *The state of the art of steering the economy in Yugoslavia*

To my best knowledge the steering functions (*a*) through (*e*) noted in the preceding section are either entirely nonexistent in Yugoslavia or carried out in an insufficient degree, often without proper knowledge of the purpose for which they should be intended.

The best evidence of this insufficiency is that even the concept of a meaningful labor-income that could be used for planning resource allocation has not been agreed on—let alone computed—by Yugoslav economists. A rough elaboration of such a concept and computation of a "planning income" has been produced (see [11]). But it is primarily an illustration of the procedure: a far more careful, firm-by-firm analysis would be called for.

VIII.3. *The course of action implied by this report*

It would take at least another study the size of this one to spell out in detail the operational implications of this report, and in particular of this part. It would also require a number of subsidiary studies to establish empirically certain key economic parameters, and to elaborate in technical detail certain "steering" procedures for the Yugoslav economy. Since such an extensive effort is impossible, I will merely sketch in a short-hand manner the various stages of the task at hand, as I see them.

(*a*) Establish as precisely as possible the true efficiency-coefficient (shadow-price) for capital for Yugoslavia. The procedures in the Vanek-Jovicic paper [9] could be used. Also, I believe, Dr. Frankovic and the Ljubljana Institute of Economic Research are working on the problem. But the rate must be based also on a planned inflation rate.

(*b*) Tax all the "current value" (or some other judiciously established measure) of capital in productive organizations at such a rate, exempting all existing debt-service payments on outstanding loans.

(*c*) Collect all depreciation allowances.

(*d*) Devote all of the funds collected under (*b*) and (*c*) to a national (or republican) investment fund.

(*e*) Except where restricted for special reasons by law, allocate the entire fund through strictly impartial and scientific price rationing to new investments. Upon scrutiny of the correctness of an investment project, a loan should be automatically granted, provided that the rate of return is in excess of the going lending rate and provided that the working collective borrowing the money assumes all the responsibilities implied by the loan.

(*f*) It is imperative in calculating the internal rates of return for all projects, that the true "alternative-use value" of labor be used (see Chapter 9 below). Only in this way can the long-range optimality of investments and the gradual equalization of incomes be guaranteed. This procedure is also the only one consistent with the individual welfare of those involved in the new projects.

(*g*) Stabilize prices at all costs, at first through controls. Gradually, once the subtle mechanism of price formation and the operation of short-term capital markets is better understood (see Section VII), controls may be relaxed, except in cases of clear monopolistic market structures (see Section I).

(*h*) Start systematically carrying out the tasks (*a*) to (*e*) outlined in Section VIII.1 using data obtained under (*a*) above.

(*i*) Allocate all interest and repayment of new loans to the national (or republican) investment fund.

(*j*) Set up a special office to promote the economic interests of those "left out" and have it create new firms, absorbing the unemployed and those willing to return from Germany, in areas of highest return (and labor incomes).

(*k*) The revenues under (*b*) and (*c*) above will leave many firms better off in terms of distributable income, many about equally well off, and some substantially worse off in the short run. In the third category, transitional alleviation must be envisaged, based on lower depreciation and interest charges, and perhaps gradual upward adjustment of prices.

(*l*) Existing resources of funds, to the extent that they are owed to depositors, should be preserved and integrated with the national (or republican) investment fund. Resources that the banks hold as an endowment (not owed to depositors) should be directly transferred to the social fund. Of course, physically, the banks would remain branches administering—under new rules—the social fund.

(*m*) Gradually synchronize market conditions in the long- and short-term capital markets, leaving rates to be determined in all markets by market forces, including in markets for housing funds as well as funds for social-overhead investments. The latter should also be financed from the social fund, debt-service obligations being covered from current budgets as a current collective consumption expenditure.

References

1. E. D., Domar, "The Soviet Collective Farm as a Producer Cooperative," *American Economic Review*, 56 (Sept. 1966) 734–757.

2. Branko Horvat, *Business Cycles in Yugoslavia*, tr. Helen M. Kramer (White Plains, N.Y.: International Arts and Sciences Press, 1971).

3. _____, "Prilog zasnisavanju teorije jugoslovenskih poduzeca," *Ekonomska Analiza*, 1 (1967), 7–28.

4. Institute of Economic Sciences, *Samoupravna Politika Dohotka* (Belgrade, 1972).

5. Miladin Korac, ed., *Osnovi Teorije Dohotka i Socijalističke Robne Proizvodnje* (Belgrade, 1970).

6. Jan Vanek, *The Economics of Workers' Management* (London: George Allen and Unwin, 1972).

7. Jaroslav Vanek, *The General Theory of Labor-Managed Market Economies* (Ithaca, N.Y.: Cornell University Press, 1970).

8. ____, *The Participatory Economy: An Evolutionary Hypothesis and a Strategy for Development* (Ithaca, N.Y.: Cornell University Press, 1971).

9. ____ and Milena Jovicic, "The Capital Market and Income Distribution in Yugoslavia," Chapter 4, below.

10. Jaroslav Vanek, "Some Fundamental Considerations on Financing and the Form of Ownership under Labor Management," Chapter 8, below.

11. ____, "The Basic Theory of Financing of Participatory Firms," Chapter 9, below.

12. ____, "The Macroeconomic Theory and Policy of an Open Worker-Managed Economy," Chapter 13, below.

13. ____, in cooperation with A. McGregor and V. Richards, "A Fully Decentralized and Fully Efficient Labor-Managed Economy," Chapter 10, below.

14. B. Ward, "The Firm in Illyria: Market Syndicalism," *American Economic Review*, 48 (Sept. 1958), 566–589.

4 | The Capital Market and Income Distribution in Yugoslavia: A Theoretical and Empirical Analysis*

With MILENA JOVICIC

I. The Theoretical Statement of the Problem

In a labor-managed firm where labor incomes are determined as a residual of sales after payment of costs, the income per worker will depend on how much of the productive services of capital constitutes a cost of production. On the one end of the spectrum, if all capital were borrowed from external sources, an important interest charge (in addition to amortization) would constitute a current cost of operation, and labor incomes would accordingly be smaller. On the other end of the spectrum, all capital could be coming from internal sources (collective savings by the working community) and not constitute a current operating cost, and labor incomes would be accordingly higher. In the second case, however, labor incomes could be viewed as composed of two parts, remuneration of labor proper, and a rent on capital previously accumulated.

The basic contention and starting point of the present analysis is that in Yugoslavia, where capital formation (enlarged reproduction) is to be performed internally by the production organizations (even bank loans having to be repaid from current income), our second broad alternative obtains, and labor incomes actually are composed of labor incomes proper and of capital rents.

If this hypothesis is correct, then a good deal of income distribution inequalities as between firms and industrial branches should be explainable by capital intensity (or more precisely the capital-labor ratio) and second by the proportion of capital financed from external sources (or more operationally, the interest costs actually paid by

* This paper appeared in *The Quarterly Journal of Economics*, 89 (August 1975), Copyright, 1975, by the President and Fellows of Harvard College. It was originally published in Serbo-Croatian in *Ekonomska Analiza* in September 1972.

the productive organizations). The first empirical objective of this article is to verify these hypotheses on data drawn from the Yugoslav economy. This will be done in Section II.

Assuming that the correlation between the capital-labor ratio and labor incomes exists, it can be further postulated that there should be some shadow price (or accounting price) of capital that would eliminate that correlation if incomes were recomputed as incomes *after* payment of such shadow prices. The study of this problem and an actual determination of such a shadow price are the second empirical objective of our study.

The utility of this objective is not only to obtain an estimator of marginal productivity of capital for the economy, but also to obtain a "purer" measure of income variability between firms or industrial branches or regions of Yugoslavia, devoid of the impact of capital intensity and devoid of the impact of the degree of actual external financing.

As a further objective of our paper, we study other determinants of the "purified" income variability, such as market structures, price controls, inflation rates, and others. But the "purified" income levels are important also for another reason. Such incomes, after correction has been made for the capital intensity, are estimates of pure labor incomes, and they should be of paramount significance for the Yugoslav policy maker in two contexts: (1) that of moving toward a distributional optimum, and (2) that of moving toward an allocational optimum. Under (1) the correcting shadow price of capital indicates the rate at which capital should be taxed if "pure labor" incomes were to be earned by workers. Under (2)—and perhaps more important—the pure incomes, unlike the actually observed incomes, indicate in which direction scarce capital resources should be allocated and which branches of the national economy should be stimulated or destimulated.

In our empirical work we restrict ourselves to the cross-sectional analysis of industrial branch variability, with only nineteen observations. But the reader should find it easy to realize the possibilities of elaboration, in the direction of time-series cross-section, in the direction of firm-by-firm analysis, and in the direction of several further explanatory hypotheses of income variability, both economic and noneconomic. We shall elaborate on these avenues for further research in the concluding section.

II. Income, Capital Intensity, and the Estimated Rent of Capital in Yugoslavia

To accomplish our first objective, that is, to verify the hypothesis of an impact of capital intensity on incomes per laborer, we estimate two simple regression lines,

$$y = a + bk_i, \tag{4.1}$$

where y is net product of industrial branch[1] per unskilled-labor equivalent, k_i (capital per unskilled-labor equivalent, being measured at its acquisition cost for $i = 1$, and at depreciated value, for $i = 2$), and a and b two constants. The underlying data for the nineteen industries, methods of computation, and sources are given in the Appendix.

The two regressions, with the standard characteristics of statistical significance are as follows:

$$y = 2.4149 + 0.0663k_1 + u \tag{4.2}$$
$$(0.0257)$$

$$R = 0.530,$$

and

$$y = 2.5050 + 0.0908k_2 + u \tag{4.3}$$
$$(0.0403)$$

$$R = 0.4797.$$

1. The precise definition of this variable is as follows: Value of total sales of an industrial branch, minus cost of material and services both from outside the firms, minus major repairs, minus depreciation. Interest and capital taxes are included in the net product because according to Marxian definitions, they do not represent costs. However, in 1969 they were a rather unimportant percentage of total capital assets. While it is impossible to obtain data exactly corresponding to the definition of industrial sectors used in this article, we can quote figures for the total Yugoslav socialist sector in 1969. Payments of financial interest were 3.3 billion new dinars and capital tax 2.4 billion. This was paid on total current value of fixed and circulating capital assets amounting to 206.4 billion. Thus, the total payments of 5.7 billion represent a rate of 2.7 per cent. Moreover, there is a strong presumption that most of the interest payments were actually effected on circulating capital, and consequently the actual interest payments on fixed capital, which concerns us in this article, must have been very small indeed. These data were taken from the *Statistical Yearbook of Yugoslavia* for 1970 and the *Statisticki Bilten*, January 1972. In this connection it may be interesting to note that the estimate in relation 4.7 below is based on income, excluding, among other tax liabilities, the capital tax, and leads to an estimate of the capital coefficient about $2\frac{1}{2}$ per cent below the estimate of equation 4.3.

In both instances our hypothesis is verified on the 5 per cent significance level.

Taking relation 4.1 as a nonstochastic relationship, it will further be noted that it can be written, L, K, and Y standing for labor, capital, and net product, as

$$\frac{Y}{L} - p_k \frac{K}{L} = a,$$

where $p_k = b$ is the shadow price of capital, which, if paid by the productive organizations, would eliminate interindustry income variation imputable to capital intensity, and where a is the "pure" labor income of an unskilled worker. The two estimates of p_k of some 7 and 9 per cent, respectively, on the two definitions of k appear as perfectly reasonable in view of other studies of marginal productivity of capital. Taking the higher estimate as more representative because it is based on the depreciated (not used-up) value of capital assets, we come out about 3 per cent below a figure obtained by Frankovic for the marginal productivity of capital for all Yugoslavia for the early 1960's.[2]

In Table 4.1 we show the key results of the first step of our econometric analysis. We do so, relating to capital valued after depreciation, that is, basing ourselves on equation 4.3. In column 1 we show the nineteen industries in descending order of an efficiency indicator shown in column 4 and explained presently. In column 2 we show for all industries the estimated "pure" labor income of unskilled labor in 1970 in thousands of new dinars for all nineteen Yugoslav industries. In column 3 we find the imputed rent of capital per unskilled worker, as estimated through our procedure. In column 4 we present the residual variation of income per unskilled worker, unexplained by capital intensity. The order of industries as given in column 1 is based on these residuals, starting from the highest (positive) and ending with the lowest (negative). These figures can be taken as average efficiency—or total productivity—indicators of the different industries. It is these indicators that could serve the Yugoslav planners in deciding on resource allocation.

2. The 12 per cent is an unpublished estimate of the marginal productivity of capital, based on a Cobb-Douglas function fitted to industries, by Vladimir Frankovic of the University of Ljubljana.

Table 4.1. Composition of income per unskilled-labor equivalent

Industry (1)	Estimated pure labor income (2)	Imputed rent of capital (3)	Residual variation in labor income (4)	Observed income 2 + 3 + 4 (5)
1. Oil	25.050	8.160	31,690	64.900
2. Tobacco industry	25.050	2.424	13.326	40.800
3. Printing	25.050	1.498	7.352	33.900
4. Chemicals	25.050	3.785	2.665	31.500
5. Shipbuilding	25.050	2.287	2.263	29.600
6. Rubber	25.050	1.307	1.843	28.200
7. Building materials	25.050	2.387	1.163	28.600
8. Nonferrous metallurgy	25.050	3.831	119	29.000
9. Food processing	25.050	2.950	− 1.300	26.700
10. Metals industry	25.050	1.398	− 2.448	24.000
11. Leather and footwear	25.050	1.062	− 3.512	22.600
12. Electrical industry	25.050	1.352	− 4.602	21.800
13. Wood products	25.050	2.478	− 4.828	22.700
14. Nonmetal	25.050	2.505	− 5.855	21.700
15. Electrical power	25.050	24.262	− 6.012	43.300
16. Ferrous metallurgy	25.050	4.919	− 7.169	22.800
17. Textiles	25.050	1.389	− 7.539	18.900
18. Paper	25.050	6.499	− 8.349	23.200
19. Coal	25.050	3.758	− 8.808	20.000

It may be interesting to observe that the imputed capital rent is equivalent to some 13 per cent of the net product (*neto dohodak*) of the nineteen industries. If such rent were collected and entirely invested together with the amortization funds of these industries (16 per cent in 1969), this would yield some 29 per cent of net product of gross investment, a truly considerable percentage. In fact, it would suffice for a highly dynamic development of the industrial sector of the Yugoslav economy, without any need for savings by productive organizations or individuals of any other kind; and if such savings were forthcoming, this would only enhance the development effort of Yugoslavia. The structural effect of a more correct factor pricing and an improved capability of national planning would also contribute in a significant manner to the performance of the economy.

III. Other Factors Affecting Income Distribution

The differences in income per worker between industrial branches (after adjusting for the skill differences) are a result of the use of other factors of production or monopolistic situations. Since in Yugoslavia the means of production are socially owned in each of their uses, at least a certain minimum social rentability has to be realized. In the second part of the paper the concentration was on the determination of that part of income by industrial branches, which is a result of the use of the means of production, and on determination of that level of interest on these means, which reduces the difference in income to the greatest degree.

The rest of the differences in income per worker can be explained by the presence of natural monopoly, market and technological monopoly (considering the fact that the organizational advantages of firms, the differences in intensity of work, and so on probably average out on the level of the branches). Natural monopoly occurs as a result of market imperfections and represents a possibility for control of the price by the firm in order to realize the extra profit. And, finally, insofar as the market conditions are such that the differential increase in productivity by individual branches is not compensated for by the corresponding changes in price, the branches with the higher than average increase in labor productivity have a chance of appropriating the extra income.

Since the study of the effect of capital intensity has shown that capital intensity leaves unexplained a large part of the variation in the income per worker of individual industrial branches, what remains to be studied is the effect of other factors. In accordance with the previously listed possible differences in obtaining the income, we have considered the influence of the following variables:

X_1 = producers' price index (1960 = 100) with turnover tax excluded, relative to the price index as a whole—a measure of inflationary tendencies and changes in relative prices due to other causes (e.g., productivity);

X_2 = the value of output of the four largest producers in a branch as a percentage of the total output of the branch—a measure of supply concentration in the branch (the data are for 1969);

X_3 = the percentage of production with controlled prices in total value of production of branches (in 1969)—a measure of price controls; and

X_4 = the present value of fixed assets as a percentage of the purchasing value of fixed assets—or measure of "newness" of fixed assets.

The dependent variables are the residuals of our equations 4.2 and 4.3, that is, the positive and negative deviations from the computed values of income per worker:

$$Z_2 = -1.0274 - 0.0103X_1 + 0.0118X_2 + 0.0029X_3 \qquad (4.4)$$
$$ (0.0106) \qquad (0.0099) \qquad (0.0062)$$
$$+ 0.0246X_4$$
$$(0.0407)$$

$$R = 0.4700$$

$$Z_3 = -1.1982 - 0.0093X_1 + 0.0132X_2 + 0.0040X_3 \qquad (4.5)$$
$$ (0.0108) \qquad (0.0101) \qquad (0.0062)$$
$$+ 0.0240X_4$$
$$(0.0413)$$

$$R = 0.5021.$$

Due to the high standard errors of regression coefficients, all coefficients are insignificant at the 10 per cent level of significance but in general the signs are as expected. It is obvious that to a certain extent the measures of supply concentration and newness of fixed assets confirm the existence of the market and technical monopoly; it seems that the price controls do not succeed in eliminating it, while the changes in relative prices seem to be in accordance with the movement of labor productivity (higher growth of productivity— higher capital intensity and newer means of production—growth of prices relatively slower).

Relatively low coefficients of correlation and high standard errors of equations 4.4 and 4.5 point to the fact that the variables used do not explain sufficiently the differences in incomes. Since this is only preliminary research, we did not enter into the analysis of the effect of others and into a search for other variables that would (at least statistically) explain these differences best.

However, it would be interesting to find out to what extent the effect of all these factors is affected by the existing distribution, or how the effect of capital intensity in equation 4.1 changes, starting from total net income and going to the various income magnitudes as defined by the distribution of income in business enterprises. For this purpose we used statistical data for 1969, and we obtained the following regression equations:

$$Y = 2.1337 + 0.0980k_2 \qquad (4.6)$$
$$(0.0479$$

$$R = 0.4447,$$

where Y and k_2 are defined as in equation 4.3;

$$Y_r = 1.6762 + 0.0654k_2 \qquad (4.7)$$
$$(0.0161)$$

$$R = 0.7014,$$

where Y_r represents the net income per unskilled-worker equivalent after the deduction of all kinds of tax liabilities; and

$$Y_1 = 0.9321 + 0.0161k_2 \qquad (4.8)$$
$$(0.0065)$$

$$R = 0.5109,$$

where Y_1 is defined as personal take-home income and other personal receipts per unskilled-worker equivalent.

It is seen that when income remaining in the hands of the working collectives after taxes is considered, the effect of capital intensity is diminished, but the higher value of the correlation coefficient and a lower standard error indicate a diminished effect of all other factors except of k_2. The increase in R between relations 4.6 and 4.7 is remarkable and seems to indicate that the Yugoslav working collectives in making business decisions are more concerned with income after taxes than with total net income (before-tax payment). Relation 4.8 also contains a very interesting result. The effect of capital intensity on personal incomes, while remaining statistically significant, becomes very small. It means that in their internal income distribution capital-intensive sectors allocate far more to investment funds and other nonpersonal incomes (collective consumption) than do capital-poor sectors. But of course it must be stressed that from the point of view of efficiency of resource allocation the comparative equalization of incomes occuring in relation 4.8 does not imply a correct scarcity pricing of capital. The funds allocated to investment still will be used in incorrect proportions as long as effective underpricing of capital, notorious in Yugoslavia, is perpetuated.

IV. The Likelihood of a Downward Bias of Our Estimator of Price of Capital

A more subtle theoretical argument strongly suggests that our estimators of the shadow price of capital in fact are lower limits of the true value of such prices, the true values most likely being higher. This can be explained using Figure 4.1. With labor measured in terms of unskilled-labor equivalents along the horizontal axis, and both production processes expressed per one unit actually observed of such labor, the ordinates of points a_1 and a_2 express, respectively, the observed output per worker (y) of two industries. The first is highly capital-intensive, the second relatively labor-intensive.

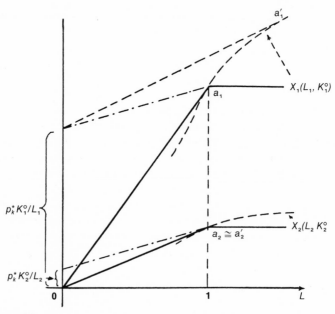

Figure 4.1

The slopes of the solid lines passing through a_1 and a_2 also express incomes per worker y_1 and y_2 if, as is roughly the case in Yugoslavia, no effective payment is made for the use of capital. The process of finding our shadow price of capital now can be seen as a clockwise rotation around a_1 and a_2, the intercept with the vertical axis measuring the hypothetical costs of capital $p_k K_i/L_i$ ($i = 1, 2$), to the point where the lines become parallel. At such a point, for p_k^*, the hypothetical (pure) incomes of labor (after allowance is made for capital cost), expressed by the slopes of the dashed-and-dotted lines, are equalized. It is p_k^* that we have estimated in the earlier sections with the only difference that we dealt with nineteen instead of two industries.

It is apparent that the construction crucially depends on the kinks in the (solid) production functions of x_1 and x_2 at the points a_1 and a_2. If, as can be expected in the intermediate or long run, substitutability of capital and labor becomes a possibility, as shown by the dashed production functions passing through a, the estimate p_k^* almost certainly becomes too low. The capital-intensive industry seeking the maximal income for workers, with the same capital stock K^0, would seek to increase employment and produce at point a_1'. On the other hand, given a certain regularity of convexities, the second industry would barely move away from a_2, the new point a_2' roughly coinciding with a_2. But if such is the case, the procedure of equalization of slopes, i.e., equalization of labor incomes, would call for further increases in the hypothetical p_k, beyond the level of p_k^*. In terms of our empirical analysis this would mean, for example, that the true value of the shadow price of capital is above 9 per cent, as high as the 12 per cent estimated by Dr. Frankovic.

V. Conclusions and Suggested Further Research

The area of possible research opened up by this study is considerable, so much so that we have decided to publish it as an interim report before covering the entire ground. In this concluding section we shall first sum up briefly our main findings and then discuss the principal further avenues of investigation that we have either entered on already in a preliminary manner or that we feel ought to be explored.

The key findings are that capital in Yugoslavia is seriously underpriced in the sense that labor earns considerable imputed rents of capital, such rents, and correspondingly incomes, being significantly higher in activities with high capital intensity. Our theoretical and statistical analysis, moreover, permitted us to produce estimates of the scarcity rental (price) of capital, and the corresponding pure income (i.e., income devoid of capital rents) of labor. The econometric procedure also leads to efficiency indicators for various branches of Yugoslav industry, which could be of interest to the planners and policy makers of the country.

The avenues that we feel ought to be explored further are as follows (those marked by an asterisk indicate that we have already done some preliminary work):

1. Cross-section time-series analysis on a firm-by-firm basis (instead of sector-by-sector).

2*. Exploration of other functional forms, e.g., log or log-log functions.

3*. Use of other definitions of income, e.g., after turnover tax incomes, after-interest actually paid income, distributable income, take-home income, etc.

4*. Analysis of other economic factors affecting income and product distribution, after the impact of capital intensity has been taken into account, preferably on the firm-by-firm basis. Some sectoral work along these lines was reported on in Section III.

5. Analysis of noneconomic, sociological, cultural-regional, and other possible effects on income formation.

Appendix

The basic statistical series used in the study are given in Tables 4.2 and 4.3. In converting the number of employed workers to unskilled labor equivalents, we used the methodology developed in the Popov and Jovicic study.[3] From the same book we took the following data: relative base indices of producer prices with turnover tax excluded, three-quarter average, 1970 (X_1); value of output of four biggest producers in a branch expressed as a percentage of total value of output of the branch for 1969 (X_2); percentage of output with controlled prices in 1969 (X_3). The source of the rest of the data was *Statistical Yearbook of Yugoslavia* for 1970 and 1971.

3. Sofija Popov and Milena Jovicic, *The Effect of Personal Income on Movement of Prices* (Belgrade: Institute of Economic Sciences [Works 20], 1971).

Industry	Net product per unskilled-labor equivalent	Undepreciated value of fixed assets per unskilled-labor equivalent	Depreciated value of fixed assets per unskilled-labor equivalent	X_1	X_2	X_3	X_4
Electrical power	4.33	39.91	26.73	109.0	28.2	100,0	67.12
Coal	2.00	7.45	4.14	119.7	46.7	14.0	55.61
Oil	6.49	17.19	8.99	76.8	100.0	91.0	52.28
Ferrous metallurgy	2.28	10.20	5.42	94.0	83.2	100.0	53.14
Nonferrous metallurgy	2.90	8.75	4.22	124.9	67.6	100.0	48.20
Nonmetals	2.17	4.34	2.76	95.0	31.4	37.0	63.62
Metals	2.40	3.08	1.54	76.0	18.9	59.0	49.96
Shipbuilding	2.96	4.66	2.52	80.0	81.2	0.0	54.18
Electrical	2.18	2.59	1.49	71.6	40.5	57.0	57.32
Chemicals	3.15	7.04	4.17	80.4	22.8	82.0	59.25
Building materials	2.86	4.90	2.63	133.2	29.7	23.0	53.67
Wood products	2.27	3.75	2.73	125.3	9.8	1.0	72.01
Paper	2.32	10.86	7.16	97.0	32.6	6.0	65.93
Textiles	1.89	2.75	1.53	89.8	9.4	15.0	55.55
Leather and footwear	2.26	1.98	1.17	100.3	23.3	0.0	59.22
Rubber	2.82	2.79	1.44	73.9	87.1	46.0	57.69
Food processing	2.67	4.95	3.25	143.6	15.2	30.0	65.58
Printing	3.39	2.59	1.65	115.0	15.0	0.0	63.65
Tobacco	4.08	4.01	2.67	72.2	21.4	94.0	66.54

ble 4.3. Data for 1969, in millions of old dinars

Industry	Undepreciated value of fixed assets per unskilled-labor equivalent	Net product per unskilled-labor equivalent	Income for distribution per unskilled-labor equivalent	Take-home pay and other personal income per unskilled-labor equivalent
. Electrical power	25.38	3.77	3.24	1.28
. Coal	3.70	1.56	1.43	0.90
. Oil	9.44	6.89	3.04	1.30
. Ferrous metallurgy	5.23	2.00	1.77	1.00
. Nonferrous metallurgy	5.76	2.33	2.07	1.05
. Nonmetals	2.38	1.77	1.57	0.86
. Metals	1.56	1.96	1.75	0.97
. Shipbuilding	2.52	2.60	2.38	1.30
. Electrical	1.57	2.14	1.95	0.97
. Chemicals	3.94	2.57	2.25	1.05
. Building materials	2.24	2.21	1.88	0.94
. Wood products	1.24	1.77	1.54	0.84
. Paper	6.67	1.85	1.59	0.97
. Textiles	1.46	1.62	1.39	0.76
. Leather and footwear	1.02	2.06	1.61	0.88
. Rubber	1.34	2.66	2.11	0.99
. Food processing	2.89	2.21	1.88	0.96
. Printing	1.57	2.75	2.35	1.28
. Tobacco	2.30	3.88	1.42	0.73

5 | Explorations into the "Realistic" Behavior of a Yugoslav Firm*

With PETER MIOVIC

In an article thus far unknown to English-speaking economists [2], Branko Horvat offers an explanation of behavior of the Yugoslav firm that differs from those of Ward [4] and Domar [1]. After going over the main aspects of the work of the last two mentioned authors, Professor Horvat suggests that in fact a Yugoslav firm plans for each period in the future a certain increase of the wage rate and beyond that behaves like a capitalist firm maximizing its profit (at that wage rate). This hypothesis seems to be of significant value because, contrary to the hypotheses of Ward and Domar, it is based at least to a degree on an actual observation of economic behavior.

In this paper we propose to explore some of the key implications of the "realistic" hypothesis. Our first task, to be carried out in Section I, will be to complete the hypothesis by an operational hypothesis determining the rules of wage adjustment from period to period. Section II will then discuss the short- and long-run implications of what we may refer to as the *socialist model*,[1] where the (maximized) profits are returned to society and where the labor-managed firm pays a fixed price for use of its capital. Sections III and IV turn to the model which reflects most closely (if not entirely) the reality of Yugoslavia, namely, where profits generated in each period are used to expand the capital stock of the firm; we may refer to this model as the *self-financing model*. Whereas in Section III the underlying wage-determination function (developed in Sec-

* Cornell Department of Economics Working Paper no. 7, April 1970. The research was made possible through the funds of the Program on Participation and Labor-Managed Systems at Cornell University.
1. We felt that this term was not entirely satisfactory but used it for lack of a more accurate and concise term.

tion II) calls for a wage-rate adjustment whenever profits are different from an objective defined in terms of nonwage income per worker, in Section IV we analyze the case where the objective is stated in terms of nonwage income per unit of capital. Section V studies the relation between solutions obtained under the operationalized "realistic" rule on the one hand and those produced by (Ward's and Domar's) maximization of income per laborer on the other. Supply responses to changing product market conditions are our concern in Section VI. Finally, Sections VII and VIII consider the effects that the behavioristic rules discussed in this paper would have on interfirm efficiency of resource allocation, and the case of technological progress, respectively.

Although our principal concern here is to study the behavior of a Yugoslav firm, it may be useful to note that our analysis and results have some bearing on the possible behavior of Western corporations operating in a labor market dominated by strong unions. For example, the self-financing model of Section IV can be taken as descriptive of a corporation which plows back its profits into its capital stock, and at the same time is constrained by the union to adjust wages in relation to the profits per unit of capital invested in the preceding period of operation.

I. Some Operational Hypotheses Related to Adjustment in Wage Rates

While Horvat's approach does seem to bring some realism into the picture, the results, as we shall see, depend crucially on how wage increases are determined.

To begin with, if the worker-managers simply increased wages by a fixed percentage every year (say, $W_t - W_{t-1} = 10$ per cent per year), and beyond that maximized profit, profits would eventually become negative unless productivity increases kept up with the wages. This would be untenable. One is thus led to ask what would be a reasonable operational hypothesis for adjusting wages.

In this paper we examine basically two operational alternatives. In one, the firms increase (reduce) their wages in the current period, $W_t > W_{t-1}$ ($W_t < W_{t-1}$), if profits per worker in the previous period, $\emptyset_{t-1}$, turned out to be larger (smaller) than some target profit per worker. It is reasonable to suppose that the target will be zero or positive.

The other wage adjustment rule is based on the hypothesis that the firms increase (decrease) their wages in the current period depending on whether profit per unit of capital, X_k, is greater (smaller) than some target. Notice that in this case the target is defined as profit per unit of capital, not labor. As before, we will assume it to be zero or positive.

The specific forms that these wage adjustment rules take will be defined in subsequent sections.

II. The Socialist Case

As indicated earlier the socialist model is one where the firms operate totally with society's capital and pay a fixed price, p_k, for its use. In addition, at the end of each period they turn over their profits, P_t, to society, if profits are positive, or receive a subsidy, if profits are negative. These profits represent all income not paid out to factors of production as remuneration and thus differ from the profits in the self-financing alternative, which include the implicit factor payments to capital (although at an unspecified price).

Given this model, let us consider the following wage adjustment hypothesis:

$$W_t - W_{t-1} = AP_{t-1}. \tag{5.1}$$

In other words, current wages are adjusted upward (downward) if profits in the previous period were positive (negative).[2] Parameter A is positive and represents a behavioristic constant determined by the worker-managers. The target profit discussed in Section I is assumed to be zero. This is reasonable in the socialist model since the firms already pay a price for the use of capital and thus have no need for some minimum permanent profit.

Let us postulate that the firm's output is produced according to a smooth neoclassical production function

$$X = F(K, L), \tag{5.2}$$

where X is output and K and L are capital and labor inputs. We will deal with situations (1) where F is a technology subject to increasing and then decreasing returns to scale, and (2) where F is

---

2. Notice that P_t are total profits, whereas $\emptyset_t$ defined in the previous section were profits per worker.

subject to constant returns to scale. Also we assume that p, the price of X, p_k, the price of capital, and the initial wage, w_o, are all fixed, and that p is unity by a suitable choice of the units of measurement.

Following a customary procedure we will first speak about the equilibria occurring in our system and then turn to the problem of dynamic adjustment to equilibrium, and to the problem of stability. It is clear from relation 5.1 that a stationary state, that is, a state in which all variables remain constant over time, is possible only if P_{t-1} is equal to zero, that is, if profits at the prevailing price of capital and at the prevailing wage are zero. In that case there will also be no inducement to change the prevailing wage.

Two situations must now be distinguished depending on whether the capital stock is permitted to adjust or not, that is, depending on whether the underlying static equilibria are of the long-run or short-run variety. In the first situation the equilibrium in relation 5.1 implies, with marginal pricing of factors of production,

$$P_t = 0 = X - X_L L - X_K K, \tag{5.3}$$

where X_L and X_K are marginal physical products of labor and capital, respectively. This is nothing but the well-known Euler equation, and thus we find that the dynamic stationary equilibrium of our socialist firm that is permitted to adjust its capital stock optimally is found on the production function at a point where constant returns to scale are realized. Thus, for the case where F is a function subject to increasing and then diminishing returns, the dynamic equilibrium must be found along the contour dividing the increasing returns zone from the diminishing returns zone. This contour is referred to as the locus of maximum physical efficiency and is extensively discussed and explained by Vanek [3, chap. 2]. Such a locus is illustrated in the capital-labor plane of Figure 5.1 as the locus EE'. When the production function F is subject to constant returns to scale, of course, relation 5.2 simply says that the equilibrium point can occur anywhere on F, i.e., anywhere in the capital-labor plane of Figure 5.1.

To determine further the location of the equilibrium point on the production function another restriction is necessary. Obviously, with marginal factor pricing and equilibrium adjustment of capital

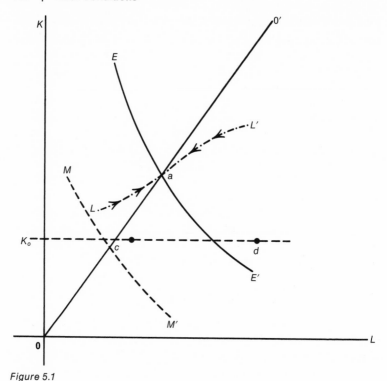

Figure 5.1

stock, such a relation is given by

$$X_K = p_k, \qquad (5.4)$$

stating the condition that the marginal value product of capital must be equal to the price of capital (recall that p equals one by assumption). Relation 5.4 is one between two variables K and L and is depicted as the locus LL' for the case where F is subject to increasing and diminishing returns. Obviously the dynamic equilibrium of the firm will now be found at the intersection of EE' and LL', that is, at the point a in Figure 5.1.

When F is subject to constant returns to scale the locus of constant marginal products of capital is a ray through the origin such as $00'$ in Figure 5.1. Because there is no other restriction on the position of the equilibrium the dynamic equilibrium of the firm can exist anywhere along $00'$ if the technology is subject to constant returns to scale.

Turning now to the dynamics of the situation it is immediately apparent that in the case of increasing and diminishing returns the equilibrium at point a will be a stable one. For example, starting from anywhere along La in Figure 5.1 the employment point must move toward a because in that zone of LL', with increasing returns, profits must be negative, and thus by relation 5.1 wages must be declining. With declining wages and correspondingly declining marginal products of labor, as indicated by the arrows in Figure 5.1, we must move toward point a. An analogous argument, with positive profits and increasing wages, can be used to show that to the right and above a the input point will also be moving toward the dynamic equilibrium.[3] To sum up, with both capital and labor inputs variable, the dynamic stationary state is at point a in Figure 5.1, which is a point of maximal factor productivities for that set of factor proportions, and that point is dynamically stable.

If we retain the assumption of variable capital and labor but now postulate technology subject to constant returns to scale, the problem of dynamic adjustment becomes more complicated. The solution now can be termed a degenerate one because with p_k and the initial wage w_o leading to positive profits, the firm ought immediately to expand output to infinity, and vice versa, with negative profits, contract output to zero. The only reasonable solution now is to say that the initial wage w_o would have to be selected by the firm in such a way as to nullify profits. In that case any initial equilibrium along the ray $00'$ would be possible, and it would be just on the borderline between dynamic stability and instability. Of course, as soon as we drop the assumption of variable capital and postulate a fixed capital stock (note that in any real situations capital cannot be infinitely variable), the problems of indeterminacy and dynamic stability disappear. It is to such situations that we now turn.

3. In view of the fact that Section III deals with profits per laborer, it might be noted that if in relation 5.1, P_{t-1} were replaced by P_{t-1}/L_{t-1} (i.e., profits per worker), the end result would be convergence to the same long-run dynamic equilibrium except that the speed of adjustment would be greater when profits are positive and smaller when negative. This follows directly from the fact that P/L increases faster than P as labor is cut back from some point LL' to the right of a, and is slower when L is increased from some negative profit point to the left of a.

Assume that the capital stock is given once and for all at the level K_o in Figure 5.1. For equilibrium, P_{t-1} in relation 5.1 still must be equal to zero. However, relations 5.3 and 5.4 no longer hold because the capital stock is constant. With profits (that is, P_t) equal to zero, we now have, with marginal product hiring of labor,

$$P_t = 0 = X - X_L L - p_k K_o. \tag{5.5}$$

It is a relation in L only and can be expected to have a single solution which is the dynamic equilibrium state of the socialist labor-managed firm endowed with a fixed amount of capital K_o. The equilibrium employment point now can be at a point such as c or d in Figure 5.1. With F subject to increasing and diminishing returns the equilibria must be to the right of locus MM', which is the locus of maximum average products of labor for prescribed levels of capital. In the case of constant returns to scale the locus MM' in Figure 5.1 degenerates, so to speak, into the origin 0; and thus all points along the line $K_o d$ are conceivable dynamic equilibria. Of course, the dynamic equilibria will be moving to the right along the line defined by cd for higher given prices of capital, p_k.

From the nature of the production functions and relation 5.1 it is immediately apparent that any dynamic equilibrium such as c or d in Figure 5.1 must be dynamically stable. For example, when c is a dynamic equilibrium, to the right of that point there will be positive profits and thus wages must be increasing, and to the left of the point profits will be negative and thus wages must be declining; consequently, in either case the solution point will converge gradually toward the dynamic equilibrium at c.

Although we will return to the subject in Section V, it may be useful to point out that all of the dynamic equilibria, whether with or without adjustable capital stock, whether the production function is subject to increasing and diminishing returns to scale or constant returns to scale, actually are the same as those obtained, *ceteris paribus*, for labor-managed firms maximizing income per worker. In other words, the dynamic stationary states of what we have referred to here as the socialist model are exactly the same as the corresponding solutions obtained by the firm maximizing its income per worker. For example, it will be recalled from Vanek's work [3, chap. 2] that a labor-managed firm maximizing its income per worker in the long run will find its equilibrium at the locus of maximum physical efficiency EE' at the point corresponding to the prescribed cost of capital, p_k.

III. The Self-Financing Alternative with a Target Profit per Worker

In this section we are turning from what we have termed the socialist model to the self-financing model. Moreover, we postulate that the working community will adjust its wages in relation to profit per worker in the preceding period.[4] The specific form of this adjustment rule is expressed as

$$w_t - w_{t-1} = A\varnothing_{t-1} - B, \tag{5.6}$$

where A and B are behavioristic constants determined by the self-management process of the enterprise.

We will first consider briefly the case where the technology employed by the enterprise is subject to increasing and then diminishing returns. Afterward we will study more extensively the case of constant returns to scale.

In Figure 5.2 we find the capital-labor input plane of our labor-managed firm and in it the all-important locus of maximum technical efficiency EE'. Along this locus, as shown in the previous section, the production function is instantaneously subject to constant returns to scale and to the left and below that locus we have increasing returns while on the other side of EE' we have diminishing returns to scale. It will also be recalled that marginal factor pricing along the locus EE' will exactly exhaust the firm's product.

Consider first the case where B is zero, that is, wages will be adjusted upward or downward according to whether profits per laborer are positive or negative, and an equilibrium wage rate presupposes zero profits. The first important result that can be immediately derived is that for this case an equilibrium can exist only at an inefficient point below and to the left of the locus EE' at a point such as a. This is immediately seen, for example for a capital stock K_o, from the fact that at point b the production is subject to constant returns to scale and consequently the marginal physical

---

4. While total profit, P_t, of Section II was computed exclusive of (or after) capital charges, $\varnothing_t$ includes them implicitly. This, in fact, is the essence of the self-financing model.

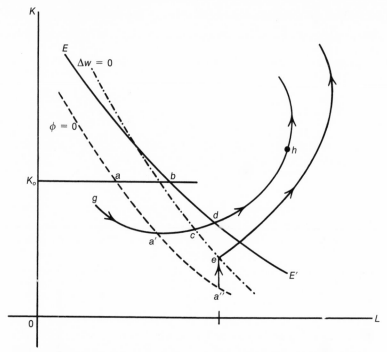

Figure 5.2

product of labor as well as the average product must be declining at *b*; and because in equilibrium profits must be equal to zero—that is, the marginal and average products of labor must be equal—the equilibrium must be found to the left of point *b* at a point such as *a*. Our first finding, then, for the technology subject to increasing and diminishing returns and *B* equal to zero, is that an equilibrium must be technologically inefficient. There will be an entire locus of points such as *a*, below the *EE'* locus, containing all the equilibria of the labor-managed firm on the assumptions made. Another such point corresponding to lower capital stock than K_o is *a'* in the diagram.

The stability of points such as *a* or *a'*, still assuming *B* equal to zero, is a precarious one. For points slightly to the right of the *aa'* locus, given equation 5.6, wages must increase together with accumulation. And this will keep moving the input point (i.e., the point reflecting the current labor and capital inputs) away from the aa' locus toward the locus of maximum physical efficiency and beyond. On the other hand, for points slightly to the left and below the locus aa', equation 5.6 tells us that wages must be declining together with the accumulation, which will tend to produce convergence back to the locus aa'. Of course, it will be futile to spend too much time on the analysis of the case of input points below aa' because once the firm pays out to its labor force more than its total value product it becomes extremely nonviable and it probably would adopt some other policy of adjustment besides the one expressed by equation 5.6.

Let us now consider the more general and very likely more realistic situation where B in equation 5.6 is a positive constant. In that case, in Figure 5.2 in addition to the aa' locus and the EE' locus we will have a third significant locus of input points, namely, the locus passing through c and e along which the change in the wage rate is zero. To the left of that locus wages must be declining and to the right of it the wages must be increasing according to relation 5.6. A typical path of inputs now will begin to the left of the aa' line at a point such as g, then proceed with decumulation and expanded labor employment, toward a point such as a', at which decumulation ceases but wage declines still continue. Beyond a' the direction with respect to the capital axis reverses; accumulation takes place but wages continue to decline, and thus employment experiences significant increases. At point c even wages start increasing as we move toward d, at which total product is exactly exhausted by the marginal factor shares of capital and labor and the rate of accumulation equals the marginal productivity of capital. Beyond d much the same happens, but with diminishing returns the excess of value of output over the wage is increasing and thus accumulation occurs at an increasing rate. Moreover, wages now are rising and therefore there is less impetus to expand employment. In fact, there will be a point such as h at which finally the expansion of employment will cease altogether; from there on the expansion path will proceed in the northwest direction. Of course, starting from some point to the left of a' and going well beyond h, the output of the labor-managed firm will be expanding. Whereas in the early stages of this path the capital-labor ratio will be declining, beyond a certain point the capital-labor ratio will be increasing indefinitely.

The important economic conclusion for this case of increasing and diminishing returns with self-financing and a positive target rate of profit per worker B is that the firm eventually is bound to move beyond a point such as d into the region of inefficient production. In fact, it is only at point d that the firm will maximize its factor productivities for the corresponding factor proportions. Another conclusion deserving notice is that while the EE' locus and the aa' locus are independent of the behavioral relation stated in equation 5.6, the locus of stationary wages will move to the right and to the left with increasing or declining B, i.e., the target rate of profit per worker. Consequently, an increase in B will move a point such as c to the right, and the entire path such as $a'h$ will become horizontally more spread out, that is, the firm on the whole will employ more labor per unit of capital at each stage of its evolution.

Before leaving the case of increasing and diminishing returns, as represented in Figure 5.2, one set of realistic remarks is called for. It is quite unlikely that relation 5.6 would effectively apply during the period of declining wages. There is no reason to believe that a workers' collective that cannot produce its desired surplus (i.e., B divided by A), which would allow it to increase wages, would actually keep on hiring larger numbers of workers with declining wage rates. Rather, as long as there is positive accumulation—that is, in terms of Figure 5.2, as long as the firm finds itself to the right and above the aa' locus—the collective would probably prefer to keep its membership unaltered and wait until, through accumulation, the desired target rate of profit per worker is attained. Only from that point on would the dynamic rules of wage adjustment expressed in relation 5.6 apply, and from then on the expansion of the firm would proceed along the lines already discussed with relation to the path gh. Such an altered path is illustrated by the one passing from a'' through e and then turning in the northeast direction. Of course, for initial points below aa' where decumulation of capital occurs, wage reductions might be the only alternative for a labor-managed firm which wants to avoid failure. Of course here again, it might be preferable in some situations to hold the size of the working collective unchanged and simply reduce wages and thereby produce accumulation and hence growth to more efficient levels of output.

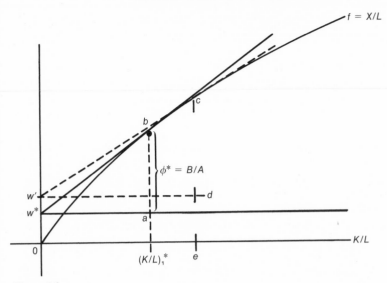

Figure 5.3

But let us now turn to the more interesting and very likely more realistic case of constant returns to scale.[5] In Figure 5.3 we find the well known and very important function f expressing output per worker as a function of the capital-labor ratio for a technology subject to constant returns to scale. It will be recalled here that with technologies of this kind the important independent variable is the capital-labor ratio and not the scale of production. It is for this reason that we use the function f. As is well known and as the reader may verify through a simple exercise in calculus, f', that is, the slope of the f function, measures the marginal productivity of capital. This is stated as

$$X_K = f'(K/L) = d(X/L)/d(K/L). \qquad (5.7)$$

The portion of output per worker not paid out as wages now becomes

$$\varnothing = X_K K/L, \qquad (5.8)$$

5. By "more realistic" we mean here that at least beyond a certain point of production, technology in the real world can approximately be expected to be of the constant returns to scale variety.

and thus in terms of Figure 5.3 $\varnothing$ becomes the distance cd. The remaining portion of output per worker measured by ed in the diagram or by $0w'$ is the income per worker, that is, the wage paid out by the working collective producing with a capital-labor ratio $0e$.

Putting the left-hand side of relation 5.6 equal to zero, we obtain an equilibrium level of $\varnothing$ (call it $\varnothing^*$) which may be stated as

$$\varnothing^* = B/A. \tag{5.9}$$

Such an equilibrium $\varnothing^*$ is shown by the segment ab in Figure 5.3 for the equilibrium capital-labor ratio $(K/L)_1^*$ and an equilibrium wage rate w^*. Because our firm accumulates all that is not paid out to workers as income, the rate of growth of capital, k, becomes $\varnothing$ multiplied by L, which measures the absolute level of accumulation, divided by K; but as stated in relation 5.10 that is nothing but the marginal productivity of capital X_K:

$$k = \varnothing L/K = X_K. \tag{5.10}$$

And this, we know already, is the slope of the f contour in Figure 5.3. Thus, when it is in equilibrium, our labor-managed firm will be expanding its capital stock at the rate measured by the slope of f at b. Consequently, with unchanging capital-labor ratio and constant returns to scale employment and output will also be growing at the same rate X_K.

To study the nature of our equilibrium let us turn to Figure 5.4. In it we have plotted on the vertical axis the equilibrium capital return per worker $\varnothing^*$ ($=B/A$) together with three alternative forms of the $\varnothing$ function. Probably the most common is where $\varnothing$ is indefinitely increasing. The Cobb-Douglas function and a wide class of other linearly homogeneous functions would reveal such a pattern. The equilibrium is obtained at point E_1 where $\varnothing = B/A$. From the behavioral rule stated in relation 5.6 it immediately follows that when we are to the right of E_1 in Figure 5.4 the wage rate must be increasing, and consequently, as is easily seen from the construction of Figure 5.3, the capital-labor ratio must also be increasing. On the other hand, to the left of E_1 the reverse will happen and the capital-labor ratio must be indefinitely declining. In other words, the equilibrium shown at E_1 in Figure 5.4 is an unstable one. Given our behavioral rule stated in equation 5.6, once the capital-labor ratio falls short of $(K/L)_1^*$ it must decline indefinitely

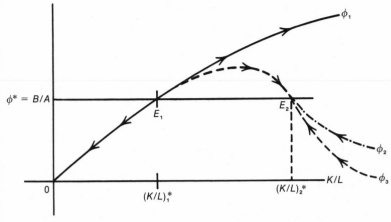

Figure 5.4

together with declining wages. Of course, this does not say anything about the absolute level of output of the firm, the subject to which we will turn presently.

To the right of E_1 wages and the capital-labor ratio must be indefinitely increasing in the case of contour $\emptyset_1$, which we have already termed the normal situation. On the other hand, if the marginal productivity of capital declines significantly with increasing capital-labor ratios and perhaps even reaches a level of zero marginal productivity of capital—that is, the situation of isoquants parallel to the K axis—another equilibrium E_2 in Figure 5.4 will be reached for the equilibrium capital-labor ratio $(K/L)_2^*$. In contrast to the first equilibrium, this will be a stable one. All this is shown by the arrows along the contours $\emptyset_2$ and $\emptyset_3$.

Of course, as was argued earlier for the case of increasing and diminishing returns, if the firm found itself to the left of E_1, it could always keep its labor employment constant, and with accumulation which must be taking place as the marginal productivity of capital is positive, wait until the equilibrium capital-labor ratio at E_1 were reached—and in fact such behavior would be more realistic. Only at that point, or slightly beyond it, would the behavioral rule 5.6 become operative. And constrained or unconstrained growth, depending on the specific form of the $\emptyset$ function, would be guaranteed beyond that point.

We may now turn briefly to the absolute level of output and the absolute level of capital and labor inputs corresponding to the growth patterns identified thus far with respect to the capital-labor ratio. The alternative possible outcomes are illustrated in Figure 5.5. Two equilibrium capital-labor ratios found in Figure 5.4 are now reflected by the two rays in Figure 5.5 marked E_1 and E_2, respectively. If the firm finds itself on the first of the two rays with a relatively low capital-labor ratio, at a point such as a, it will remain on that ray indefinitely and move to the right along it indefinitely at a rate equal to the marginal productivity of capital. On the other hand, if the firm has a capital stock somewhat smaller than that required by the ray E_1, we will have a pattern illustrated by the locus ad, with a continuous increase in output, a continuously declining capital-labor ratio, and continuously increasing stock of capital and labor employment. The indefinite decline in the capital-labor ratio will be generated by a faster growth of employment than that of the

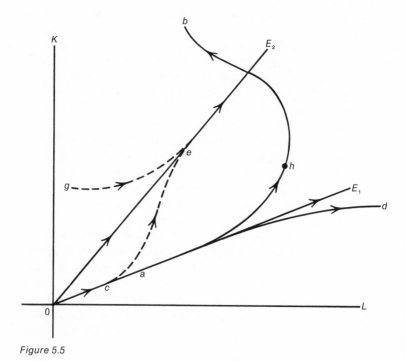

Figure 5.5

capital stock. This is so because below E_1 in Figure 5.4 the rate of growth of capital must be increasing (recall relation 4.10, and thus the rate of growth of employment must be growing even faster to reduce the capital-labor ratio.[6]

On the other hand, if the firm finds itself slightly above the ray $0E_1$ the normal outcome will be a contour such as *ahb*, corresponding to indefinitely increasing capital-labor ratios. At first the firm will increase both capital and labor in absolute value, then beyond point *h* labor employment will be reduced but output will continue to increase and will eventually reach the stage of declining absolute level of output. Of course, wages will be growing throughout this process. Alternatively, corresponding to the second equilibrium in Figure 5.4, we can find a path such as *ce* or *ge* in Figure 5.5 leading the firm from one equilibrium capital-labor ratio to another or from a disequilibrium high capital-labor ratio to an equilibrium lower capital-labor ratio along $0E_2$.

Turning now to what is probably the most relevant and realistic path, the one illustrated by *ahb*, it is not difficult to see that in the vicinity of point *a* both the capital stock and the labor employment will be increasing. This is so because if the firm is in the first equilibrium, both capital and labor must be increasing at the same rate. A small deflection from the ray $0E_1$ will only make these rates of growth unequal; it certainly could not reverse their sign. Only after a period of substantial accumulation and an increasing capital-labor ratio will the behavioral rule 5.6 lead to such substantial increases in wage rate that the rate of expansion of the labor force will turn from positive to negative.

This conclusion—that is, the existence of point *h* in the diagram—calls for additional proof and clarification. Using our notation, the wage rate is defined as

$$w = f - f'K/L. \tag{5.11}$$

Differentiating relation 5.11 defined for the change in the wage rate results in

$$dw = -f''K/Ld(K/L). \tag{5.12}$$

6. Of course it is necessary to recall that adherence to the behavioral rule stated in relation 5.6 in this situation may be highly unrealistic and the working collective may prefer not to hire any new laborers and wait until, with accumulation, a point on the ray $0E_1$ or beyond it (Figure 5.5), is reached.

If at a certain point in the evolution of the firm the labor force is to be stationary, then this change in the wage rate stated in relation 5.12 must equal the change in the wage rate given by the behavioral rule of relation 5.6. This is so because, with a stationary labor force, the accumulation per laborer, $\emptyset$, will be translated exactly into an increment in the capital-labor ratio by the amount $\emptyset$; if the wage for the new capital-labor ratio, as constructed in Figure 5.3 is exactly the one predicted by the behavioral rule (5.6), the new wage equilibrium will not require any adjustment in employment. Consequently the labor force will be stationary. The condition for a stationary labor force can thus be stated as

$$-f'' \cdot K/L = +A\emptyset - B. \tag{5.13}$$

The geometry of this condition is depicted in Figure 5.6. From the law of diminishing marginal productivity of capital the locus $-f''$ is an indefinitely decreasing one, with the increasing capital-labor ratio adding to the steepness of the combined $-f''K/L$ locus. On the other hand, for the function $\emptyset_1$ in Figure 5.4 we have a locus such as $A\emptyset - B$ in Figure 5.6 There will be one intersection such as the

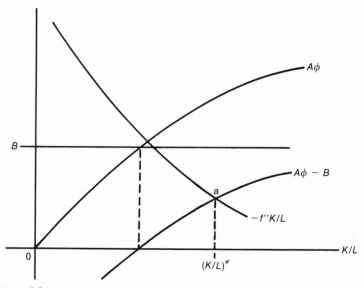

Figure 5.6

one at a for the capital-labor ratio $K/L^{\#}$ (see Figure 5.6 for notation). It is at this level of the capital-labor ratio that equation 5.13 is satisfied and for which labor employment will be stationary. For capital-labor ratios higher than that ratio, the labor force will be declining, for levels lower than this critical capital-labor ratio, the labor force will be increasing.

It is immediately apparent that an increase in the target profit rate per worker, B, will increase the critical capital-labor ratio, which will reverse the trend in employment and thus in a sense postpone reductions in employment. A reduction in A—that is, a diminution in the share of profit rate per worker of the preceding period that the workers want to appropriate in terms of current wages in the current period—will have the same effect, although in this case the function will be rotated about the origin rather than shifted.

These considerations of the changes in the two behavioristic parameters A and B suggest other interesting results regarding the entire growth process. One not entirely self-evident result is that a reduction in the target profit rate per worker, B, will increase, for any prescribed capital-labor ratio, the likelihood that the firm will find itself in the output range to the right of point E_1, the range in which the capital-labor ratio keeps increasing indefinitely together with labor incomes. In fact, if the target level B is reduced all the way to zero, the firm will normally be guaranteed indefinite growth in the capital-labor ratio provided that it starts with any level of capital and a finite labor force. This is immediately apparent by considering Figure 5.4 and realizing that with B tending to zero, equilibrium E_1 will converge to zero. If this happens, the equilibrium such as E_2, if it exists, would, of course, also have to move indefinitely to the right or disappear altogether.

Because reasonable values of A are between zero and one, no alterations in that parameter by the workers' council can produce a similar collapse of E_1 into the origin. However, increases in A can again increase the firm's chance of finding itself in the zone of increasing wages and capital-labor ratios. On the other hand, with A tending toward zero the critical level of $\varnothing^*$ in Figure 5.4 will tend to increase indefinitely, and consequently equilibria such as E_1 will also move indefinitely to higher and higher capital-labor ratios. This implies that for very low or zero A, that is, with a very austere policy of wage adjustment, any reasonable initial capital-labor ratio must fall within the unstable zone below E_1. This means that the behavioral rule stated in relation 5.6 must necessarily lead to continuing reductions in the capital-labor ratio and a convergence of that ratio toward zero. At the same time, wages would have to be declining indefinitely and the size of the working community increasing continuously. Of course, one can again invoke at this point the argument used twice before to the effect that under such conditions the working community would prefer to arrest employment expansions and concentrate on increased labor income through accumulation.

IV. Wage Adjustment with a Target Minimum Return to Capital

In this section we will explore briefly an alternative rule of wage adjustment by the labor-managed firm. We retain the assumption of the self-financing model but we postulate that wages will be adjusted upward or downward depending on whether profits, that is, value of output in excess of the wage, correspond to a satisfactory return to capital or not. From the point of view of a labor-managed firm, this objective may be a less realistic one. At the same time, as we will argue in the subsequent section, it may be more consistent with a social optimum. In fact, the rule explored here applies much better to a large capitalist corporation which has to rely on self-financing for accumulation and which is under continuing pressure from the labor unions to adjust wages upward if the return on capital exceeds a certain level considered normal or satisfactory by the union and perhaps by the economic community at large. Restricting ourselves exclusively to the case of constant returns to scale, we may express this behavioral rule as

$$w_t - w_{t-1} = A[(K/L)(X_K - B)]_{t-1}, \qquad (5.14)$$

where A and B are behavioral constants. B now reflects the desired or adequate return to capital. On the other hand, the capital-labor ratio appears on the right-hand side of relation 5.14 to make a transition from excess profitability per unit of capital to excess profitability per unit of labor; it is the latter that is relevant for any wage adjustments. Putting the left-hand side of relation 5.14 again equal to zero, we obtain a new equilibrium condition which simply is contained in the requirement that the marginal productivity of capital effectively be equal to the target level B—or, alternatively, that $\emptyset$, as defined in the preceding section, be equal to B times the capital-labor ratio, i.e.,

$$\emptyset^* = B(K/L). \tag{5.15}$$

Diagrammatically the equilibrium levels of $\emptyset$ and the capital-labor ratio are found at point E in Figure 5.7. At E the profit rate per worker equals the target rate per worker. To the left of E, as indicated by the arrows, the solution point will now converge toward E, and the same holds for points to the right of E along $\emptyset$. This must be so because for capital-labor ratios falling short of $(K/L)^*$ the marginal productivity of capital must be increasing, and vice versa for capital-labor ratios exceeding $(X/L)^*$. The equilibrium E in Figure 5.7 is thus a stable one which follows from the concavity of $\emptyset$. Of course, once point E is reached, the firm's output and employment and capital stock will all expand at the constant rate equal to the marginal productivity of capital, that is, to B. Wages will remain constant over time.

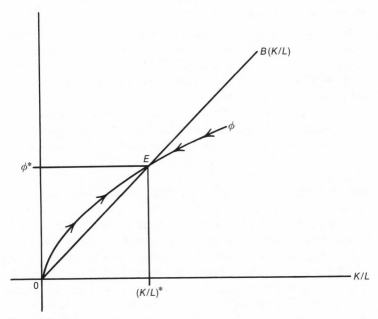

Figure 5.7

If we take the case illustrated by the path *ahb* in Figure 5.5 as the most typical of the target set in relation to profitability per worker, we come out with a comparative set of conclusions paralleling some others found by Vanek [3, chaps. 2 and 19]. The target setting in relation to profits per worker, which we consider more consistent with self-management, will tend to produce, as compared to target setting in relation to profits per unit of capital, (1) higher capital-labor ratios in the long run and (2) a comparatively lesser tendency toward concentration and bigness. We may paraphrase the second conclusion and say that the corporate-cum-union rule of linking wage changes to returns to capital will be much more conducive to the indefinite growth and expansion often associated with large Western corporations than the other behavioristic rule stated in relation 5.6. Although throughout this paper we are dealing with situations where product prices are constant, this conclusion is relevant for the comparative assessment of market structures in capitalist and labor-managed economies, respectively.

V. The "Realistic" Behavior of Yugoslav Firms and Maximization of Income per Worker

We have now completed our exploration of the various forms of wage setting in conjunction with Professor Horvat's "realistic" hypothesis. Because some of the earlier hypotheses—including those made by Ward, Domar, and Vanek—claim maximization of income per worker, we ought to make an attempt to relate the two kinds of hypotheses or, more exactly, to set some additional hypotheses.

To begin with a general statement let us say that upon closer examination the difference between the income-maximization-per-worker hypothesis and the "realistic" hypothesis of Professor Horvat is much less significant than one would have thought. In fact, most of our work in the present paper indicates that, stated with proper qualifications, the short-run profit maximization criterion with prescribed subjective wage rates leads in most situations in the long run to a state involving maximization of income per worker.

But let us now turn to the detail underlying this statement. We recall first that in what we have called the socialist case, where the firm adjusts wages, pays a fixed price for capital to society, and returns any profits to society, the long-run solution is maximization of income per worker. We recall that in that case the long-run solution must always be found at the locus of maximum physical efficiency, which is the locus of long-run equilibria of labor-managed firms that maximize income per worker.

For the two self-financing models it is of central importance to distinquish two cases: (1) where the target rate of profit is zero, that is, in our equations 5.6 and 5.14, B is equal to zero, and (2) where B is a positive constant. In the first situation what we usually refer to as equilibrium is effectively possible because wage rates and capital stock can simultaneously be held constant. For the technology with increasing and diminishing returns such an equilibrium state effectively is one of maximization of income per worker for the capital stock at which it is reached. It is another matter that the equilibrium involves disbursement of the entire value of product and that once the firm's factor inputs are displaced from the equilibrium positions the firm very likely will never return to the equilibrium.

On the other hand, when the technology is subject to constant returns to scale—still retaining the assumption that the target rate of profit is zero—the static equilibrium at which all variables remain unchanged is impossible because accumulation can never cease as long as the marginal productivity of capital remains positive. However, with B equal to zero in both cases, the one discussed in Section III and the one discussed in Section IV (see the constructions of Figures 5.4 and 5.7), income per worker or the wage rate in the context of our present analysis must be increasing indefinitely as long as the marginal productivity of capital remains positive. Thus we can say that in the two cases just noted income per worker still is maximized in the very long run, the wage rate converging at all times to an equilibrium maximum state which has, so to speak, escaped to an infinite capital-labor ratio.

Let us now take up the more general case where B, the target rate of profit, is positive. In the context of the self-financing model, where the target is stated in terms of a return to capital per worker, we know for increasing and diminishing returns that, starting from any reasonable factor input mix and level of output, short-run equilibria of the labor-managed firm must be changing and must eventually reach a stage in which the capital-labor ratio will indefinitely be increasing together with an increasing wage rate. Again we can refer to this as income maximization per worker in the very long run with an elusive target maximum.

With self-financing, a positive target return on B, and constant returns to scale, we have steady-state solutions both where the target is stated in terms of return to capital per worker and where the target is stated in terms of return to capital per unit of capital. In all these steady-state equilibria, income per worker in effect is maximized at the corresponding target return to capital, whether per worker or per unit of capital, in the sense that for the actually realized return per unit of capital in the steady state the income per worker could under no circumstances be increased by changes in production.

In the case where the target is stated in terms of a return to capital per unit of capital we know from the preceding section that the equilibrium steady state will be a stable one and that consequently, starting from any initial conditions, the firm will converge toward a solution involving maximization of income per worker in the sense just stated. If instead the objective is stated in terms of the return to capital per laborer, that is, in the context of our analysis of Section III, the situation is somewhat more complicated. However, the overall conclusion need not be altered: again with proper qualifications the firm operating under constant returns to scale with a positive B is in the long run aiming at maximization of income per laborer.

We have already covered the situation of steady states such as those corresponding to E_1 and E_2 in Figure 5.4. The second equilibrium is a stable one and thus the firm in the vicinity of that equilibrium, if such an equilibrium exists, will converge with maximization of income per worker. On the other hand, the more normal and necessary equilibrium E_1 is, as we know, unstable. However, to the right of it for capital-labor ratios exceeding the equilibrium level, the firm, as we have shown, will keep increasing its capital-labor ratio either to the point where stable equilibrium such as E_2 is reached or indefinitely. In the latter case also the income per worker will be indefinitely increasing and this again we can speak of maximization of income per worker at an elusive, infinitely high capital-labor ratio. Only if the initial equilibrium were to be found at a point to the left of E_1 would the capital-labor ratio tend to decline indefinitely with indefinitely declining income per worker. This is the only case where our results lead to a significant departure from a solution maximizing income per worker. However, as we have argued before on several occasions, it would be extremely unlikely to find a firm behaving in the way indicated by the path to the left of E_1 in Figure 5.4; rather, the working community realizing returns to capital per worker less than the stated target level would prefer not to hire additional workers but rather to keep employment constant, and with (necessarily) positive accumulation wait until the return to capital per worker reaches the desired level. At that point the firm would find itself at or to the right of E_1, in one of the situations maximizing income per worker described earlier.

VI. The "Realistic" Rule and Elasticities of Supply

It seems that one of the reasons Professor Horvat suggested his new hypothesis was to show the absurdity of a negatively sloped short-run supply curve of the labor-managed firms originally obtained by Ward. While we certainly agree with the proposition that labor-managed firms' supply functions in the short run or otherwise cannot be expected to be negatively sloped, it seems to us that Horvat's argument can be pushed further in the direction of a realistic representation in the light of our present results.

The first difficulty we have to deal with is the concept of the "short run." The theorists of labor management, like all economic theorists, usually fail to specify what they mean by the term "short run." Unless duration is specified very little can be said. In the context of our present work we feel that the most appropriate short run is a period of about one year, the period for which short-run plans of the worker-managed firms are made and also the period for which profits or residue income are computed and wage rates, in the sense of Horvat's paper, are determined.

It is not realistic to expect that the working community would vary the size of its membership over periods as short as a year in response to changes in market prices. And thus in what we have identified as our short run probably the most realistic conclusion is that elasticity of supply actually is zero on account of a short-run fixed level of employment and fixed capacity. Of course, once we depart from a model including only primary factors and include intermediate goods, the elasticity can be expected to be other than zero on account of the equilibrium adjustment of use of intermediate goods. However, the existence of such goods now will turn the elasticity from zero to positive rather than from zero to negative, as is the case in the Ward model of labor adjustment.

Over longer periods of time a lasting change in the price of the product in competitive product markets will affect the entire dynamic processes described in the preceding sections of this paper. The static equilibria, the steady states, and the disequilibrium path of adjustment will all be affected by such changes in prices. The static long-run equilibrium of the socialist model will be adjusted in very much the same way as the equilibrium of a conventional labor-managed firm maximizing income per worker, as shown by Vanek [3]. The equilibrium steady states of the self-financing models, to the extent that they exist, will adjust to changing market prices along the lines analyzed in the same study, for technologies subject to constant returns to scale. Specifically, noting that profits per worker $\emptyset$ will vary with the price at which the product of the firm can be sold, we note immediately from Figures 5.7 and 5.4 that an increase in price from its thus far assumed unitary level will move stable equilibria to the right, that is, to higher capital-labor ratios, and unstable equilibria to the left to lower capital-labor ratios. At the same time, during the dynamic adjustment from the original equilibrium to the new state in each period output, profits and wages will be higher with the increased price than they would have been without a price increase. In this sense of dynamic adjustment we still can speak of a positive supply elasticity, and thus confirm Horvat's general hypothesis.

Moreover, in the context of general equilibrium interindustry and intraindustry adjustment, we will have the desirable effect of resource reallocation toward higher relative prices. We will consider the efficiency of structural adjustment in the following section.

VII. The "Realistic" Rule and Efficiency of Resource Allocation

It is obvious that what we have called the "realistic" behavior of the Yugoslav firm will have definite effects on resource allocation and on its efficiency compared to an absolute standard of optimality. We can organize this subject under two distinct headings: (1) efficiency of resource allocation within a firm and (2) efficiency of resource allocation among firms and among industries.

The first heading need not detain us for very long because we have gone a long way in the direction of answering the questions raised in the preceding sections. In what we have termed the socialist model in Section II, the long-run equilibrum of the firm will be found at the point of maximum physical efficiency consistent with the prescribed price of capital. In this case, then, resource utilization from the point of view of the firm itself is as efficient as can be.

The conclusions with respect to intrafirm efficiency for the self-financing model with target return to capital per worker and increasing and diminishing returns to scale are less optimistic. In that case if an equilibrium exists it must be internally inefficient, as we have seen in Section III. If an equilibrium does not exist and the firm finds itself in perpetual motion, it must sooner or later pass into the zone of diminishing returns and declining average factor productivities. And this in itself is technologically inefficient, at least from the point of view of the individual firm.

On the other hand, with constant returns to scale and self-financing under either of our rules, factor productivities are always maximized for the prevailing capital-labor ratios, and thus any inefficiencies of resource allocation can arise only in the interfirm context. In this context the "realistic" rule will have quite different implications for the socialist model than for the self-financing model. The implications of the former will on the whole be more favorable than those of the latter. Let us turn first to the socialist model.

When society charges all individual firms the same price for capital, in the long run the marginal value products of capital will tend to be equalized and thus no reallocation of capital assets will exist that would increase total national product (given the existing distribution of employment among firms). Moreover, if technologies accessible to all firms are the same, it is obvious that with equalization of marginal value products of capital the marginal value products of labor will also tend to be equalized through the process of long-run adjustment discussed in Section II, somewhere along the locus of maximum technical efficiency. In fact, the "realistic" rule will converge, under free entry in the long run, toward the same Pareto-optimal solution (of course we are assuming competitive conditions throughout) as does the pure labor-managed system based on maximization of income per worker (see Vanek [3]), and as does the ideal capitalist solution with zero excess profits.

By contrast, the self-financing models—at least in their strict interpretation—imply economies composed of individual firms which act as microcosms in themselves unrelated to one another on the side of factor markets. Each firm generates all its capital assets without regard to some external or objective conditions of capital market, and each firm, at least implicitly, can draw on an unlimited pool of labor resources. In this strict interpretation, of course, there is no reason for marginal value products of factors to be equalized. Thus we can have quite significant departures from an efficient allocation of resources. Of course, by design, instruction from a planning office, or government regulation, the target rates of accumulation (expressed by the coefficient B in our earlier discussion) could be set in such a way as to lead, in the case of technologies subject to constant returns to scale, to steady states in which the marginal value of products of capital are equalized. Especially in the model where the target is stated in terms of a desired return per unit of capital, B could simply be required to be the same for all firms. But this might be only a partial or an entirely inadequate solution because with B identical for all firms the long range steady states would involve rates of growth identical for all firms and also identical to the rate of growth of employment and the capital stock. Obviously such a phenomenally golden age is not likely over any long period of time if national capital resources are expected to grow at all at a rate higher than that of the labor force.

In the self-financing model with a target return to capital per worker, equalization of marginal returns to capital among firms may be much more difficult, if not impossible, especially in view of the fact that, as we have seen, the most likely outcome is a continuing nonsteady state of dynamic disequilibrium in which capital-labor ratios are indefinitely increasing. However, that alternative may prove comparatively more efficient in the context of matching a growing national capital-labor ratio with the primary proportions of the individual labor-managed firms. Also, as we have argued already, self-financing with a target return to capital per worker may have the comparative advantage of keeping the size of the firm within bounds and thus reducing the danger of oligopolistic concentration.

The single most important conclusion from the discussion of this section, and in fact from the discussion of this entire paper, is that if self-financing is the dominant rule of the game, as it would appear to be in present-day Yugoslavia, some safeguards are necessary to preserve some minimum degree of contiguity of factor markets among individual firms. There are many tools that can be used to accomplish that aim; some of them will be clear from the present analysis. Of course, this should not detract from the fact that, as far as we can judge from economic analysis, the pure labor-management model with effectively operative factor markets, or, for that matter, the socialist model discussed in Section II, should prove to be structurally far more effective. Self-financing has the important advantage, especially for countries in early stages of development that are incapable of mobilizing investment resources at a high rate in other ways. However, as one of the present authors has shown [3], there is no difficulty in generating equal rates of capital formation and growth of national product through a national effort which at the same time is consistent with a high degree of structural efficiency of resource allocation.

VIII. The "Realistic" Rule and Technological Progress

Up to this point we have neglected one important fact of real life: namely, that in the real world technologies and production functions are not invariant, as we have assumed thus far, but tend to change over time. As is well known from the economic literature, the problem of handling adequately the phenomenon of technological progress is by no means a simple one. And thus we will restrict ourselves in this section to some general observations based on a highly streamlined and simplified set of assumptions regarding technological progress.

First, we will deal with only one firm, and, second, we will assume technologies subject to constant returns to scale only. The technological progress that we want to speak about is of the disembodied variety and moreover is Hicks-neutral, that is, augmenting productivity of both factors at the same rate. Also we will deal only with the case which we identified earlier as more consistent with labor participation in management, that is, where the wage-increasing target is based on return to capital per worker rather than return to capital per unit of capital.

The key behavioristic equation now can be written as

$$
\begin{aligned}
(dw/dt)/w - a &= AX_k K/L - Be^{at} \\
&= e^{at}(Af' \cdot K/L - B),
\end{aligned}
\tag{5.16}
$$

where a is the autonomous rate of Hicks-neutral technological

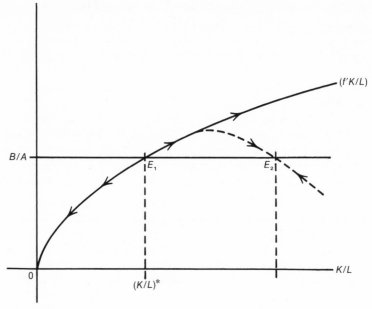

Figure 5.8

progress, (hence $X_k = f'e^{at}$), where A and B are behavioristic constants, and where f again is a function of the capital-labor ratio. We
have now dropped the difference-equation form and for simplicity
are relying entirely on first differentials with respect to time. The
left-hand side of equation 5.16 implies that the working community
considers the autonomous rate of technological progress a as the
normal rate at which wages ought to grow, and the actual changes
in the wage rate, which depend on the fulfillment or nonfulfillment
of the target of profitability, are to be measured from that autonomous rate of increase, a. The new behavioristic equation also implies
that the target rate of profit per worker ought to grow at the exogenous rate a. The equilibrium steady states are now found, similarly
to Section III, in Figure 5.8. For equilibrium—that is, for a constant
capital-labor ratio and for a wage rate growing at the constant rate
a—the key function f' times the capital-labor ratio must again equal
B/A:

$$(f'K/L)^* = B/A. \tag{5.17}$$

At the capital-labor ratio $(K/L)^*$ the firm will find itself in a steady state with respect to its factor proportions. However, the wage rate now will be growing at a constant rate a and so will the marginal physical product of capital. That product being equal to the rate of growth of capital itself within our model, the rate of growth of capital when the firm operates at the equilibrium E_1 in Figure 5.8 will continuously be accelerating at the rate a. And because the capital-labor ratio is constant at E_1, the size of the working community will also be growing at that accelerating rate. As before, for capital-labor ratios in excess of $(K/L)^*$, the capital-labor ratio will be increasing, and vice versa to the left of E_1 in the diagram. In other words, the equilibrium E_1 then, as before, is found to be unstable. Again as before, an upper stable equilibrium may or may not exist at a point such as E_2. If normally such an equilibrium E_2 does not exist at a finite capital-labor ratio, the continuing increase of the capital-labor ratio along the solid contour to the right of E_1 is highly plausible. Although at E_1 the rate of growth of capital is accelerating, as we move in the northeast direction, to the right of E_1, indicated by the arrows, the declining value of f' ought to be offsetting the basic acceleration of growth of capital stock. By and large it can be expected that when the firm finds itself in the range to the right of E_1 and proceeds to higher and higher capital-labor ratios, it does so at a more or less stable rate of growth of capital. Moreover, while this is happening, the capital-labor ratio must be increasing, which implies that the rate of growth of labor also may be fairly stable but definitely lower than that of capital. As we move to higher and higher capital-labor ratios, along the solid contour, of course, the wage rates must be increasing, and they are increasing for two reasons: first, because of the diminishing slope of the locus $f'K/L$ (see the construction in Figure 5.3), and, second, because of the autonomous technological progress at the rate a.

To the left of E_1 in Figure 5.8, on the other hand, the conjecture about stabilizing behavior of the working collective no longer can be made as it was in Section III. The working collective may see its wages now growing at a rate less that that implied by the negative effect of the right-hand side of equation 5.16. And since the firm is not hurt by declining wages, the continuous decline in capital-labor ratio indicated in Figure 5.8 is more of a real possibility.

The effects of autonomous changes in the behavioral constants A and B on the dynamics of the participatory firm are quite analogous to those established in Section III. Probably the most important one is that if the target B is reduced to zero, the equilibrium E_1 in Figure 5.8 collapses into the origin, and thus the entire solid locus f' times K/L in Figure 5.8 corresponds to infinitely growing capital-labor ratios. The firm now must progress on an expansion path in the capital-labor plane such as the path $0ahb$ in Figure 5.5 as long as the initial capital-labor ratio assumes any positive value.

For similar reasons an increase in B can change a dynamic process of adjustment from one involving collapsing capital-labor ratios to one corresponding to increasing capital-labor ratios. The effect of a change in A, that is, in the proportion of the return to capital that the community wants to appropriate in the form of wages in the following period, is just the opposite. An increase in A will shift downward the horizontal line in Figure 5.8 and thus lead to a continuing increase in the capital-labor ratio from a situation of gradual decline in that ratio.

References

1. E. D. Domar, "The Soviet Collective Farm as a Producer Cooperative," *American Economic Review*, 56 (Sept. 1966), 734–757.

2. B. Horvat, "Prilog zasnisavanju teorije jugoslovenskih poduzeca" (A Contribution to the Theory of the Yugoslav Firm), *Ekonomska Analiza*, 1 (1967), 7–28.

3. J. Vanek, *The General Theory of Labor-Managed Market Economies* (Ithaca, N.Y.: Cornell University Press, 1970).

4. B. Ward, "The Firm in Illyria: Market Syndicalism," *American Economic Review*, 48 (Sept. 1958), 566–589.

PART III

INCOME DISTRIBUTION

6 | The Equilibrium of the Labor-Managed Firm and a Variable Income Distribution Schedule*

In a recent study[1] I examined the equilibrium of a labor-managed firm, that is, a firm maximizing income per employee, on the assumption that there is a variety of skills and types of labor operating in the enterprise. The key assumption underlying the analysis was the so-called income distribution schedule on which the worker-managers agree collectively, and which assigns to each job category certain constant relative wages reflecting the share of total income to be assigned to a member of the particular job category. Thus, for example, the unskilled laborers' coefficient might be equal to one and that for the skilled laborer equal to two, this implying that whatever the final outcome of the operation of the enterprise the skilled worker will always receive twice as much per week, month, or year as the unskilled laborer.

Judging both from the practice of the Yugoslav economy and on grounds of a priori reasoning, however, it is perfectly possible that the wages-shares assigned to individual job categories would not be constant but could vary with the level and success of performance of the enterprise as a whole. Thus, for example, it is perfectly imaginable that the higher-echelon administrative workers and the general manager of the labor-managed firm might be given a progressive income wage and the unskilled workers a regressive one, although one that permitted increases in income with improved performance of the enterprise. Alternatively, the firm which recognizes the necessity of income differentiation in the short run but aims at income equalization in the long run might have strongly progressive coefficients for the lowest income categories and regressive ones for the

* Cornell Department of Economics Working Paper no. 48, 1973.

1. *The General Theory of Labor-Managed Market Economies* (Ithaca, N.Y.: Cornell University Press, 1970), chap. 11.

highly paid workers. The purpose of this brief paper is to derive the equilibrium conditions for the labor-managed firm which has such a generalized income distribution schedule.

To be more precise, using y to express the basic remuneration unit in terms of which everyone is paid and a_i to express the income coefficient assigned to the i'th job category, we thus can write the variable a_i as a function of y as follows:

$$a_i = a_i(y); \qquad a_i' \gtreqless 0, \qquad (6.1)$$

a_i is a continuous function of y and can be increasing or decreasing; or it can be a constant, which is the simpler case dealt with in my earlier study. The production function used by the labor-managed firm is a conventional neoclassical one depending on n different types of labor L_i as well as on the input of capital, K. Thus, using X to express the physical level of output, we have a production function:

$$X = X(L_i, \ldots, L_n; K). \qquad (6.2)$$

The basic remuneration unit y is defined as

$$y = (pX - p_k K)/\sum a_i L_i, \qquad (6.3)$$

where p and p_k stand for constant prices of product and of the use of capital, respectively.

Clearly the objective of the firm is to maximize the basic remuneration unit y.[2] Using the standard procedure, that is, differentiating y with respect to all the variable factors of production, we obtain the first-order conditions for a maximum remuneration unit. In relation 6.4, using subscripts of X to express partial differentials,

$$\partial y/\partial L_i = [pX_i \sum a_i L_i \\ - (pX - p_k K)(a_i + a_i' L_i \, \partial y/\partial L_i)]/(\sum a_i L_i)^2, \qquad (6.4)$$

we have computed the first partial differential of y with respect to L_i.

2. Of course, with strongly regressive income coefficients, a_i, it could happen that with an increasing basic remuneration unit y, the actual income assigned to the i'th labor category per worker would be declining. In that case the objective of income maximization by the labor-managed firm would become ambiguous because maximization of y would not necessarily mean maximization of corresponding income for every member of the enterprise. But we can safely eliminate such cases of strongly negative slopes of the a function as absurd.

Rearranging and putting 6.4 equal to zero we obtain relation 6.5:

$$\partial y/\partial L_i[1 + (px - p_kK)a_i'/(\textstyle\sum a_iL_i)^2]$$
$$= 0 = [pX_i \textstyle\sum a_iL_i - a_i(pX - p_kK)]/(\textstyle\sum a_iL_i)^2. \qquad (6.5)$$

From this, finally, we obtain the important requirement for equilibrium in the employment of the i'th labor category:

$$pX_i = a_i(pX - p_kK)/\textstyle\sum a_iL_i = a_iy. \qquad (6.6)$$

Perhaps surprisingly, the result is no different from the one obtained for constant a_i's. The actual remuneration of the i'th labor category per unit of labor supplied, a_iy, must be equal in equilibrium to the value of marginal physical product. Using the same procedure for the input of capital—a procedure we have omitted for reasons of simplicity—we obtain the same result as before:

$$pX_k = p_k. \qquad (6.7)$$

Relation 6.7 requires that in equilibrium the price of capital must equal the value of marginal physical product of capital.

To sum up what we have established here: Whether the income distribution schedule is composed of constant coefficients a_i or of coefficients changing with the basic remuneration unit, the objective of the labor-managed firm attempting to maximize income per worker is to bring in as many laborers to each labor category as necessary to make them earn their respective values of marginal product, and to hire sufficient capital to render its cost equal to its marginal value product.

7 | The Subsistence Income, Effort, and Developmental Potential of Labor Management and Other Economic Systems*

With JUAN G. ESPINOSA

In a recent study [2] one of the present authors has argued that a significant advantage of labor management is its capability to produce efficient allocations—or combinations—of real income on the one hand and effort (producing that real income) on the other. The argument concentrated primarily on an advanced economy where the incomes earned and produced are far in excess of what we might call subsistence income.

In developing countries, where incomes—especially the incomes of those who have not yet been incorporated into the modern developmental sector—are usually very low, not far from subsistence levels, the problem is quite different and deserves special attention. In fact, real income, subsistence, effort, and incentives may be variables most central to the question of economic development, and the choice of an economic organization for development should depend heavily on them.

In this paper we will attempt to show that if labor management is a suitable system from the standpoint of choosing an optimum of labor effort in general, its comparative advantage with respect to other economic systems is even greater in the context of developing countries. To show this a set of short- and long-run *subsistence-effort functions* is developed in Section I, relating various levels of real income to maximum effort producible consistent with that income. Section II combines that analytical tool with the effort-

* Cornell Department of Economics Discussion Paper no. 14, June 1971. A revised and shortened version of this paper appeared in *Economic Journal*, 82 (September 1972), with Juan G. Espinosa, who was then a graduate student in the Department of Economics at Cornell, as co-author. An elaboration of one point, bearing on labor unions in capitalist countries, was incorporated in the revised version.

income possibility locus[1] in showing the long-range adjustment of a labor-managed firm in typical developing countries. Section III contrasts the solutions shown for the labor-managed firm (or economy) with solutions likely to occur under capitalist conditions. Section IV discusses more thoroughly the concepts of short run and long run in the context of our analysis and gives them two alternative interpretations, both very relevant for the problem at hand. Section V integrates the analysis into a more general setting of theory of economic development. Finally, Section VI summarizes the results and draws general conclusions.

I. The Subsistence-Effort Loci

The key notion on which we would like to elaborate in this section is that what we usually refer to loosely as the substance minimum wage or subsistence minimum income, in the context of developmental analysis, is by no means an unambiguous and easily observable or determinable magnitude. The primary emphasis here is on the fact that the subsistence minimum or the real income necessary to sustain a human being will depend heavily on the amount of effort which he is supposed to supply. A man who can be completely idle can survive on real income far below that of a man who is supposed to work hard for eight hours a day.

This notion is by no means new, not even in economic theory, where normally the real world penetrates with a considerable time lag.[2] For our purposes we will distinguish between the *short-run* (or short-range) subsistence-effort locus and the *long-run* (or long-range) subsistence-effort locus. We will elaborate on the distinction in greater detail in Section IV, when a precise definition of the length of each time period will make more sense. For the moment let us simply remember that the short run is significantly less than the long run.

In Figure 7.1 along the vertical axis we measure real income, y, while from the origin 0 to the left we measure the amount of effort

1. I have used such a locus, comparable to the traditional production possibility function, in deriving the equilibrium output of a labor-managed firm.
2. For example, it underlies T. C. Koopmans' *consumption set* in his first essay [1]. Also it has been used in a seminar at Cornell University by J. Mirrlees. It is his presentation that helped me in the extension of my earlier work [2 and 3, pp. 30, 31] and I should like to express hereby my gratitude to him.

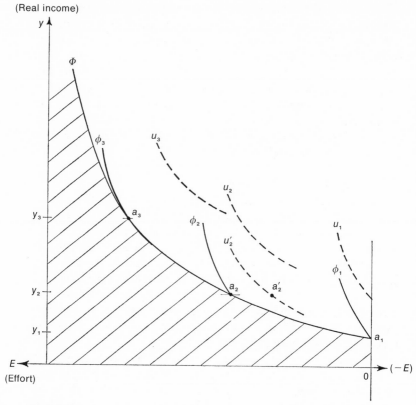

(Real income)

Figure 7.1

supplied by a representative individual. The distance between the two vertical axes is the maximum effort that ever could be supplied by the individual. The locus marked $\emptyset$ dividing the shaded from the unshaded area is what we will refer to as the *long-run subsistence-effort line* or locus, showing for each prescribed level of real income (such as y_1, y_2) the maximum amount of effort that a person living on such a level of real income *for long periods of time* can supply over *long periods of time.*

The shaded area below our locus $\emptyset$ is a "no-man's-land," so to speak, or impossibility zone in the sense that any person who would be required to supply an effort in excess of that given by $\emptyset$ for a given real income could not survive. Clearly locus $\emptyset$ starting from point a_1, corresponding to the subsistence minimum for complete idleness, is upward-sloping as we move to higher levels of effort; the positive slope itself increases with E and reaches very high levels in the vicinity of the y axis.

In addition to the long-run subsistence-effort locus, Figure 7.1 shows three short-run subsistence-effort loci, $\varnothing_1$, $\varnothing_2$, and $\varnothing_3$, originating at points a_1, a_2, and a_3, respectively. The meaning of these loci can be explained in the following manner. Suppose that the individual considered has been working at the subsistence minimum level of income y_2, supplying the amount of effort corresponding to a_2 for a prolonged period of time. If he now is expected to increase his supply of effort in the short run he will not be able to proceed on $\varnothing$ but will have to proceed along a much steeper path such as $\varnothing_2$. This simply indicates that a person living at subsistence for the effort supplied—in our example, living at and operating at a_2—will not in the short run be able to expand his effort except stimulated by substantial increments in real income. If such increments become lasting, of course, over long periods of time, he will be able to supply an increased amount of effort and will eventually reach points on the long-run subsistence-effort locus $\varnothing$. (As has been pointed out, we will specify more exactly at a later stage in the argument what is meant by these short or long periods of time involved in constructing the two types of loci.)

Another set of questions remains to be discussed in this section. Clearly loci $\varnothing$ and $\varnothing$ are somewhat reminiscent of the more conventional indifference curves used in economic analysis. In some sense it can be said that the locus $\varnothing$ is the ultimate, extreme, or iron-rule indifference locus between income and effort, beyond which life ceases and along which one is indifferent in the sense that one can survive. More generally, in the unshaded area to the right of $\varnothing$, it is possible to think of alternative indifference maps—we should think of them as short-run indifference maps—corresponding to or defined by alternative levels of real income experienced over long periods of time.[3] Thus, for example, the locus marked u_2 corresponding to an

---

3. Formally, what we are postulating here is a short-run utility function of the form $U = U(y, E; Y)$, where Y is some average income experienced in the past over a long period of time. Alternatively, and more precisely, Y could stand for income of the preceding period, that is, Y_{t-1}. Still another interpretation of Y would be some index of the distance of the actual point in the y-E plane from the $\varnothing$ locus. But with any of these interpretations, the findings for very poor countries would essentially remain the same as those obtained in this paper.

entire convex nonintersecting indifference map is conditioned by a long-range experiencing of real income, y_2. Of course, only points at the level of real income, y_2, on the second indifference map could ever become lasting solutions of income-effort allocation. Points a_2 and a_2' on u_2' belonging to the second indifference map are such consistent or long-run feasible points.

In a sense the short-run indifference maps corresponding to the three levels of real income are linked to (or are germane to) the short-run subsistence-effort loci, which also are conditioned by the long-range experience of such levels of real income and which also should be thought of as the ultimate short-run in difference curves.[4] As the loci $\varnothing_i$ move upward to the left, so do the indifference maps. This merely expresses the fact that as our individual moves to higher and higher levels of real income—each level being experienced over a long period of time—his marginal rate of substitution between effort and income in the short run is declining at any given point in the sense that an extra unit of real income becomes worth more and more of additional amounts of effort.

What happens to the short-run subsistence curves beyond the points a as we move in the southeast direction? For the purpose of our analysis, we simply assume that in that region they coincide with the long-run locus $\varnothing$. In other words, we are postulating that if over a short period of time (i.e., in the short run, as defined in Section IV) real income were to be reduced in the vicinity of a point such as a_2, beyond that level individual effort would have to decline along with the locus $\varnothing$. Some might argue that below a_2 the continuation of $\varnothing_2$ ought to be a prolongation of the steep locus $\varnothing_2$; but this is not really essential for our argument. In either case, we will not later the alterations in the analysis that such an assumption would require.

It may also be interesting to note, even if only briefly and without much rigor, that as we move to higher and higher levels of real income—that is, from the zone of developing countries living near subsistence to the zone of advanced, wealthy countries with incomes some ten or twenty times higher, where the whole subsistence-effort locus becomes irrelevant except for "inhuman" levels of effort—the

4. Professor Koopmans [1, p. 19] draws his nonintersecting curves reaching the frontier of the consumption set at an angle. But this would imply preference of situations just on the brink of death by starvation over points with considerable excess of income and non-effort (or leisure) above subsistence.

short-run indifference maps would just about merge with each other within the relevant levels and become the same for all real incomes.[5] And thus with no significant change in the short-run maps as we move from one level to another of real income (all incomes being very high in comparison with the incomes considered in Figure 7.1), the single (common) map becomes a long-run map corresponding to all high levels of income experienced over long periods of time. In our opinion it is this unique short- and long-run indifference map which has become, culturally, the standard tool of Western economists. Academic economists have traditionally been members of rather opulent income groups, to whom the multiplicity suggested here for the neighborhood of starvation levels of income never occurred as a real possibility.

II. The Labor-Management Solution of Production in the Light of the Subsistence-Effort Function

In the preceding section we have explained the analytical concepts regarding absolute ability to supply effort and also regarding the preferences in effort and real income. In a summary manner we can say that we have discussed the conditions of labor supply. In this section we will expand the analysis to introduce demand for effort, or more generally to introduce the production possibility resulting from alternative levels of effort.

Figure 7.2 shows, first, the long-run subsistence effort locus $\emptyset$ together with some short-run loci for selected levels of income. In addition it introduces the concave locus, P,[6] comparable to a conventional production possibility function and expressing the maximum level of real income producible by an *average* or *representative* worker using alternate levels of effort, E. To simplify our analysis we assume that in the production process the capital per worker is fixed at the level K_o, and so is the price of capital p_K. Consequently, if our representative does not supply any effort, his maximum attainable real income will be the negative amount $p_K K_o$ indicated in

5. We will argue in Section V that, for one type of short and long run (as defined in Section IV), even at very high levels of income there may be distinct short-run preference maps.

6. I have discussed the locus in more detail and defined the concept of effort elsewhere [2, chap. 12]. Normally one can think of effort as of some index combining three main attributes of labor, namely, duration (in hours per day), intensity of work, and quality of work.

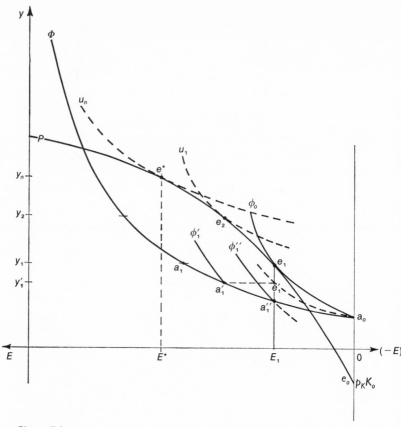

Figure 7.2

Figure 7.2 by the point e_o. The number of workers in the enterprise (for the scale of operation) can be assumed as either fixed or optimally adjusted for each level of E.

As the representative worker moves toward higher and higher levels of effort, the value of real output per man will be increasing indefinitely. In our diagrammatic representation we have postulated that such increases will be at diminishing rates so that the possibility locus P is strictly concave. However, this assumption is by no means essential for our analysis and we could just as well have postulated the locus P to be a straight line or even slightly convex to the origin.

The central point of our argument concerns how in the short and in the long run a labor-managed firm will adjust, or keep adjusting, in finding its equilibrium level of operation and output. Let us re-emphasize that because we are dealing throughout with situations in the vicinity of the subsistence-effort locus, the present case most closely approximates conditions in poor countries. Leaving aside problems of income distribution among the various members of the labor-managed firm and problems of collective decision making within such a firm (see Vanek [2, chap. 12]), we postulate that the representative worker faces a possibility locus P.

To start from the most rudimentary and in some sense most destitute conditions (conditions which are experienced by many millions in the developing countries), suppose that at first our representative worker is unemployed, supplying zero effort, or at least zero productive effort, and is kept alive—at least temporarily—at the level of real income given by the point a_o through government subsidization, receiving alms, or the charity of his relatives or acquaintances. Because he has been living in this state of destitution for a long period of time, his short-run ability to increase effort is rather limited, and any increase of effort would require considerable increase in real income.

All this is reflected in Figure 7.2 by the short-run subsistence-effort locus $\varnothing_o$ originating at point a_o. As we have drawn the locus, at point e_1 it is just tangential to the possibility locus P. In more human terms this means that in a world of labor management there is hope for our unemployed and destitute worker. With organizational and institutional assistance from a national or local labor-management agency[7] he can start producing at point e_1 in Figure 7.2, while paying his fixed capital cost, and in fact can produce well above the long-range subsistence minimum for the corresponding equilibrium level effort E_1.

But this is only the first step in the process of advancement. If he were to stay at e_1 for a substantial period of time, not only would his maximum producible effort eventually move to point a_1, but he would acquire tastes for real income and effort given by a new short-run preference function characterized in Figure 7.2 by the short-run indifference curve u_1 corresponding to real income y_1.

7. I have discussed this type of agency and its functions elsewhere [2, chap. 15].

And this, in turn, in a labor-management setting where the workers can decide on their effort-income combination, would lead to an optimum solution at e_2. From the shifting of preference fields with increasing real income explained in the foregoing section it follows that the point e_2 must be at a higher level of real income and a higher level of effort than was the initial point e_1. Moreover, e_2 is well above the long-run subsistence-effort locus or any short-run locus corresponding to that level of real income. In other words, figuratively speaking, the income-effort combination has taken off from the runway of subsistence given by the $\emptyset$ function.

But obviously at point e_2 and real income y_2 the preference map will again shift in the northwest direction and the process of readjustment just described will keep repeating itself, but in what we may term a converging manner. It follows from the configuration of the $\emptyset$ and P functions and the fact that the $\emptyset_i$ functions are also nonintersecting short-run indifference curves that (1) the process of readjustment will converge until at a specific point the equilibrium levels of effort and income determined by the short-run indifference map will be exactly consistent with the long-run level of real income determining the specific indifference map and (2) that the solution will be above $\emptyset$. In Figure 7.2 this happens at the point e^* for equilibrium level of effort E^*. The corresponding income y_n is now precisely the income conditioning the short-run indifference curve u_n. And of course the final equilibrium is far above the initial state e_1 which constituted the original and in fact sole opportunity of our destitute representative worker.

Although we have started our "narrative" from point a_o, it is descriptive for the labor-managed situation of any intermediate solution. For example, if we had first observed a labor-managed firm operating at the level of effort E_1, in Figure 7.2, the firm would have been producing at e_1, and proceeded thereafter to e^*, as described already.

III. The Capitalist Solution

Let us now change the assumption of economic organization from labor-managed to capitalist. More specifically, workers now are not free producers deciding on alternative levels of effort and income: rather they are hired by a capitalist entrepreneur who, within limits to be specified presently, determines some of the key production variables. We will again start from zero, so to speak, considering a representative man who finds himself initially at the subsistence point with zero effort a_o in Figure 7.2.

Suppose that the relevant data in the initial situation are the same as those considered in the preceding section, that is, we have a possibility locus P and an initial subsistence effort locus $\varnothing_o$. Quite obviously—and this is our first important finding—a capitalist entrepreneur cannot engage in production under such conditions. At best, he could produce at point e_1, where he would have to disburse all of his net income to his workers and there would be no profit left for him. In fact, under realistic conditions, with the considerable degree of uncertainty and scarcity of entrepreneurial talent which is likely to prevail in developing countries, the entrepreneur would be unwilling to engage in production even if the locus $\varnothing_o$ were somewhat below the position shown in Figure 7.2.[8]

Only at the position indicated by the broken line passing through e_1', with a profit margin per worker equivalent to the distance $e_1 e_1'$, might the capitalist entrepreneur contemplate entering production.[9] Of course, in the short run he would be paying his workers a real income y_1' for an effort per laborer equal to E_1. In the long run, if the workers kept receiving income at the rate y_1' operating at the point e_1', the maximum attainable effort per worker, as we have argued, would increase, moving as high as the level corresponding to a_1' in Figure 7.2. In other words, in the long run, the point e_1' would no longer be at the subsistence effort.

Three alternative further solutions now are conceivable:

Solution 1: The entrepreneur, realizing that there are large numbers of unemployed (under the windows of his factory, as Marx would say), might threaten workers with dismissal unless they increased their effort while receiving the income y_1'. Thereby he might get his entire working force operating in the long run at the point a_1', and this of course, as the diagram indicates, would give him a considerably increased profit. If we realize that what we are calling *effort* has at least three composite dimensions—length of working

8. It is also important to realize in this connection that entrepreneurial *excess* profits by those in business already are normally far above zero in developing countries.

9. We have drawn the diagram in such a way as to have the capitalists profit at maximum for E_1. But this is by no means necessary or essential for our argument.

hours, quality of work, and intensity of work—it becomes quite obvious that many instances of this type of adjustment could be found in history, in the early stages of industrialization.

Solution 2: Using very much the same threat or argument as in solution 1, the entrepreneur, alternatively, over longer periods of time, could seek to depress the real income of his workers from the level y_1' as low as the level consistent with the long-run subsistence-effort line, that is, to the point a_1''. Of course, any combination of results between points a_1' and a_1'' would be conceivable, containing elements of both solutions 1 and 2.

The important characteristic of both solutions is that eventually the entrepreneur gets to the long-run subsistence-effort locus and realizes considerably increased profits. Some might call it an increased rate of exploitation. Analytically, the most important fact is that wherever the long-run point of production on $\emptyset$ may be—at a_1', a_1'', or in between—none of the dynamics of expansion described in the preceding section can occur for the simple reason that the decision maker, the capitalist entrepreneur, is completely oblivious of the preferences of his workers and is simply concerned with maximization of his own profit. The fact that he considers his workers as like any other factor of production, that is, like a raw labor force, backfires in the social sense by stifling the development, expansion, and advancement for men at a very rudimentary level of existence, such as that corresponding to the range a_1', a_1''. Moreover, the workers (the majority of the population) live at subsistence, that is, under very difficult conditions. Some might argue rather cynically that the high profits made by the entrepreneur can serve the development effort through accumulation. But let us not forget that the amount $p_K K_o$, which represents the cost of the use of capital, can under certain conditions itself constitute considerable resources for investment and capital accumulation.[10] Also it must be noted that even in the labor-management solution discussed in the preceding section, the income earned by the representative worker might be diminished from the very high levels indicated by the locus P by appropriate taxation or mandatory saving, the proceeds of which would then be used for accumulation.

10. The importance of such resources in the national economy I have considered elsewhere [2, chap. 18].

Solution 3: In situations of modern underdevelopment—as contrasted with the underdevelopment in industrialized countries after the industrial revolution—we often find a solution conditioned by the existence and often considerable power of labor unions which have been introduced partly as a result of an international demonstration effect and partly in a desperate attempt to combat situations like those described in our solutions 1 and 2. That solution is one where the workers, through the power of their labor union, resist over long periods of time a movement from e_1' in Figure 7.2 toward a_1' or a_1'' and thus retain their position at e_1'.

Staying there over longer periods of time of course makes their condition somewhat less deplorable than in the first two situations. However, the dynamic inefficiency—let's refer to it as the stifling effect—still is present, production normally remains frozen in the initial point, and the changing preferences and ability to work of the workers with an increased living standard have no effect on further adjustment of the equilibrium of the firm.[11] While the situation is, so to speak, frozen in solution 3, one might argue that solutions at points such as a_1', a_1'', in Figure 7.2, could not be solutions of long-range equilibrium because, given the loci $\varnothing$, the private entrepreneur is not maximizing his profit; such an objection is not correct. Take, for example, the situation where the entrepreneur has, in the way explained above, reduced the real income of his workers to the absolute minimum and is operating at the point a_1''. In the short run, which normally will be the more relevant time horizon for him, he can increase the effort of his workers only along a locus such as $\varnothing_1''$, and this would not add much, if anything, to his profit. On the contrary, in the "good" capitalist tradition of the nineteenth century, he might try even to reduce real income below a_1'' taking the broken prolongation of $\varnothing_1''$ below $\varnothing$ mistakenly as the relevant locus. But, of course, sooner or later, he would have to learn from his mistake and thus remain on $\varnothing$ at a_1'' or somewhere in its vicinity.

We can sum up the principal findings of this section in the following manner. In developing countries where there is a substantial pool of employed and unemployed workers living at subsistence, the capitalist solution is far inferior, both in the context of

11. As has been pointed out by Juan Espinosa, under some conditions the solution need not be entirely frozen at e_1'.

our analysis and in general, to the labor-managed solution because of two stifling effects that we have described. The first is that in many cases production will not even be undertaken under capitalist conditions, whereas it would have been under labor management. The second is that even if production is started by capitalist firms, the production solution normally becomes frozen at rather rudimentary levels of labor income, effort, and output, whereas under labor management a long-range expansion, advancement, and self-improvement (note that quality of work is one of the components of E) would have been a necessary result.

IV. Interpretation and Clarification of the Concepts of Short Run and Long Run

Although discussion of the short run and the long run has played an important role in our analysis, we have not thus far exactly defined the two concepts. The purpose of this section is to remedy this deliberate omission and also to suggest that the two concepts in fact have alternative sets of interpretation, both relevant for the argument of the present paper.

First, it is possible to argue that what we have referred to as the short run is a period of some one or two years, whereas the long run represents a time span considerably longer than that, perhaps five or ten years. Thus it can be said that what we have termed in Figure 7.2 the short-run subsistence-effort locus $\varnothing_o$ indicates that within one or two years an idle worker living at subsistence cannot increase the level of his effort beyond point e_1 at the corresponding level of real income. If, however, he is allowed to stay at the income y_1 for some five or ten years, his overall health, strength, familiarity with his job, and in fact also his acquisition of better skills will allow him to reach maximum levels of effort as high as those corresponding to a_1 in Figure 7.2. Of course, it is another matter that, as in many of the situations discussed in the preceding two sections, he may no longer need to live at the subsistence-effort locus $\varnothing$.

Although the entire analysis thus far can be understood in terms of short and long runs of some one and five years, respectively, the concepts can be given entirely different interpretations and our analysis still can make a good deal of sense—perhaps more sense using the following alternative interpretation than using the first one. Suppose that what we have called the short run corresponds to a generation and that what we have termed the long run corresponds to intergenerational transitions and movements. Of course, what we have termed short-run indifference maps now will largely correspond to different groups of individuals, but this does not have to bother us because what we are after are not comparisons of social welfare for alternative generations but rather the positive real solutions reached by a firm or the productive sector of an economy.

The long-run subsistence-effort locus $\emptyset$ still can be taken as given by some biological minimum requirement for human beings, and the possibility locus P can be taken as a hypothetical production relationship which in a more complete analysis would have to be permitted to shift with changing capital stocks and technologies over time. But this does not much change the essence of our argument.

This intergenerational interpretation of our concepts of short and long run seems logical in view of recent biological and medical research on populations living under subsistence conditions. Children born in families living under such conditions in the Andean mountains or in India will at best be able to increase effort in relation to real income according to a locus such as $\emptyset_o$ in Figure 7.2 and not along the long-range intergenerational locus $\emptyset$. If, however, two or more generations of families can live at the income y_1, such a living standard would permit them to supply a maximum effort corresponding to a_1 on $\emptyset$.

With the intergenerational interpretation of the concepts of short and long run—by contrast to the other, more conventional interpretation—going from a point such a_o in Figure 7.2 to a final equilibrium at a point such as e^* might of course involve long periods of time, perhaps a hundred years or so. But this can only bring into focus the true dimensions and seriousness of the problem of economic development in the context of human effort, capacity to work, and real earning power. The intergenerational interpretation of short and long run also underscores the enormous benefits that developing countries might secure by adopting more humane forms of economic organization that permit a direct translation of the desires and preferences of the majority or totality of men into decisions regarding output income and intensity of work.

V. Some Related General Considerations Regarding the Developing and Advanced Countries

Thus far we have proceeded in a systematic manner in explaining and developing our argument for the case of an individual firm. From this point on our exposition of necessity will be less systematic because we want to move onto a broader and more general ground and discuss some selected topics that help to further illuminate and substantiate our theory. We will also be able to show the theory's utility in analyzing certain well-known phenomena of both developed and underdeveloped countries.

In Sections II and III we have attempted to compare the solutions obtained in developing countries by the labor-managed system and those obtained (or, more precisely, not obtained) by the capitalist system. A highly relevant question is, how does the third alternative—namely, a Soviet-type centrally planned (command) economy—compare in the context of our analysis with the other two systems? For very poor countries where the majority of men initially finds itself in the lower portion of the $\emptyset$ function or somewhere very near or on it, the command economy can be said to occupy an intermediate position between the labor-managed and the capitalist, being inferior to the former and superior to the latter. The comparative advantage of the socialist command economies, as we know them from their performance in Russia, Eastern Europe, China, or Cuba, is evident in comparison to the capitalist solution and resides primarily in the fact that even in the very early stages of development and takeover by the centrally-planned regimes an attempt is made to employ just about everybody and to equalize the distribution of income. This, then, in terms of our Figure 7.2, brings the representative member of such socialist societies to a point such as e_1' or perhaps better, that is, above the short-run subsistence-effort line, and the force (see solutions 1 and 2 in Section III) which under capitalism tends to depress income of workers to the long-range subsistence-effort locus $\emptyset$ disappears. It disappears, first, because there are no large numbers of unemployed who could compete with those who are employed for their jobs and, second, because the profit motive, which under capitalism would tend to bring the workers back to the $\emptyset$ locus, disappears. On the other hand, the comparative disadvantage of the socialist command economy is that as much as the capitalist economy it excludes the majority of the population, that is, all the workers, from translating their preferences with respect to efforts and real income into actual production decisions, and thus the beneficial and spontaneous long-run movement toward solutions such as e^* in Figure 7.2 becomes most unlikely.

We can thus conclude that the socialist command economies avoid the problems of unemployment and income distribution together with the problem that some might refer to as exploitation, but they retain in large measure the stifling effect. It is true that all sorts of programs, such as the Stachanov and similar schemes after World War II, have been employed in the socialist economies in attempting to move workers from points such as e_1 in Figure 7.2 to points such as a_1 through exhortation, appealing to patriotic feelings, and other methods. But these, in the long run, perhaps with the outstanding exception of China, were at best faint substitutes for the spontaneous process which we have described in Section II and which leads to the equilibrium e^*.

A second point concerns the actual level of workers' efficiency in the developed as compared to the less developed countries. Although most theories of economic development and progress rely heavily on capital accumulation as an explanation of such progress, empirical studies usually fail to reveal that the productive contribution of capital is very significant in aggregate growth. Often it is argued that investment in human capital explains wide differences in labor efficiency. This explanation comes closer to what we have been discussing in this paper, but it is still a half-way house in that it shifts the emphasis of accumulation from physical assets to human capital. Our theory, by contrast, explains quite clearly—even without reference to any accumulation of human capital—that the advanced countries might be operating at a level of effort somewhere near the point e^* in Figure 7.2 or beyond (owing to technological progress, which has not yet been introduced into our discussion), whereas the developing countries would be operating somewhere in the vicinity of E_1.

And all this has little or nothing to do with education but rather is linked to the biological and psychological and physical facts of human existence both within and between generations. Indeed, the extremely productive workers in American mass production often require lesser skills and less education than do some craftsmen in the least developed countries. It may also be useful to recall at this point that one of the most plausible explanations of the so-called Leontief paradox is precisely the significant differential in labor efficiency between the United States and the rest of the world.

As a third illustrative point, our analysis also seems able to explain the comparative success and rapidity of economic development in the United States throughout the nineteenth and twentieth centuries as compared to other countries, including those of Western Europe. In a nutshell, it can be said that the extreme abundance of natural resources and the comparative abundance of capital relative to labor, even in the early stages of American industrialization, never permitted in this country what we have referred to above as the stifling effect. First, real incomes, at whatever level of effort E, were always well above the long-range subsistence-effort line $\emptyset$ because labor was comparatively scarce, and thus the preference fields as explained in Section I could keep moving to the left and upward with increasing real incomes. It is true that a substantial portion of the productive sector was operated in a rather ruthless capitalist way, with the workers' preferences not directly considered. In the long run, however, what substituted for this was a high degree of social mobility, the ethic of the self-made man, and a willingness to risk entering business on one's own.

In England and other Western European industrialized countries, by contrast, the period where the working man remained at the subsistence-effort line from generation to generation lasted well into the nineteenth century, and in some parts of Europe—such as Ireland, Portugal, or Spain—this state, roughly speaking, lasted well into the twentieth century, perhaps until today. This, together with a basically capitalist economic organization, then, can explain a good deal of the comparative backwardness of these countries with respect to the United States and the considerably lesser effort and labor intensity encountered there.

Our fourth point concerns the most advanced countries in connection with the phenomena of accumulation and technological progress which we have not yet discussed. Of course, technical progress and growth of capital stock could on their own shift the transformation locus P upward in Figure 7.2. For countries which find themselves already well on the road to development with incomes in the vicinity of y_n and levels of effort and productivity of the order of E^*, technical progress and accumulation thus can constitute quite considerable—in some sense, windfall—gains in national income per man and, with labor scarcity and strong labor unions, also in real wages. The short-run preference maps—where short-run is interpreted as belonging to specific generations and long-run to intergenerational comparisons—then allow considerable increases in real output and real income in the span of a single generation with a basically unchanged supply of effort. But such very high levels of income for those who experience them can lead to backward, or downward and rightward, shifts of the preference maps between generations, just the opposite from what we have argued for the very poor countries. It seems to us that the comparative lethargy and lack of vitality or ambition on the part of the third generation of wealthy Americans—today even of the third generation of middle-class Americans—is precisely a reflection of this phenomenon. Their relevant indifference lines, while far above the $\emptyset$ locus in Figure 7.1, tend to shift with exogenously increased incomes back in the southeast direction, that is, toward preference for more leisure and less real income and output.

Our fifth point bears on countries in the early stages of economic development and on the phenomenon usually referred to as the *dual economy*, or *noncompeting groups*. This can best be understood in the context of the intergenerational interpretation of our concepts. Suppose that the process of development is underway, and a certain portion of the population not only has been hired by capitalist entrepreneurs at a point such as e_1' in Figure 7.2, but over long periods has been induced to work to the left of that point. The children of the industrial workers in the second and third generations, stronger and better fed, accustomed to new cultural conditions, perhaps assisted by a labor union, have been able to move to points to the left of the broken lines passing through both e_1' and $\emptyset_1''$. The latter locus reflects, hypothetically, the ability to supply effort by those actually working in the traditional sector of the economy. This is nothing but the creation of dual economy or of noncompeting groups of the industrial labor force on the one hand and those in the traditional sector of the economy on the other.

The industrial workers and their children staying over generations considerably to the left of $\emptyset_1''$ no longer compete with those in the traditional sector at far lower real incomes. This guarantees their comparably high real incomes and at the same time produces for those in the traditional sector a certain state of frustration of under-development in the sense that no capitalist entrepreneur will hire them. He prefers to hire those from the pool of existing industrial labor (which is usually expanding at a high natural rate) those who can conform to superior performance standards, even if at higher real incomes; and this allows him to derive a considerably greater profit.[12] The strength and validity of this argument must be clear to anyone who has traveled, say in Southeast Asia or Latin America, and contemplated the physical and social dividing lines between the modern and traditional sectors of the respective economies.

In the context of our fifth point, it again should be clear that labor management offers far greater versatility and flexibility in solving such problems. For example, even if somewhere in São Paulo workers are performing well beyond point $\emptyset\,''_1$ in Figure 7.2, it would still be possible for workers in some newly industrializing or mod-ernizing sectors (or regions) of the economy to start working under labor management (as we have argued in Section II) at points such as e_1 in firms competing with the more traditional firms. This could possibly mean lower incomes in the labor-managed sector than in the established industrial sector in the short run, but in the long run the labor-managed sector would have to overtake the traditional capitalist firms for reasons explained in Sections II and III.

The rationale behind our fifth point also offers a possible explana-tion for the existence of higher labor incomes in the modern indus-trial sector of developing countries, as compared to traditional agriculture.

Our sixth point relates to a very well known phenomenon. It is often observed that in developing countries in traditional primitive farming an increase in price leads to a reduction of gross output. But this, in the context of Figure 7.2, can be translated as a reduc-tion in the effort supplied with an upward rotation, so to speak, of the possibility locus P around the point e_o. Given the configura-tion of the short-run preference maps (which we recall are linked to and conditioned by the long-run level of income preceding the price change) this appears to be the most natural short-run outcome. On the other hand, if the higher prices of farm products are sus-tained over long periods of time, perhaps even generations, then our

12. In fact, nothing guarantees that he would make any profit using the labor force from the traditional sector.

theory of adjusting short-run preference maps explained in Section I will quite clearly lead to the conclusion that the elasticities of supply of goods and effort in the context of our analysis ought to be a good deal higher, and very likely ought to assume positive values. This is precisely what is observed over longer periods of time in the traditional sectors of the developing countries.

In our seventh point we return to the problem of entry of industrial firms by capitalist entrepreneurs in the developing countries, but we do so recognizing the existence of a traditional sector coupled with some degree of unemployment or underemployment. Before any industry is introduced, the effort-income possibilities of an economy, presumably in traditional farming, are represented for a typical or average individual by the broken line P_a in Figure 7.3.

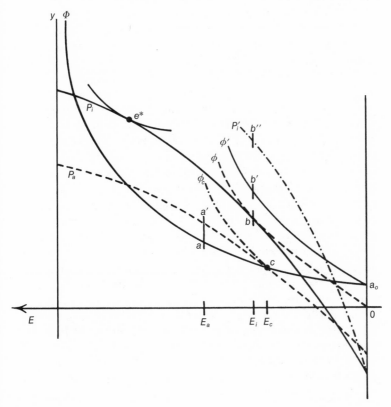

Figure 7.3

Supplying the effort E_a the economy produces per man a real output given by a', and each man employed earns a real income given by point a. The surplus per man employed, equivalent to the distance aa', is then distributed to the unemployed, who operate at the level of effort $E = 0$ and find themselves also at subsistence at point a_o. Since the distance aa' is about one-half of the distance $0a_o$, it is assumed that those employed are about twice as numerous as those unemployed.

Now suppose further that the best industrial activity technically possible in the country is represented by another effort-income possibility locus P_i. Postulating a short-run subsistence-effort line $\varnothing'$, obviously, the new sector could not absorb the presently unemployed under capitalist conditions because even at the most efficient point of operation the capitalist would be making a loss equivalent to bb'. Given the configuration of loci in Figure 7.3, industrialization absorbing the unemployed would be possible under liberal capitalism only if the production-possibility locus assumed the position of the dashed-and-dotted line P_i'.

Under what we might call liberal labor-management in the present case, however, the unemployment-absorbing industrialization could not begin because the locus $\varnothing'$ never even touches the income-possibility line P_i. However—and this is the main content of our seventh point—if the social cost of keeping one-third of the population alive at point a_o could be internalized through collective social decision by the state, by a national labor management agency, or within a smaller unit such as a farm cooperative, the applicable short-run subsistence-effort locus would lie below the line $\varnothing'$ and assume a position of $\varnothing$ in Figure 7.3, originating at point 0. With this alternative, of course, industrialization could begin, with the first short-run production taking place at b. Then, in the manner described in Section II, the expansion process of the labor-managed industrial sector could get underway and lead eventually, in the manner understood already, to a point such as e^* on P_i. And after a while the subsidy which shifted $\varnothing'$ to $\varnothing^-$ could be discontinued.

The attempts being made in Chile or Peru to establish second-level cooperatives or second-level processing firms on or related to traditional first-level farm cooperatives are illustrative of what has just been said. If what we might call the survival transfer equivalent to $0a_o$ in Figure 7.3 can be continued for a time by those actively employed in the first-level cooperative, then the process of industrialization can get underway under labor management where individualistic capitalism or individualistic labor management would have to fail.

A policy implication of our seventh point is that unemployment subsidies, or whatever the transfer which keeps those at a_o alive, should be always guaranteed and continued for a time even after the unemployed have found some productive employment in a new industrial sector.

Our eighth point is that within a society—presumably a small society such as a cooperative or a village—it may be preferable not to perform the transfer that we have spoken about from those optimally employed to those unemployed, but rather to have everybody employed at a low level of intensity of work at a point such as c in Figure 7.3. Here everybody earns exactly his subsistence but everybody is employed. Besides the advantage of distributional equality there is the strong advantage of having the relevant short-run subsistence-effort curve originating at point c. It is clear now that the production possibility P_i is not only consistent with the development of the industrial sector in the short run, but it could even immediately take those who would be engaged in the industrial sector away from the subsistence locus and thus start the long-range expansion toward e^* in Figure 7.3 even more promptly. At the same time, as soon as the industrial sector provided new employment, those remaining in agriculture could move to points of effort-supply superior to E_c, possibly helped temporarily by small transfers from those in the industrial sector. The moral of points seven and eight is that it pays to cooperate—that cooperation between firms of the type described here may be the *sine qua non* of economic advancement in very poor countries or regions.

The solution at point c also indicates, as our ninth point, that in very poor countries a national policy of full employment, even with a temporarily low level of output and effort supplied per individual, may be highly beneficial for long-range industrialization and development of the country. For example, what some might call the overcrowding of cooperatives following agrarian reforms, such as those of (pre-Pinochet) Chile or Peru, securing the maximum employment of peasant families even at the cost of considerable reductions in productivity per family, may be the wisest policy as long as the labor force available within the traditional sector has not been absorbed by industrialization and the development process in general. In some sense also the solution at point c supports the wisdom of full employment policies in the very poor socialist countries irrespective of the obvious equity argument for full employment.

In the context of labor-managed economies which are very poor and, so to speak, just beginning the development process, the solution at point c also indicates the strong desirability of full employment policies. These should be made possible by the government or a national labor-management agency that retains for a time the right to control the numbers of employed in labor-managed firms. An active policy of stimulating entry of new labor-managed firms may also be highly desirable for the purpose of bringing employment to a maximum.

Our tenth point is related to the definition of effort. As used throughout our analysis thus far the variable effort, E, was considered to be, in all of its aspects—duration, quality, and intensity of work—what we might call a "choice" variable. By this we mean that its precise level is subject to a deliberate choice on the part of the person supplying the effort. By contrast, it is possible to think of some aspects of effort—especially in connection with intensity and quality of work—which are not subject to deliberate choice and which do not affect utility but rather assume a certain specific level related to the time spent by a person on a particular job. If we now define our variable E as involving strictly the choice aspect of effort (perhaps the term "degree of application" would be preferable here to the term "effort") changes in the other, nonchoice, effort can be seen as exogenous shifts in the transformation locus P upward over time.

Clearly there will be a good deal of difference between how such a shift in the income-possibility locus will affect the development process in a labor-managed system on the one hand and in the capitalist system on the other. In the labor-managed developing economy, the result will be an additional increase in income per worker at each period of time and thus an accelerated and a more pronounced movement over long periods of time comparable to the movement which led to the point e^* in Figure 7.2. By contrast, in the extreme capitalist case, where there are no labor unions, workers operate at the locus $\emptyset$ in Figure 7.2 and the autonomous shifts over time in the income-possibility locus will only increase the capitalist profits, and thus further accentuate the distributional imperfections, without reducing in any significant manner the stifling effects explained in Section III. As the reader may visualize, if the labor force is organized in a labor union, the adjustment to the autonomous shifts here considered may be more advantageous to the workers in the distributional sense, but the stifling effects will, by and large, remain unaffected.

The eleventh and last point is perhaps the broadest in its implications: it can be sketched here only in very general terms. As has been argued elsewhere [2, chap. 13], income is by no means the only thing into which a labor-managed firm can transform its effort. Many variables also enter the utility function of the members of the enterprise and of the collective taken as a whole, such as all kinds of collective consumption by the working community, education, rendering the work more pleasant and less strenuous, or action toward the community in which the enterprise finds itself. Choosing the variable z to represent all such other factors entering the function next to real income and the degree of effort, we can thus construct in Figure 7.4 a new generalized possibility locus in three dimensions, one of which is our new variable z. The other two dimensions, as previously, are real income and effort.

Assuming that the degree of the variable z does not affect the subsistence-effort relation, we can also construct in our three-dimensional space a new locus $\varnothing$ generated as a cylinder by lines parallel to the z-axis and passing through the original long-run subsistence-effort locus in the y-E plane. This gives us the new feasible possibility locus which has the shape of a shield and is shown in perspective in Figure 7.4.

To reiterate our analysis and begin again from subsistence and zero effort at point a_o, a newly-formed labor-managed firm can contemplate in the short run to start producing at a point such as e_1 consistent with the earlier explained short-run subsistence-effort curve $\varnothing_1$. As before, remaining at e_1 for an extended period of time will start shifting the indifference map of the typical worker, but this shifting characteristically will not be along the old possibility locus but rather upward and into the three-dimensional space, increasing the equilibrium levels of the variable z. After many years, through a process illustrated in Figure 7.4, a final equilibrium will

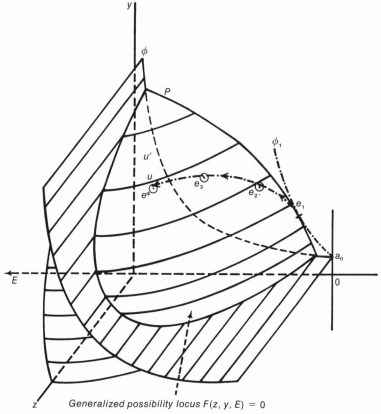

Generalized possibility locus $F(z, y, E) = 0$

Figure 7.4

normally again be reached at a point where all three—the variable z, real income (distributed to workers), and the degree of effort not expended—will be in excess of what would be permissible on grounds of the subsistence-effort function. Of course in this way the satisfaction level of social welfare of the working community in the long run will generally be far higher than it would be if only a movement along the two-dimensional P function in the y-E plane were permitted.

It is quite obvious that in a capitalist firm or in a Soviet state-capitalist firm such a movement in the z space is just about impossible because the preferences of the members of the working collective are largely left out of the decision-making process of the firm.

That what we have just shown is not a mere invention of economic theorizing cannot be overstressed. For example, the process of development and advancement as we have suggested it for the United States earlier in this section, that is, a movement along the P locus in the y-E plane, remains largely unchanged without any movement taking place into the z dimension. The well-known American dictum "time is money" is perhaps the best reflection of this comparative nondimensionality of working life in the United States. Indeed, time, as a proxy of our variable E, is primarily understood as transformable into money, the latter then being transformed by individual workers and salary earners into private consumption and utility. But a transformation of money and effort into a score of variables characterized by our variable z on the level of the enterprise is unknown. It is possible to say in the context of our analysis that the average American through the last one or two centuries, while becoming extremely rich in terms of money, has become impoverished in terms of the number of dimensions which he was able to introduce into his life as a worker or employee. For this reason it may be appropriate to rename our two-dimensional locus P the "time is money" locus.

Some might object that there is nothing wrong with this because if one generates a good deal of money in the working place, one can then go on transforming it at home or on one's own into consumption; but this is certainly not so. This has only become the understanding in our highly individualized society. First of all, there is something that we might call economies of scale of consumption. There are many types of consumption that one cannot undertake on one's own but which can easily be undertaken by the working collective. For example, education, or education on the job, or acquisition of a summer place on the seashore, or a decent insurance scheme, or a swimming pool, or a collective transportation facility, or a housing development. It is not true that all this could be done on another plane than that of the enterprise.

The overcrowding of our streets and highways by individual cars, the desire of everyone to have his own motorboat or yacht or an estate on the shore is only the other side of the same coin. Not only cannot everyone reach these levels of luxury consumption but the consumption by those who can individually afford it is extremely inefficient.

Our theory can also be substantiated on the other side of the spectrum, that is, at the other end of the $\emptyset$ locus, and by the very poor countries. It is well known that after self-management was introduced in Yugoslavia, enterprises became perhaps as important in providing satisfaction of the type of our z variable as they were in generating real income to be distributed to the workers and employees. Housing developments, schools, education facilities, vacation places, sports fields, and the like were developed. In Peru, where the participatory form of management was introduced since 1968 in the large sugar estates, one of the first preoccupations of some of the self-managing bodies was basic education and elimination of illiteracy. The same is true of some of the farm cooperatives created by the agrarian reform in Chile; there, I have also found in one instance construction of a football field in the middle of a projected village (community) far higher on the priorities list than increase in cash income.

It can also be argued that the recent movement among many young people in the United States toward separation from conventional society is in large measure a result of frustration with a society that is constrained by its capitalist or neocapitalist rules of conduct to move only along the time-is-money locus in Figure 7.4 and not permitted to move into the third dimension. The communes and living communities founded by dissident young Americans are precisely to be associated with our third dimension. But note that with very few exceptions they are not also communities of work, and this renders them both vulnerable and lacking a genuine and lasting character.

VI. Summary and Conclusions

In this paper we have combined the theory of production in relation to variable effort with a theory of supply of effort in discussing the comparative merits of alternative economic systems as a vehicle for advancement in countries at a low level of economic development with a significant portion of the labor force in a traditional sector. All things considered, under such conditions an economic system based on self-management by workers and employees appears superior to centrally-planned socialism, and even more so to liberal capitalism. Whereas in the latter two systems various inefficiencies and shortcomings arise from imperfect motivation or the absence of self-expression in determining economic variables, the participatory economy suffers very little from such difficulties and is likely to promote human and economic development *pari passu* at a rapid rate.

The theory offers a satisfactory explanation of the comparative lack of success of capitalist less developed countries in promoting economic progress and advancement for the majority of their populations. It also explains the comparative state of destitution and hopelessness, especially among the nonunionized "lower strata" of the labor force, not only in the less developed countries but even in some advanced capitalist economies.

In Section V we were able to establish, at least approximately, the consistency of our theoretical analysis with many broader phenomena observable in both the developed and the less developed countries. Among these we may note a possible explanation of the insignificance of capital accumulation in increasing productivity, the far greater efficiency of the American labor force compared to that of the rest of the world and the higher per capita income in this country, and the dual economy or noncompeting-groups phenomenon so well known from the experience of many developing countries.

References

1. Tjalling C. Koopmans, *Three Essays on the State of Economic Science* (New York: McGraw-Hill, 1957).

2. J. Vanek, *The General Theory of Labor-Managed Market Economies* (Ithaca, N.Y.: Cornell University Press, 1970).

3. ____, *The Participatory Economy: An Evolutionary Hypothesis and a Strategy for Development* (Ithaca, N.Y.: Cornell University Press, 1971).

PART IV

INVESTMENT AND FUNDING

8 | Some Fundamental Considerations on Financing and the Form of Ownership under Labor Management*

Self-management and economic self-determination are without doubt steps in a secular evolutionary process. But these new forms, akin to the biological evolution of species, need their own new environment, as mammals need air—and not water—to live in. If the production cooperative and other democratic forms did not flourish in the past, it was because we were, unwittingly, forcing mammal babies into water in which they were bound to drown.

I. Introduction

The questions of property rights and the form in which production is financed under labor management are quite central to that ecomic system. Actually the success and efficient operation of a labor-managed economy will, to a considerable degree, depend on the answers to these questions.

In this paper I will first attempt to show, in Section II, that the proper way for a labor-managed firm to be financed is not from within, that is, by retained earnings, but from outside the firm, or at least that self-financing ought to be kept a clearly separate and individualized operation. Using these arguments I will argue in general terms in Section III that it would be desirable for any labor-managed economy or labor-managed sector of an economy to give a new definition to ownership or to the rights of property, different from both the rights as conceived in the Western economies and the rights of social ownership as we know them in socialist countries. In Section IV, finally, I will define and explain my new concept of property for the participatory economies.

* Cornell Department of Economics Working Papers no. 16, June 1971. This paper appeared in *Economic Structure and Development*: *Essays in Honour of Jan Tinbergen* (Amsterdam: North-Holland Publishing Company, 1973).

II. Arguments for External Financing of Labor-Managed Firms

Although they are traceable to different historical origins, the Yugoslav worker-managed firm and the traditional worker-managed producer cooperative as we have known it in Western Europe and the United States, and more recently in Latin American agriculture, have a good deal in common when it comes to the position that capital and accumulation have in these productive organizations. In the Yugoslav worker-managed firm, primarily owing to the concept of enlarged reproduction introduced by Marx, firms basically are called on to reproduce their capital in ever-increasing amounts as an integral part of their productive process. It does not matter whether the law states that the factories in Yugoslavia are socially owned or not; from the point of view of the working collective, capital assets must be taken as collectively owned investments. Such investments are determined from some subjective profitability calculation of the collective. Similarly, in what we have termed the traditional co-operative capital is also owned collectively, and accumulation generally takes the form of collective savings or undistributed earnings of these firms.

This state of collective ownership, collective accumulation, or, in the case of Yugoslavia, quasi-ownership or quasi-accumulation, will generally have undesirable economic effects both on the firm itself and on the allocation of resources within the economy. It is the purpose of this section to identify such undesirable effects. At the same time I will attempt to show the advantages of the labor- (or worker-) managed firm being financed externally, that is, through an explicitly recognized external body or institution, such as a state bank in the case of socialist countries, or a savings association partly or fully formed by members of the enterprise, or what I have termed elsewhere the National Labor Management Agency [3]. But let us now turn to the specifics of our discussion.

II.1. Suppose first that we have a producer cooperative or a Yugoslav worker-managed firm in a hypothetical environment where funds can be deposited by anyone into a banking institution and an interest rate equal approximately to the productivity of capital in the economy can be earned, say 10 per cent. The real assets of the firm have been accumulated over a long period of time as collective ownership and the firm is not in debt to anyone. Consider now a situation where there is no law or other impediment to prevent the members of the firm from converting the value of real assets into money, depositing that money in a bank, and earning the corresponding interest income. Everyone employed by the enterprise now can become a collective rentier earning a share of the interest on funds deposited. Provided that there are sufficient resources, he may never work again. This is certainly an undesirable situation from the national point of view, whether we take the position of a socialist country or any other. It is true that if the real assets—machinery and buildings—were marketed and sold to someone, someone must use them for production and thus they would not be idle. However, we have the undesirable effect of idleness among the original users of the capital assets. Now contrast this with a situation under financing external to the firm where any decision to realize the value of physical assets and deposit the corresponding amount into a bank at interest would simply mean liquidation of the original loan to the firm through which it was financed, and no income could accrue to the participants. In consequence, the decision to liquidate and realize the real value of assets would be completely irrational on the part of the employees unless there were true economic reasons for liquidation of the firm.

II.2. The case underlying my second point is in all respects identical to the case just discussed under point 1, except that the law now prohibits the cooperative or worker-managed firm to sell its real assets and transform them into financed assets which would permit the working collective to transform itself into a rentier group. In fact we find a situation approximately of this kind today in Yugoslavia. The important point here is that such legal restriction does not prevent the anomaly or inefficiency of the internal financing of the firm. Note that at all times the firm is transforming itself physically by using up its capital assets and replacing them with new ones. Now our firm over time can reduce by attrition the number of its members and gradually transform its physical plant and equipment into one which is highly automated, that is, it can use factor proportions entirely unwarranted by the degree of capitalization of the economy. As a *reductio ad absurdum*, after many years the firm could end up with only a janitor and a director, both millionaires, sitting together on the workers' council of a completely automated labor-managed factory. Again consider the contrast of a situation where financing is external to the firm and some considerable real return must be paid on the financial assets. In that case the extremely high, virtually infinite, capital-labor ratio (implied by full automation) would be warranted only if at that ratio the marginal productivity of capital were still very high, equal to the rate of interest which must be paid for the use of borrowed funds. In a developing labor-managed economy, the social undesirability of a completely automated firm to which the situation discussed here leads must be obvious. Without enough capital to go round, we would have a few highly automated firms with a few employed rich people and an enormous army of unemployed. In fact, the tragedy of the situation is that what we find today in Yugoslavia has a good deal to do with precisely this situation.[1]

II.3. A third point has to do with the all-important phenomenon of entry into and formation of new firms in a labor-managed economy. The basic proposition is that self-financing as a general rule will be an important impediment to the formation of new firms, and thus may considerably undermine the dynamics and long-range development of a labor-managed or cooperative economy. My reasoning is as follows: Suppose that all capital assets must be generated by existing firms and that there is no external source of financing for new or old firms. Under such conditions it must be obvious that the natural procedure will be for an existing firm to retain some of its income and invest in its own expansion, which ultimately will benefit its membership. There will be very little impetus for an existing firm to create a new firm because thereby it would be giving additional income to the men newly employed in the new firm without partaking of that output themselves. Of course this is so because we have eliminated external financing by assumption, but even if external financing were permitted and the old parent firm created a new one by creating an interest-bearing debt between the two, we would have very much the same problem as we had under our points 1 and 2, the parent firm becoming in part a financial institution. Nothing could stop the parent firm in the long run from creating new firms until the income to itself was sufficient for the members of the old parent firm to stop working entirely and become

---

1. In fact the reforms and legislation of the early 1970's provide for mandatory accumulation in enterprises, which then makes our point 2 also applicable to new funds; these funds can also, like depreciation, be used for most capital-intensive projects, unrelated to national factor endowments.

a new rentier class. One does not have to elaborate the absurdity of this situation. The important moral of the story is that without external financing, one way or another, there will be very little entry and formation of new firms.[2] Again this situation may be contrasted with the case where external funds are available (say in something like the National Labor Management Agency) and where, typically, young people just entering the labor force, perhaps together with capable upcoming executives of existing firms, can together form new enterprises beneficial for everyone including the society at large.

II.4. My fourth point was first pointed out and developed by Professors Furubotn and Pejovich [1]. If a firm is to rely on self-financing to generate additions to its productive capacity, the net returns from new investments must be very high indeed in order to appear profitable to the working collective. This is so because an individual worker can count only on the returns from the new investment in the form of increased future income, and not in terms of a final claim on the assets generated. The latter are merely an addition to the collective ownership over which no individual has a right of disposition. More specifically, if at the same time the workers can deposit realized income as private individual savings at a local bank or elsewhere, they will have to have an expectation of returns far above the rate paid by the savings bank in order to decide on a collective (self-financed) investment. Moreover, this differential between the market rate of interest and the rate of return required on internal investments will vary with the expectation of number of years of employment and in consequence with the average age of the members of the working collective. The confusion and the inefficiency that this will generate in the allocation of scarce capital resources throughout the economy will be easily realized by anyone with even a rudimentary training in economics. By contrast, again with predominantly or entirely external financing, there will be an overall tendency to equalize returns to capital on the margin throughout the economy and thus, for a given allocation of labor, generate an optimal allocation of capital.

II.5. My fifth point contains one-half of an argument very central to the theory of labor management which I have termed elsewhere

2. As shown by Mr. Sacks [2], such appears to have been the case since about 1964 in Yugoslavia—a period when hardly any new firms were created.

"the dilemma of the collateral" [3]. It is a point which in my opinion goes a long way in explaining the comparative lack of success of traditional producer cooperatives throughout history. With self-financing and collective ownership of productive assets, the early comers, or, even more restrictively, the founders of a cooperative, may always feel that they have given more to the enterprise than the newcomers, and this in most cases will lead to the situations of first-, second-, and third-class citizens within the firm. Often even shares proportional to the contribution to the firm, however measured, will be given to the participants to reflect their years of participation and relative status in the enterprise. But this can only gravely undermine and sometimes destroy the true spirit of equality and cooperation within the firm and lead to an internal human situation not much different from that which we find in conventional capitalist firms. Again it will be noted that with financing from the outside, that is, in a situation where capital is hired at a given price from an external market (in very much the same way as any other factor of production), all such problems will disappear; the philosophical and real foundation of the participatory firm will remain the work in common.

II.6. My sixth point is an elaboration of something that has just been said. It is of truly fundamental importance that the basis of the cooperative worker-managed firm be the work in common and not ownership in common or a combination of work and ownership in common. The pure form of a participatory firm must be based entirely on participation in work. The Marxist writers' concept of alienation comes into play here. It is the mixing of participation by work and participation by ownership that injects the poison of alienation into an otherwise pure labor agreement of a participatory firm.

II.7. The seventh point has already been alluded to in passing. By external financing, that is, absence of self-financing, capital is assimilated to any other nonhuman factor of production. This is very important, as it should be. Just as under capitalism labor was degraded to the position of other productive factors, under a participatory economy capital ought to be put on the same level with all other nonlabor factors of production. The only difference is that the latter solution is correct, desirable, and moral because capital is as physical and inanimate as raw materials, fuels, and other inputs in production. By contrast, self-financing or the Marxian "enlarged reproduction" on the level of the firm gives the capital factor more of a status and preserves more of the anomalies of capitalism than what Marx himself would have liked it to preserve.

II.8. My eighth point is based on the notion that the act of investing is one in which both the investing firm and society at large are jointly involved, both in terms of the benefits to be derived and in terms of the responsibilities to be assumed. This being so it is proper to have each investment project scrutinized and judged not only by the investing firm but also by society represented by some institution, perhaps the National Labor Management Agency referred to earlier. Clearly such is the case with external financing where the impetus to invest originates with the potential investor but must be submitted to the lending agency for scrutiny and verification. By contrast, under self-financing the firm which covers the entire cost of the investment project normally is perfectly free to invest and need not consult anyone nor conform with any national development plan. Inefficiencies arising from this one-sided solution can be quite considerable, especially when we realize that an individual firm may have limited access to information on what other firms in the economy are doing and on what are the general trends of the economy for the future.

II.9. The ninth point is germane to the point just made. Because the act of investing involves both the firm and the society, both should also share the risks of possible failure of operation. And indeed, with external financing, if the investment turns out unproductive, those who will lose are not only the workers in the firm, in terms of loss of job and income, but also society through the loss of the value of, or of income from, the assets which have been invested. By contrast, with full self-financing the burden of risk is entirely on the shoulders of the enterprise, and this is obviously undesirable because the success, or lack of success, of the operation based on the new investment also in part depends on actions taken by the society, such as providing information, stimulating demand through economic or commercial policy, and the like.

II.10. One form of investment, a very important one in modern industrial economies, is investment in the inventive activity, "research and development" as it is sometime referred to. Of course, for any firm short of giant firms (which are very rare under the participatory solution) such investment in research and development may be quite risky. If it were to be undertaken entirely from owned funds, the rate at which research and development activity would proceed might be quite low in a labor-managed economy. By contrast, with external financing, we have a dual advantage: first, the external lender acts as a reinsurance against major losses from failures of research and development attempts; and second, there is an external observer, that is, the lender, who, together with the firm undertaking research and development, passes judgment on the reasonableness and viability of the project.

II.11. One of the greatest strengths and most attractive features of the participatory firm is that it can and usually will include in its objective function a variety of variables, not only income but also all kinds of collective consumption, action toward the community, and variables which normally are classified under the heading of external economies. With internal self-financing, such financing becomes one of the focal variables of decision-making processes of the labor-managed or participatory firm. Because of its major importance it will detract considerably from the deliberation or action on other objectives. And thus, by and large, a self-financed firm will tend to restrict its objectives to a limited number of variables, perhaps only (1) the monetary income from which the payrolls are paid; and (2) the new investments to be developed. By contrast, with external financing the process of deliberation and decision-making can become a much more subtle and multivariate procedure establishing a precondition for a truly humanist productive organization and economic system in general.

II.12. My twelfth point was also noted previously in passing, but it is so important that it deserves a specific elaboration. With a perfect capital market in which everybody can borrow and lend approximately at the same rate of interest and in which all productive firms are borrowers of funds for their physical productive assets, the marginal productivities of capital by and large can be expected to be equalized among themselves and also to the rate of interest in the capital market. This will, as is well known, for a given allocation of labor, produce an optimum allocation of scarce capital resources. By contrast, with self-financing, for many of the reasons outlined earlier, no such equalization of productivities among users will be obtained. And thus the capital allocation is bound to be inefficient.

II.13. The thirteenth point is linked to the twelfth and bears on the efficiency of allocation of the human factor throughout the participatory economy. Provided that the equalization of returns to capital on the margin pointed out in the preceding paragraph is fulfilled, then a very simple criterion for full efficiency of the economy, that is, for the efficiency of allocation of all resources, is the equalization or at least approximate equalization of incomes of labor of equal quality throughout the economy. And thus external financing which leads to equal returns to capital also, by implication, gives a simple tool to the policy makers of the participatory economy leading to full allocational efficiency: the tool is the adoption and design of such policies (primarily allocation of new investments into and expansion of the high-income industries) as to equalize returns to labor of identical nature and quality. Of course, it goes without saying that this policy which guarantees allocational efficiency is also desirable on distributional grounds.

II.14. Here I do not intend to say anything new over and above what is contained in the preceding thirteen points, but rather to transpose the analysis which has thus far been cast in terms of and in connection with capital and capital accumulation to assets which are not capital, that is, which are not produced but rather given to men by nature—specifically land and the corresponding production organization, such as a farm cooperative of the type of a Chilean *asentamiento* or a Peruvian sugar plantation. To self-financing and accumulation of capital now corresponds collective ownership of the land used by the participatory firm. Given such collective ownership, the same difficulties and inefficiencies can arise as those described under points 1 and 2 above. Specifically, if the cooperative can sell its land, it can transform itself into a financial lending institution and its members may become idle rentiers. Otherwise, if they cannot sell the land—as can normally be expected under any real conditions—the collective ownership, as in the case of physical assets, can lead to completely inappropriate factor proportions; for example, a very large cooperative farm, as measured by its acreage, can be supporting only a very small number of families or members of the cooperative, each family earning very high incomes and only the best land on the farm being utilized for production. If, moreover, it is possible to hire second-class wage-earning labor, the few participating families in the cooperative certainly will do so to increase their incomes further and thereby transform the farm cooperative into something akin to a partnership with a large number of hired laborers at a fixed wage. But this is no different from a traditional capitalist enterprise. By contrast, the case of external financing here would correspond to either leasing of land to the cooperative at a price or collective ownership of land by the cooperative accompanied by a substantial tax on land levied to extract the scarcity rent of that land. In either situation, for some rent (or tax) high enough the number of families on the farm would become sufficient to conform with the requirements of nationally efficient resource allocation.

III. The Need for a New Concept of Ownership under Labor Management

As we have seen in the preceding section, it is of paramount importance that the labor-managed firm be externally financed and that it pay in one way or another for the use of its capital resources. To attain these objectives in practice, we can envisage two avenues of approach. One of them I have described elsewhere [3]. It is based on the creation of a special agency which guarantees the external financing, as well as many other efficient characteristics for the participatory economy.

The other approach, by contrast to the first institutional solution, is legal, or juridical, involving a fundamental redefinition of rights of property, quite different from the conventional concepts of either the Western law or that of the socialist countries. In the remainder of this section I will attempt to give the reader an overall impression of what I have in mind, and in the subsequent and concluding section I will go into greater detail in developing the definition. Of course, the reader should be aware of the fact that the subject is new and in addition that the author is not a legal expert. Consequently, all the remainder of this paper ought to be taken as a preliminary sketch in need of subsequent improvement, not only by this writer but also, hopefully, by some legal experts.

First we must point out that we do not want to speak about all kinds of assets, only about a special type of assets that we may refer to as *social* and *productive*. More exactly, the assets for which we want to redefine the concept of ownership and property are social, that is, more than one person must be involved in one or another of the several possible attributes of property. Second, the assets must be productive, that is, they must be used in a productive activity. A more precise definition of "productive activity" will be necessary, but this ought not to detain us at this preliminary stage of our argument.

The fundamental ingredient of our new definition of ownership for what we have just defined as the social productive asset is that with any such asset we always must have two distinct owners, physical and legal persons, each of whom possesses one but not all of the attributes (or rights) usually associated with the concept of ownership. Thus, for example, a factory in productive use in which a large number of workers are employed would have two owners. The first we may refer to as the usufruct owner or U-owner, and the second is referred to as the basic owner or B-owner. The U-owner always and unalienably must be all those who collectively use the asset in production. The B-owner, on the other hand, can be anyone, and its principal function and right is to extract what we may call the scarcity rent (but not any kind of surplus or profit) of the productive social asset.

IV. The U-B Ownership Analyzed in Greater Detail

The essentials of what we want to present in this section are summarized in Table 8.1 below. We will organize our discussion according to that table and explain one by one each of its eight entries.

As indicated by the headings on top of the table, the four columns correspond to the four important aspects of the U-B ownership. The first column indicates who can own under the two alternative types of ownership. The second column summarizes the most important rights of ownership. The third column summarizes the obligations imposed on the owner. The fourth column indicates the type or nature of transferability of ownership and its taxability. The two horizontal rows of the table correspond to usufruct (U) ownership and basic (B) ownership. For easy reference we have numbered the eight positions in the table, the numbering running horizontally, row by row.

Turning first to position 1, we note the most important aspect of the U-B ownership, namely, that the U-owners must be collectively all those who work with the productive assets. There can be absolutely no exception to that rule.

Table 8.1. Summary of U-B ownership of social productive assets

	Who can own	Rights	Obligations	Transferability and taxability
Usufruct ownership	(1) The total collective working with the asset, exclusively and unalienably	(2) Collective demo-cratic management of activity Nobody can take away asset from U-owner fulfilling his obligations Appropriation of all net income of activity except for rent (see "obliga-tions")	(3) Preserve value of asset or compen-sate B-owner, if value is changed (with + or − compensation) Preserve specific use or uses Pay to B-owner scarcity rent (objectively determined)	(4) Is taxable Can be transferre without pay to oth collective assumi same obligations and rights. The agreement of the B-owner may be required to cover against increase risk.
Basic ownership	(5) Anyone, but if B-ownership overlaps U-owner-ship, this is a separate and indi-vidualized position	(6) Scarcity rent and compensation for depreciation or depletion Nobody can take away B-ownership from B-owner Prosecution of U-owner in case of default on debt service	(7) In some cases, re-finance fully de-preciated assets	(8) Is taxable Can be sold to another B-owner without agreemer of U-owner

In position 2 we summarize the principal rights of the U-owner. The first is the collective democratic management of the activity involving the asset. Of course, in this connection it is necessary to introduce a concept of natural or functional unit. It would be absurd to say that each machine in the factory must individually be managed by those who work on it; rather, the integrated process of production involving the factory—or perhaps a department, itself defined by the self-managing and self-determining function—ought to be taken as the unit being democratically managed and U-owned by the working collective. The next important right is that the U-ownership cannot be taken away from the owner, who is protected by law. Of course, customary exceptions can be made on grounds of eminent domain. Finally, the U-owner, after paying the scarcity rent, has the right to appropriate all net income of the activity linked to the productive asset.

Position 3 shows the principal obligations of the U-owner. First, he must preserve the value of the asset he is using. If the value is increased through addition or improvement[3] or is reduced through use or depletion, such a change must be compensated. More concretely, in the case of physical capital assets which are depreciating over time, restitution should be made of the depreciation allowances to the B-owner or held on deposit by the U-owner with the appropriate financial return from these deposits going to the B-owner as a form of scarcity rent. Another obligation of the U-owner may be imposed regarding the nature of use of the asset. For example, a piece of land may be restricted in use only as farm land and can be used in no other way. Clearly, this obligation is very closely related to zoning rights as we find them in most countries. The third important obligation already implied in the first is the obligation of the U-owner to pay to the B-owner a scarcity rent for the use of the productive asset. Of course, in some cases such a rent may be zero. The rent ought to be, as much as possible, objectively determined and changed from time to time to reflect changing economic conditions.

Turning now briefly to position 4 we first note that the U-ownership is taxable by the public authorities. Second, the U-ownership of the entire asset (e.g., a factory) or part thereof (e.g., a piece of machinery) can be transferred from one U-owner to another, that is, from one working collective to another. This has to be done without compensation, but the new U-owner must assume all the obligations. Of course, in practice, the first case may not be very important, as it would happen only rarely that the entire collective working on a farm or in a factory would change at a single point in time.

Turning now to the B-ownership, at position 5 we first note that anyone can be the B-owner. In a socialist economy it would be the state represented by the government or public authorities. In case of national ownership, as noted above and discussed elsewhere, it

---

3. Of course there is no question here of an increased market value of stock. There is no marketable security endowed with controlling power whose value would vary with the success of the firm, and all net income after payment of rent (or rental) to the B-owner belongs and is attributable to the working community.

would be the National Labor Management Agency. In other cases it would be an individual or group of individuals, a bank, a saving cooperative, or a similar group. The only specific requirement is that if there is an overlapping between some or all of the U-owners and the B-owners, then the B-ownership should be individualized. By this we mean that the portions of the B-ownership assignable to individual members of the B-owning group are clearly and precisely defined. In practice, for example, this would mean that if the B-owners of a farm are some or all of those working on the farm, such an ownership should be in the form of something like a saving co-operative where the ownership share of each individual is stated clearly in terms of its value on which the individual B-owner would receive the scarcity rent proportionately. Also such a portion of ownership would be negotiable individually. Of course, one has to realize here that such a negotiability would not carry with itself the usually undesirable effects under the normal type of ownership, because the U-owners of the farm are all those working on the farm irrespective of who the B-owners are or how they are distributed.

At position 6 we note that the B-owner has the right to receive the scarcity rent noted already in position 3. Of course, how such a rent is determined would depend on circumstances. For example, in situations where the asset in question is a factory the link or contract between the U- and the B-owners can assume the form of negotiable bonds, and in that case the scarcity rent would be the interest return on such securities. Moreover, the B-owner has the right to receive compensation for depreciation of the asset, which in turn can take the form of debt repayment.[4] In case of default on the rent or repayment obligations by the U-owner, the B-owner has the right to initiate legal action, under national legislation designed for that purpose. An essential part of such legislation would be the defini-tion of bankruptcy of the U-owner. Still another right of the B-owner similar to that of the U-owner is that nobody can take away the B-ownership from him.

Turn now to position 7. Especially when the supplier of funds (i.e., the B-owner) possesses a strong monopoly power, as would be the case with socialist or national B-ownership, the B-owner should be obligated to refinance those who fulfill all previous debt-service

4. As in the case of a mortgage, interest and repayment might consist of a constant annuity with declining interest and increasing repayment components over time.

obligations. The obvious aim of this would be to limit the power that the B-owner might exercise over the U-owner.

In position 8 we note that the B-owner is taxable and that the B-ownership can be sold at a price to another B-owner. We note that such a sale is not contingent on agreement by the U-owner. Similarly, the transfer of U-ownership is not contingent on the agreement by the B-owner.

References

1. E. Furubotn and S. Pejovich, "Property Rights and Behavior of the Firm in a Socialist State: The Example of Yugoslavia," *Zeitschrift für National-ökonomie*, 30, 3–4 (Dec. 1970), 431–454.

2. Stephen Sacks, "Changes in Industrial Structure in Yugoslavia, 1959–68," *Journal of Political Economy*, 80, 3 (1972).

3. J. Vanek, *The General Theory of Labor-Managed Market Economies* (Ithaca, N.Y.: Cornell University Press, 1970), chap. 15.

9 The Basic Theory of Financing of Participatory Firms*

I. Introduction

In the last chapter I assembled a large number of arguments to explain in simple terms—primarily to the noneconomist or practical policy maker—the desirability of having labor-managed firms always financed from the outside and not through self-financing and collective ownership. The purpose of this paper is to provide a unified theoretical basis on which the argument for external financing and against self-financing and collective ownership is based. We will primarily concentrate on the latter aspect, namely, the analysis of the drawbacks of self-financing, the advantages of the opposite form of financing through a capital market external to the firm being quite self-evident by implication.[1]

The arguments which follow are of considerable real relevance. All the actual forms of self-management that we encounter today in the world, be they the Yugoslav worker-managed firm, an Israeli kibbutz, a Western industrial producers' cooperative, or a Latin American farm cooperative, are much closer in their design and actual operation to the case of self-financing and collective ownership than to that of external financing. That these productive organizations rely heavily on their own funds, primarily in the forms of initial contributions or retained earnings which are largely irrecuperable (except in some instances, and only partially, at retirement), is not difficult to understand. Not only are—especially in

* Cornell Department of Economics Working Paper no. 27, July 1971. This paper was published in *Self-Management*: *Economic Liberation of Man* (New York and London: Penguin, 1975).

1. In our concept of external funding we also include redeemable savings deposits of members, bearing a market rate of return paid, as to other creditors, prior to the distribution of labor incomes. To the extent that our analysis comes out in favor of external funding, it also favors this type of individualized funding by members.

the Western world—banks and other external creditors unwilling to finance the totality, or even a major portion, of a labor-managed firm's assets, but, and this is more important, the firm itself will generally not want such financing because this would jeopardize its autonomy and thus undermine its very nature and *raison d'être*.

In my opinion (with which some will disagree) the arguments presented hereafter are so powerful in explaining the shortcomings of traditional or conventional forms of producer cooperatives and participatory firms that they offer an ample explanation of the comparative failure of these forms in history, ever since they were first conceived of by the writers of the eighteenth and nineteenth centuries. The development of this analysis was to me personally most gratifying. It had always puzzled me how it could have been possible that a productive organization based on cooperation, harmony of interests and the brotherhood of men, so appealing and desirable on moral and philosophical grounds, could have done so poorly when subjected to a practical test. It seems to me that we now have both an explanation and a way of remedy.

II. Assumptions

As is customary in theoretical arguments, we will consider in most of this discussion a "pure" or "extreme" case, where, if a firm wants to invest, it must do so from its own resources, as a matter of a collective saving effort, the title to which remains in the hands of the working collective and not in the hands of individual members who would earn a given return on the capital and could recuperate the principal part of the investment at some point.[2] Later at the end of the fourth section we will generalize this discussion and permit some degree of external financing.

To simplify the analysis further, we will speak about a single firm, labor-managed, selling its product x at a constant price, for simplicity equal to unity, and using only capital K and (its members') labor L. Capital has an infinite durability, and thus there are no problems of depreciation. The production function is of the smooth neoclassical type. We will consider two cases: a linear-homogeneous function

$$x = Lf(K/L) \qquad (9.1)$$

2. In fact, this situation in many respects would approximate that of a capital market external to the firm.

and a conventional increasing-diminishing returns function

$$x = x(K, L). \tag{9.2}$$

For simplicity, we also assume that all members of the firm have the same time preference R.[3] More explicitly, in a simple case involving only two periods, each worker is willing to save and surrender from his current consumption one dollar provided that next year he will be able to receive in return at least $1 + R$ dollars.

We further postulate that the working community acts in its own self-interest and the interest of its individual members and not in the interest of those not belonging to it. This may be an incorrect assumption in some cases, where altruistic, religious, or family considerations prevail. But we will not consider such conditions here, because they are rare and because their implications for our argument are quite obvious.

III. The Case of Constant Returns to Scale

The essentials which we need for our analysis are summarized in Figure 9.1. The function $f(K/L)$ expressing output per laborer (both in physical terms and in terms of value) is plotted against the capital–labor ratio and, as is well known, this must be strictly concave on the assumptions made. It can also be easily established that the slope at any given point, such as the slope A of dc at c, measures the marginal product of capital, the segment bc measures the income share of capital per laborer if capital is paid its marginal product, and the segment ab measures the wage rate provided also that labor is paid its marginal product.

Suppose now that a firm finds itself temporarily or permanently at a point where its capital–output ratio equals a. The firm may have reached that point through an initial investment by those working in it, either through a transition from another type of firm (e.g., nationalization, as in Yugoslavia) or through prior self-financing based on current income.

When the firm finds itself at that point, the income per worker actually earned is equivalent to the distance ac. The segments de-

---

3. R can be thought of as an average taken over all the members. In that case, however, our analysis would not be perfectly rigorous because of some structural problems of decision-making which might arise.

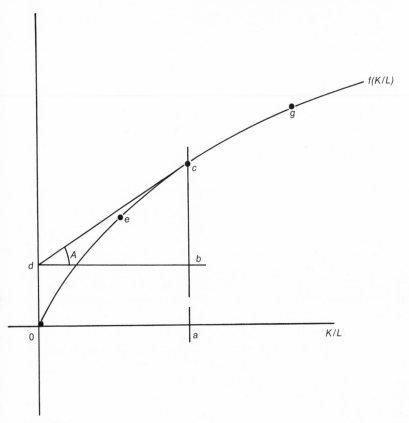

Figure 9.1

fined by point *b* and explained earlier are irrelevant because the community owns collectively its assets and does not pay for them.

Let us analyze the dynamic forces which will act on that equilibrium. First (at least on the assumptions made) there is the force that can be termed that of *self-extinction*. Irrespective of whether the point *a* is one for which the firm would be in equilibrium, given the time preferences of its members, there will be a natural tendency to reduce the number of members, for the given capital shock, and thereby move to the right of point *a*, to higher levels of income per laborer. Obviously, the working community will try to prevent this happening through prohibiting the expelling of members. But through attrition, retirement, or voluntary withdrawal, it will always be possible to reduce numbers in the long run. The full compensation of departing members which would also mitigate this self-extinction force will generally be impossible, both because of a basic unwillingness to compensate a voluntarily retiring member and because of a lack of cash with which to do so.

This first force would thus tend to move the solution point indefinitely to the right in Figure 9.1, through a reduction in membership with a constant capital stock. It would be terminated only at the point of a single member adhering to the firm.[4]

Suppose now that the initial points *a* and *c* in Figure 9.1 actually correspond to an equilibrium of time preference in the sense that the community did not have any desire to invest or disinvest over time. As the self-extinction force sets in, as explained above, and the capital–labor ratio increases (we move to the right in Figure 9.1) the marginal productivity of capital, the slope of $f(K/L)$, diminishes, and thus there will be a desire on the part of the members of the firm to return to the equilibrium point *a* through gradual disinvestment and capital consumption on the part of those who remain in the enterprise. We can now refer to this as the *second self-extinction force*, reserving for the other the term *first self-extinction force*.

But let us now turn to the forces determining the equilibrium of the firm as related to the time preference *R*. The first important conclusion, based on what we may refer to as the underinvestment force, is that if the time preference of the community is *R*, its equilibrium production will correspond to a point where the marginal productivity of capital is well above that magnitude at a level *A**, above *R* by a positive magnitude *D*, such that

$$A^* = R + D, \qquad D > 0. \qquad (9.3)$$

This must be so for the following reason. If a member of the community invests a dollar, his total return from the investment will be only the increased future current incomes and *never* the recuperation of the amount itself invested, on grounds of the collective nature of the investment. Supposing that the net addition to his income is the marginal product of capital *A* of $i = 1, \ldots, T$ years preceding his

---

4. As we will see later for the case of our second technology, $x(K, L)$, this extreme situation will disappear, but its basic and undesirable character will remain.

expected retirement, we have as the criterion for investment, for the (subjective) present value V of all these returns.

$$V = A \sum_{i=1}^{T} (1 + R)^{-i} \geqslant 1. \qquad (9.4)$$

On the other hand, if the member could have recuperated the principal part of his investment, he would have decided in favor of an investment W provided that

$$W = A \sum_{i=1}^{T} (1 + R)^{-i} + (1 + R)^{-T} \geqslant 1. \qquad (9.5)$$

By definition of subjective time preference, we know that in this case (equation 9.5), $W = 1$ for $A = R$. We thus can write equation 9.4 as

$$A \sum_{i=1}^{T} (1 + R)^{-i} - R \sum_{i=1}^{T} (1 + R)^{-i} - (1 + R)^{-T} \geqslant 0, \qquad (9.6)$$

from where, by inspection, it immediately follows that in order to invest under the criterion of equation 9.4, the return A must exceed A^*, which itself exceeds R by an amount

$$D = (1 + R)^{-T} \bigg/ \sum_{i=1}^{T} (1 + R)^{-i}, \qquad (9.7)$$

a decreasing function of T. If $A = A^*$ no investment or disinvestment will take place and thus, in connection with what we have called the *underinvestment force*, the firm will be in equilibrium. Obviously, this equilibrium is one of underinvestment because the marginal productivity of capital A^* exceeds the subjective rate of time preference. This differential D can be extremely significant, especially when the membership time-expectation T is low. In the extreme case where all members are to retire in one year, we have $D = 1$. When $R = 10$ per cent, D then is 1000 per cent of R and A^*, the critical level of the marginal productivity of capital, is equal to $R(100 + 1000)$ per cent, i.e., 110 per cent. With that A^*, of course, hardly anyone would ever invest. With $T > 1$, the results become less extreme, but still highly significant, the realistic ranges for A^* being somewhere between twice and four times the time preference rate R.

The next effect, which is just as undesirable as the preceding ones, we will refer to as the *never-employ effect*, deriving from its corresponding *never-employ force*. With reference to Figure 9.1, suppose that the firm finds itself at point e, whereas the equilibrium level of the marginal productivity of capital A^* corresponds to point c; at point g, finally, the slope, that is the marginal productivity of capital, is equal to the time preference of the working community R. Because at e the marginal productivity of capital is more than A^*, the members of the community will desire to invest and expand production with increasing K/L, as long as K/L falls short of the level indicated by a in the diagram. On the assumptions made, in particular self-financing and constant returns to scale, this is the only situation where growth of the firm occurs, of course, assuming that the membership of the firm is constant and the first self-extinction effect inoperative. But it will be noted—and this we have referred to as the never-employ effect—that under no circumstances will the firm admit new members into the community, as such action would necessarily reduce the capital–labor ratio and consequently the income per worker.

It takes only a little reflection to realize that with external financing through a competitive capital market, at a rate equal to the time preference R, all four undersirable effects would disappear, and an equilibrium at point g in Figure 9.1 would be established. The first self-extinction effect would be absent since by reducing the membership of the community the K/L ratio would increase above that corresponding to g, and with constant payment R per unit of capital, the return per worker would decline. The desire to reduce the capital stock would *ipso facto* also disappear, because this would disturb the equilibrium from its position at g, and thus the second self-extinction effect also vanishes.

The underinvestment effect disappears, so to speak by definition, as the equilibrium now is at g, precisely at the point where the marginal productivity of capital equals the rate of time preference R. Finally, the never employ effect also disappears in the sense that at any point the community can invest together with increasing employment *pari passu* without worsening anybody's condition. Actually, it is the very property of constant-returns-to-scale technology that proportional increases in both factors, with unchanged prices of capital, leave labor's condition unchanged.

IV. The Case of Increasing-Diminishing Returns

In the preceding section we have developed a simple theoretical model of a participatory firm operating under constant returns to scale, shown the equilibrium and disequilibrium behavior of that model, and indicated four important drawbacks—or negative effects—of self-financing and collective ownership of participatory (labor-managed) firms. This section will make a major step in the direction of a more realistic model by relaxing the assumption of constant returns to scale. Instead, we will assume that the technology employed by the participatory firm is that given by equation 9.2 above, subject to increasing and then diminishing returns to scale. In fact our analysis will also cover the case which is perhaps the most realistic of all, where increasing returns at first are followed, for higher levels of output, by constant returns to scale.[5] This is so because, as we will see presently, such firms can never grow to a point outside the increasing-returns range of the technology.

To start our discussion, let us turn to the capital–labor input plane of the firm in Figure 9.2 and identify in it some significant loci. First we observe the contour EE; it is the locus of maximum physical efficiency[6] along which, for prescribed K/L ratios, both average factor productivities are maximized. It may be useful to recall that a participatory firm which is externally financed will always, in the long run and under competitive conditions, operate somewhere at EE, and thus maximize its factor productivities. It is also useful to recall that along EE the technology is "locally" subject to constant returns to scale, and the left and below that locus returns to scale are increasing. To the right and above, returns to scale are diminishing, or in the "realistic" situation noted above, constant to scale. All the forces described in the preceding section for the case of constant returns to scale are "locally" valid along the locus EE, and, as we will see presently, for that reason no equilibrium of a collectively self-financing participatory firm could ever exist anywhere along that locus.

Rather, the equilibrium of the firm with collective ownership and

5. Empirical studies indicate that diminishing returns are rarely present for high levels of capital and labor employment, except where land is utilized intensively as a productive factor.

6. For a detailed discussion of this locus see my *General Theory of Labor-Managed Market Economies* (Ithaca, N.Y.: Cornell University Press, 1970), chap. 2.

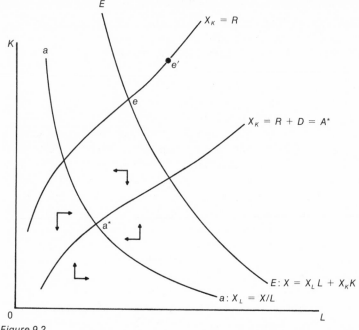

Figure 9.2

financing will have to be somewhere at the locus *aa*, which is located in the increasing-returns zone and which is technically inefficient. It is the locus along which the average and marginal products of labor are equalized (for any level of employment of capital) and along which, as is well known, the average product of labor is at a maximum. The result is obvious, because indeed it is the average product of labor that the community wants to maximize under self-financing (i.e., no payment of rental for capital) so as to maximize every member's income.

The inefficient operation at *aa* is in effect the analogue of the two self-extinction effects noted for the constant-returns technology. The difference here is that the community could never reduce itself to a single member because this would make it extremely inefficient on grounds of considerable losses due to nonrealization of economies of scale.

The underinvestment effect explained in the preceding section remains unchanged. Again, with collective ownership and savings the equilibrium marginal product of capital must fall well above the rate of time preference R, at a rate which we can again refer to as $A^* = R + D$. Corresponding to $x_K = A^*$, we have another locus in Figure 9.2. It is at the intersection of aa and $x_K = A^*$, at a^*, that we find the full equilibrium of our participatory self-financed firm, both equilibrium conditions being fulfilled at that point.

The dynamic forces of adjustment for any point away from equilibrium are indicated by arrows, leading to the conclusion that a^* is a stable position. It will be noted that to the right (left) of aa employment will be declining (rising) so as to increase the income per worker, while below (above) $x_K = A^*$ there will be accumulation (decumulation) of capital in accordance with the members' time preference.

By contrast, under external financing at a capital cost equal to the time preference R, the equilibrium of a participatory firm must be along the locus defined in Figure 9.2 as $x_K = R$. Under these conditions the income per worker will be maximized at some point on the locus of maximum physical efficiency EE. The equilibrium of a labor-managed externally financed firm thus will be at the intersection of the two loci at e. As is well known, e will also be the equilibrium of a capitalist firm provided that it operates without profit. If it makes positive profits, its equilibrium will be somewhere in the diminishing returns zone of the production function on $x_K = R$, at a point such as e'.

Comparing points e and a^* it thus becomes apparent that in the case studied in this section where the technology is subject to increasing returns to scale for relatively low levels of output—a highly realistic condition in most situations—self-financing by a participatory firm leads to both inefficient production at a low level of output and to underinvestment, as compared to a solution obtained with external financing at a price of capital equal to the rate of time preference. Undercapitalization and a small size are also the most significant drawbacks of traditional workers' cooperatives.

Before concluding this section, we may realistically relax the assumption of a 100 per cent collective internal funding and permit some external funding or individualized redeemable internal funding. The general conclusion is that such an alteration of conditions will weaken the inefficiency explained in this section—largely in proportion to the degree of external funding—but will never eliminate it altogether.

To demonstrate this, it need only be realized that if, for a portion of the capital stock, the cooperative must pay a market price (rate of interest), this will move the locus of maximum labor incomes (no longer the locus of maximum average labor productivity) from aa in Figure 9.2 to the right, but not as far as EE (the locus attained with full external funding). On the other hand, if the working collective can at all times count on a given proportion of any investment to be financed externally, at the rate R, this will reduce the necessary differential D, and thus bring A^* closer to R and shift the locus $x_K = A^*$ in Figure 9.2 upward. Thus the solution point a^* will travel, roughly speaking, toward e on account of both forces (both shifting loci).

V. The Results in Real Perspective

In Figure 9.2, the comparison between points a^* and points such as e or e' seems to offer a good deal of the explanation of why in the real world the producer cooperatives—as we have noted in the first section, basically internally and collectively financed participatory firms—have fared so poorly in a capitalist environment. The hostility and prejudice of that environment could explain only a part, and perhaps only a small part, of the difficulties of the cooperatives. The real economic reasons appear very powerful if we realize how large the orders of magnitude of the underinvestment and underproduction effects corresponding to point a^* actually can be in the real world.

To make this comparison more clear and more tangible let us contemplate a situation of two similar workers, one working in a self-financing production cooperative and the other in a capitalist firm operating (with zero profit) at the minimum average cost point, both firms producing the same product and selling in the same capitalist market. Provided that technologies are unaffected by economic organization and that both workers have the same time preference, but one saves collectively in his cooperative while the other saves individually through a capital market which finances the capitalist's firm, the situation in equilibrium can be as shown in Table 9.1 in terms of hypothetical figures.

In our competitive capitalist firm the typical worker not only earns a considerably higher current aggregate income than in the self-financed production cooperative, but he retains the command over

Table 9.1.

	Cooperative firm	Capitalist firm
Product per man	30	50
Wage	30	30
Interest income from accumulated savings	0	20
Recuperable actual accumulation of savings per worker	0	100
Irrecuperable accumulation (collective) per worker	100	0
Total capital accumulation	10,000	20,000
Employment	100	200

his accumulated savings of one hundred. As we have defined the situation, the worker's only advantage in the cooperative is the moral and psychological one, because he works in a humanly more pleasant environment with a good deal less or no alienation. What we have not considered in our example are the incentive effects of participation on productivity and effort. But these advantages, compared to the considerable drawbacks of a lower productivity and earning power and a lack of command over wealth once accumulated, in many situations were not sufficient counterweights. When in the context of, say, nineteenth-century England or Germany, the factors of a hostile environment, lack of understanding, and class resentment are added, it is no wonder that the production cooperative remained not much more than the utopian dream of a handful of idealistic men.

By contrast to the collectively financed production cooperative illustrated in the first column of Table 9.1, the economic performance of a participatory firm with external financing would lead to the pattern illustrated in the second column, for an "ideal" capitalist firm. But in addition, the human and economic advantages of participation, incentives, higher productivity, absence of alienation, and a no-conflict atmosphere of work, absent in the capitalist firm, would be added to the redesigned participatory firm.

But of course, to have full external financing (as here defined) and thereby obtain the benefits noted, one can never rely on the conventional private banking system. Conventional banks, whether in Victorian England or the modern United States, would hardly lend much to a producer cooperative, and the cooperatives themselves might shun such funding. It must take an act of political will, or a philanthropic (not profit- and power-oriented) group of men to provide the necessary characteristics of the capital market which would support the smooth and efficient operation of a participatory economy or a participatory sector. Such an economy or sector would then be optimal both humanly and in terms of economic efficiency, superior to all existing forms of productive organization.

10 | A Fully Decentralized and Fully Efficient Labor-Managed Economy*

Perhaps the most serious impediment to the rapid and successful creation of self-managed economies in the world today is the dilemma between the requirements of an efficient funding of self-managed firms on the one hand and the quest for full independence of these firms on the other. As I have shown in several places [2], [3], [4], effective functioning of the labor-managed market economy requires the predominantly or entirely external funding of labor-managed firms and conditions of a competitive capital market, if possible under the supervision of a nonprofit, semiofficial agency, call it the National Labor Management Agency. On the other hand, many practitioners of self-management in Yugoslavia, Peru, and other countries argue—and certainly not without reason—that in practice external funding and especially anything like the National Labor Management Agency must conflict with the autonomy and economic self-determination of the self-managed firms.[1]

Without disputing the argument, this paper will suggest a solution to this dilemma that will, I hope, enhance the implementation of labor management. First we will sketch the essentials of the solution in Section I. In Section II we will analyze formally the effects of the proposed solution on the behavior of the firm. In Section III we will interpret the findings for individual firms in connection with general equilibrium and the overall solution for the self-managed economy. Finally in the concluding section we will discuss the findings and their bearing on some real situations.

* Cornell Department of Economics Working Paper no. 42, December 1972. The main idea presented here emerged from a discussion seminar with Andrew McGregor and Vincent Richards, to whom I am very grateful for their collaboration.

1. In addition, even if the agency did not conflict with firms' autonomy, there might not be enough competent men in developing countries to staff it, and thus a problem would remain.

I. The Solution

To explain the idea in simple terms let us consider a concrete situation. Suppose that the government of a country which wants to introduce self-management defines a new form of enterprise in legal terms (as, for example, in the United States we have defined a corporation, a partnership, and the like) to be referred to as an *autonomous labor-managed firm*. Each firm incorporating or establishing itself under this law must fulfill the following conditions: The initial endowment of the firm is provided by the public authorities, the *government*, local or otherwise. Once the factory is built, the members of the firm are assembled, and the firm starts operating, then year after year it must pay, or more precisely, withdraw from its returns, a certain return on capital r^*. The r^* is established nationwide by the government, reflecting economic conditions and in particular and relative scarcity of capital, and is applicable to all firms defined as autonomous labor-managed firms. With amount thus obtained, which is equal to the capital of the firm times r^*, the firm is entitled either to (1) add to its own capital stock, or (2) invest in or create a new firm, or (3) deposit with some national investment institution established for the purpose. If the firm adds the capital thus obtained to its own capital and expands its operations, in the next year or the year after it will then have to pay the rate r^* on that capital also and use the proceeds exclusively in either of the three ways just outlined. The essential thing is that the r^* times capital stock can never enter the consumption resources of anyone. In the second solution, if the firm uses the funds to create a new firm, it is the new firm that will assume the same obligations on its own capital as did the mother enterprise. If the enterprise uses the third alternative and deposits the return on its capital to the national agency, it is the agency that will assume the responsibility for further channeling these funds, and the paying firm is relieved of any further obligation or responsibility for the amounts of capital paid in. The enterprise may be given the right to draw on these funds at a later date.

As with all labor-managed firms, the autonomous labor-managed firm is defined by its membership and not by its capital. The power to control and exploit the firm rests in the association of working men and not in any way in those who may have provided the capital assets. Also, the autonomous labor-managed firm just defined remains fully autonomous as long as it fulfills the capital remuneration and accumulation requirements outlined. If for reasons of serious economic difficulty it cannot fulfill its obligations, the public authorities or the initial endowing institution would have to step in, partly or completely limiting the autonomy of the firm, and attempt to restore it to its economic health. In an extreme case the firm could be liquidated, its assets sold, and the proceeds, if any, restituted to the agency or group who created it.

In Section IV we will return to some further real practical aspects of the autonomous labor-managed firm and of the economic system based on it. For the moment we hope that the outline presented here is sufficient to give the reader a rough idea of the subject at hand. And thus we can turn to the formal analysis of the behavior of the autonomous labor-managed firm. Let it also be noted here that the return r^* might be made variable along the lines of Chapter 11 below, to make the society at large participate in the risks of the enterprise.

II. The Formal Theory of Behavior of the Autonomous Labor-Managed Firm

To make the problem as simple as possible let us consider a product x produced from capital K and labor L. To approximate as closely as possible the conditions in the real world we postulate that for small levels of output the production function is subject to increasing returns to scale. This is the case in Figure 10.1, below and to the left of the locus EE. To the right and above that locus, for higher outputs and inputs the function is subject to constant returns to scale and thus can be written as a product of L and a function $f(K/L)$ depending on the capital-labor ratio only. The function $f(K/L)$ is shown in Figure 10.2.

Of course, if we believe that in the real world there are always creasing returns and the constant return zone is never reached, this would simply mean that only the results to the left of EE in Figure 10.1 hold and that the locus recedes indefinitely to the right and upward. Alternatively, if increasing returns persist to higher levels of output but are very mild, then we can think of the solutions to the right of EE in Figure 10.1 as a first approximation of the true results.[2]

2. The case of diminishing returns beyond EE is hard to handle and may be relevant in agriculture, in which context it is noted in Section IV below.

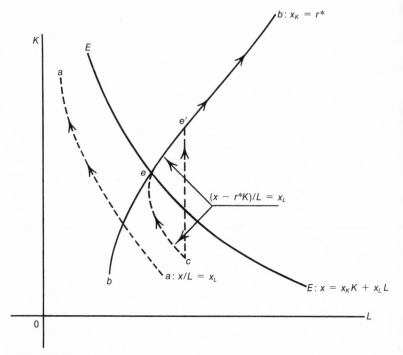

Figure 10.1

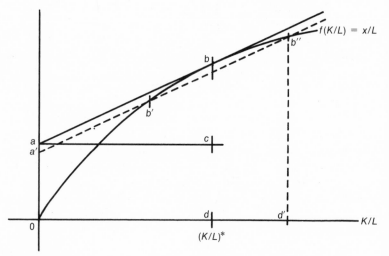

Figure 10.2

Let us look first at a firm in a competitive market, in which for simplicity the price is assumed to be equal to unity, which accumulates capital (from whatever sources), but to which the use of that capital is free. In other words, r^* is equal to zero. Such a firm would attempt to maximize the average productivity of labor and thereby the income per worker and thus always find itself at the locus aa in Figure 10.1 where the marginal and average products of labor are equal. With accumulation the firm would proceed along aa in the upward direction as indicated by the arrows. As has been shown elsewhere [4], the solutions along aa are inefficient on many accounts, among them the fact that the firm does not even maximize, given factor proportions, its total factor productivity, the latter being maximized along and beyond the locus EE.

Now consider the autonomous labor-managed firm described in the preceding section, and for the sake of an example suppose that its initial endowment and initial point of operation is that of point c where, given the corresponding amount of capital, the firm maximizes its income per member by equalizing the marginal product of labor to the average net return per laborer after payment of the required capital rental r^*.[3] Starting from c the autonomous labor-managed firm, accumulating at the rate r^*K, would proceed toward e if it could or wanted to reduce its labor force, or more likely to point e' because normally it would want to keep its labor collective undiminished. It will accumulate in its own firm and not use either of the two other solutions (i.e., forming of new firms or depositing the accumulated new funds with the agency) because at c and along the entire trajectory ce or ce' the marginal productivity of capital exceeds the rental r^*, and thus additions of capital must be adding to income per worker even after payment of the obligatory capital charge.

Once at e or e' the income per worker is maximized while both capital and labor are receiving their respective values of marginal product. And with accumulation progressing now at the rate of r^*, if the firm chooses the first alternative and expands itself, the equilibrium point of the firm will progress along the line bb. This is indicated again by arrows in Figure 10.1. With capital growing at the rate r^* and with unchanged factor proportions corresponding to

3. This condition of maximization of income per worker is carefully derived and explained by Ward [5] and Vanek [2, chap. 2].

the segment *eb*, employment must also be increasing at the rate r^* and the same must hold for output.

The equilibrium capital-labor ratio corresponding to *eb* in Figure 10.1 is illustrated by $(K/L)^*$ in Figure 10.2. As is well known from the properties of linear homogeneous functions, the income per member is given by *Oa* or *bc* in Figure 10.2, and the capital income per member for the equilibrium capital-labor ratio corresponds to the segment *cb* in that same diagram. It is immediately apparent from the diagram that as long as the working collective must pay the capital rental r^* any deviation from the capital labor ratio K/L^* would mean a reduction in income per member. For example, if at any point the working collective decided not to bring in any new members and to keep expanding capital so that the capital-labor ratio would be that indicated by b'' in Figure 10.2, the equilibrium income per worker would become only Oa'. The key factor in this construction is the slope of the lines *ab* or $a'b''$, which expresses (again, as is well known for linear homogeneous functions) the marginal productivity of capital and the rental r^*.

The important fact, of course, is that once the firm finds itself anywhere along *eb* in Figure 10.1 for the capital-labor ratio $(K/L)^*$ in Figure 10.2, it is indifferent between its own accumulation or the other two options, such as creation of new firms or depositing of the rental of capital with the labor-management agency. This is so because, as we have seen, all three alternatives are identical in the sense that the income per worker can no longer be increased by changing factor proportions or accumulation. The decisions as to which of the three options to take will now depend on other factors. For example, if the firm has a number of capable upcoming men skillful in management and organization, it may decide to form a new enterprise at no cost to itself to produce product *x*. But even more realistically it may form a new enterprise to produce a different, perhaps related product.

III. Structural and Dynamic Growth Considerations for the Entire Economy

The dynamic, structural, and general equilibrium properties of an economy based on, or composed of, the autonomous labor-managed firms are truly remarkable. We will discuss and explain them here briefly one by one.

1. The first extremely desirable property is that the economy will accumulate and expand its capital stock indefinitely at the rate r^*. That is, every year that proportion of capital stock will be accumulated. In this way the tendency toward undercapitalization, which can be shown theoretically [4], and which is notorious in the performance of all producer cooperatives which are perfectly free to decide on all matters including accumulation, is overcome. The authorities or society at large, through a vote or otherwise, can within limits decide on the rate r^* as a matter of national economic policy.

2. The second good property of the system is that all of its firms will tend to expand and increase their respective total factor productivities as long as they operate under conditions of increasing returns to scale up to the point where constant returns and maximum total productivity is reached. In other words, all firms in the atomistic (not structural) sense will either be or tend to become optimally efficient.

3. The third property is that all firms who have already reached the maximum factor productivity, as noted in point 2, will operate with marginal productivity of capital equal to r^* and thus—with an identical r^* for all—the economy will tend toward equalization of capital marginal products among firms. And this, in turn, will guarantee the most efficient allocation of capital throughout the economy given the existing location of the labor force.

4. The fourth positive property is that as long as differences exist in income per worker among firms and industries, capital will tend to flow toward new firms and/or expansions in the areas of the highest income per worker. In a firm which already maximizes its total factor productivity and produces for its members maximum labor income, the accumulations, based on the rental r^*, will tend to flow in the direction of the highest labor-income generation. And this, in turn, in a dynamic process will tend to depress prices and labor incomes in the high-income sectors relative to prices and labor incomes in the low-income sectors. And thus the entire economy will converge dynamically at all times toward a solution of income equality and thus also of equalization of marginal labor productivities.[4] But the condition of equalization of marginal product of

4. Recall that the optimizing condition for each firm is equalization of income per worker to his marginal product.

capital already being fulfilled, the tendency just noted will guarantee a convergence toward fully efficient allocations of all resources throughout the economy.

5. Of course, there should be no danger of labor unemployment because the system is capable of absorbing all factors of production including labor at the prescribed rental r^*, which under realistic conditions should exceed the rate of growth of the labor force. In fact, because normally r^* would exceed the rate of expansion of the labor force, even with technological progress, some dynamic readjustment of all factor proportions throughout the economy in the direction of higher capital-labor ratios would have to be operated in more advanced full-employment economies. But the dynamic forces of adjustment inherent in the system as described would guarantee such an adjustment.[5]

6. The fact that once in the equilibrium zone of constant returns to scale the autonomous labor-managed firms would tend to be indifferent toward choosing their own expansions over the other two alternative uses of funds would be conducive to the creation of new firms in ever increasing numbers, and this in turn would safeguard the competitive nature of the economy. In fact, built into the dynamic solution based on the autonomous labor-managed firm is an ever-improving competitiveness of market structures.

7. The seventh and last positive property is optional. In the realistic context of a world where funds are also allocated to research and development and are considered as investment funds, the capital rental of individual firms could be permitted to be used in the field of research and development. Once in the zone of constant returns to scale—or even before—the firm could utilize its capital resources, not for expansion or creation of other firms, but for research and development of new technologies and new products. If such investments were successful, yielding returns considerably in excess of r^*, they could be counted as a part of (intangible) capital stock and treated exactly the same way as all other types of capital. On the other hand, in cases where research and development activity did not lead to significant improvements of one kind or another, the corresponding capital sums could be partly or totally written off and thus not constitute part of the capital base on which r^* is levied.

---

5. r^* or the price level might have to become endogenous variables.

because there would be no public
policy parameter. For example, th
known case of the Scott Bader f
managed, could have been based frc
the autonomous labor-managed firr
successful in part because it was cap
accumulation. However, it has done
ment of a substantial portion of pr
that the r^* is a mandatory accumula
ours is linked to capital stock rathe
superior, because in any self-manage
tive and arbitrary magnitude under
body which, among other things, al

Our next practical point pertain
only could the solution offered in th
new legislation on the social prope
but it could also provide a solutior
inherent in the earlier Peruvian le
munity. Briefly, those who are fami
law and the law of the industrial c
present arguments for the autonor
be useful at the point where the ind
cent ownership of the firms. Then
legal entity could obtain a full rigl
while not transferring the assets to a
to pay the capital rental r^* to be us
in Section I.

Farm cooperatives also could be
managed firms, paying on an app
their land the same capital rental
such funds themselves or in the oth
up higher levels of food manufactu
might be very valuable for a less
primitive agricultural sector. The
rentals on both the existing landh
lated would guarantee that only v

7. Fundamentally, the arrangement is tha
up to 50 per cent of stock ownership to an
a single, democratically run social body.

Obviously such an arrangement, properly adjusted in its details to
the exact parameters of a specific economy, would act as an incentive
and promoter of technical progress. A good deal more study and
reflection would be needed to design a truly optimal arrangement.

IV. Some Real Cases and Problems

Let us now project the theory of the autonomous labor-managed
firm and of the economy consisting of such firms into the context
of some significant real situations and real problems. Since the first
impetus for this analysis came from the objections raised primarily
by Yugoslav economists and policy makers, as noted in the introduction, perhaps we ought to look first at the Yugoslav economy.

Without going into any factual detail, let it only be noted that in
Yugoslavia today the firms must rely heavily on their own retained
earnings for funding of investment and that various arrangements,
legal and otherwise [1], are used to guarantee the sufficient volume of
such self-funded investments. These arrangements are used because
in their absence the firms would have a tendency to under-invest.[6]
But in the Yugoslav arrangements there is nothing comparable to
our r^*; that is, subjectively the firms accumulating capital do not
experience any cost of that capital on the current basis. And thus as
was shown in Section II, the development of the Yugoslav firm can
be approximated by a movement along aa in Figure 10.1 in the
direction of increasing capital stock, as indicated by the arrows.
Even if in the real world things do not work out exactly as in theoretical models, the movement along aa is far different from that along
eb of the autonomous labor-managed firm discussed here. In fact,
the former will tend continuously to produce serious problems of
unemployment or labor emigration so well known in Yugoslavia,
whereas the latter, among all its other efficient properties, will have
the capacity of absorbing unemployed labor or those who are just
entering the labor force. A little reflection will reveal that the solution represented by a movement along aa thus will not guarantee a
single one of the efficient results obtained for the autonmous labor-
managed firm, as summarized in Section III. Indeed it is remarkable—and it must be entirely credited to the deeper human values
and advantages of self-management—that while operating in this

6. This is explained rigorously in [4].

inefficient manner typified
Figure 10.1 the Yugoslav
those performing best in the
in 1952.

The second point deservi
based on the autonomous
extremely well to the intr(
employment) as a new basi
firms in the economy are o
to scale in which they are m(
growth and stagnation, it v
to accept, within reasonabl(
jobs under new right-to-em]
on *aa* in Figure 10.1, by c(
almost certainly mean hard
already in the enterprise.

Our third practical point
firm would greatly facilitat
capitalist or centralized so(
cause it does not require the
or additional numbers of hi
in developing countries. F(
change the operation of its
ment could do so, so to spe
all firms from now on will :
newly prescribed nationwi(
training of new technical an(
ment agency (providing the
could be created. The abs(
would certainly not cause a
firms, even if they reached
would still have the two sig
facility or creating new firm

Moreover, the principle (
could also be used in the ent!
of a capitalist free-trade ec
namic self-managed firms. |
creators of the firm or the f
would have to decide at th(

projects would be selected. Without the $r*$ requirement accumulated funds might be misused for unproductive purposes.

But there is another, perhaps more significant argument for autonomous labor-management among farming producer cooperatives where, at least in the traditional farm operation, diminishing returns must set in at some point. When this happens and the rate $r*$ has to be paid on accumulated land and capital, the cooperative no longer will be indifferent between the alternatives of self-expansion and creation of new productive facilities, i.e., expansion into new forms of activity, other than agricultural. The latter, not constrained by land limitations, now will be preferred. And thus the rules of the game of the autonomous self-managed firm or autonomous cooperative would, so to speak, necessarily breed higher levels of development. Again, in less developed countries where nationwide institutional assistance to industrialization often is hard to come by for lack of skill and talent, these properties of the autonomous labor-managed firm might be welcome.

References

1. Institute of Economic Science, *Samoupravna Politika Dohotka* (Belgrade, 1972).

2. J. Vanek, *The General Theory of Labor-Managed Market Economies* (Ithaca, N.Y.: Cornell University Press, 1970).

3. _____, "Some Fundamental Considerations on Financing and the Form of Ownership under Labor Management," Chapter 8, above.

4. _____, "The Basic Theory of Financing of Participatory Firms," Chapter 9, above.

5. B. Ward, "The Firm in Illyria: Market Syndicalism," *American Economic Review*, 48 (Sept. 1958), 566–589.

PART V

FORMAL MICROECONOMIC AND MACROECONOMIC THEORY

11 | Uncertainty and the Investment Decision under Labor-Management and Their Social Efficiency Implications*

Practical implementation of labor-managed systems raises the important problem of the investment decision. The literature on self-management is of rather recent vintage: not much has been written on the subject of investment, and certainly what exists is not an exhaustive treatment. Benjamin Ward in his *Socialist Economy* [3] touches on the problem when he compares capitalist and labor-managed firms. In my *General Theory* [2] I deal with the problem of the investment decision in two instances: in relation to the national investment function (chapter 8) and in the formal theory of investment (chapter 14). The purpose of this paper is to fill, within the limits of a single paper, the many gaps and empty spaces which remain in the treatment of the subject and to give it more concrete operational and institutional dimensions than has been done heretofore.

Section I spells out the concrete dimensions of the capital market, identifies the most important actors or agents of that market, and discusses the investment decision-making process in practical terms; it also lists the assumptions underlying and defining the subsequent analytical sections. Section II presents the simplest and most basic element of the analysis: the process by which projects are selected and decided on by individual labor-managed firms, whether new entrants or existing ones. To keep the analysis simple and to focus on the productivity of investments, Section II hypothesizes a world of perfect certainty where variable yields or returns are left out. This

* Cornell Department of Economics Working Paper no. 83, November 1974. I should like to express my sincere appreciation to the members of the Workshop of the Cornell Program on Participation and Labor-Managed Systems, in particular to Ricardo Duhne, Carlos Corti, Alvaro Covarrubias, and Hernan Etcheto, for invaluable help in preparing this paper.

assumption is retained in Section III, which considers the capital market as a whole and the forces leading to equilibrium in that market, and in Section IV, which examines the implications of such market solutions for the efficiency of capital resource allocation through the economy.

Section V relaxes the assumptions of certainty and a single rate of return and adapts the more modern theory of portfolio allocation to the world of self-management. Because this step brings us much closer to real problems of investment decision making under self-management, the analysis is conducted here in the context of what we may regard as the most likely natural institutional setting.

1. The Process of Project Design and Institutional Setting

As an introduction to the labor-managed economy in which the investment decisions are to be taken, let us consider, first, the individual self-managed firm or investment project, and then the economy as a whole and in particular the conditions of its capital market. This discussion will introduce certain variables which will enter the more formal analysis of the subsequent sections.

In the labor-managed economy investment projects can be considered and undertaken either by existing firms (or groups of individuals contemplating formation of a self-managed firm) or by the government at different levels. Because the firms involved "must" always be fully self-managed, in all cases it can be postulated that the condition for adopting the investment project is that the totality of members of a particular group of men, which will work in conjunction with a given project, freely and democratically agree with its undertaking. Three important magnitudes can be associated with such a decision: First, the income per worker y which can be interpreted as a vector of incomes in case of a differentiated labor force; second, the minimum acceptable income y^o at which the working collective would be willing to undertake the project; and third, the income earned (and in a sense produced) in the previous occupation y^*. The last two mentioned incomes may but need not be identical. If the quality (enjoyment or lack of enjoyment) of the two jobs differs, obviously y^o and y^* will not be identical. The algebraic difference between the two, $y^o - y^*$, will measure the loss of utility or enjoyment associated with the acceptance of the new job.

The investment project is contemplated over a time span T, which we take for simplicity, without any major loss of generality, to be identical for all projects. In the first part of our discussion we will be postulating a state of perfect certainty; that is, over the given time horizon, present and future costs and benefits associated with the project can be known with perfect certainty. Later we will relax this assumption and postulate that with each expected income, y, is associated a coefficient of risk S_y—normally taken to be measured by a variance—and that that coefficient can be estimated. With each project we further associate its initial capital outlay c and the total labor force involved L. L again could be thought of as a vector of different types of labor skill, but we will not consider such situations here explicitly.

Let us turn from the individual firms and/or projects to the economy as a whole, which includes a large number of projects, each of them discrete (noncontinuous) and perfectly well defined in all of its aspects and dimensions. If a group of men contemplates more than one mutually exclusive project, we may understand that the choice of the one final project associated with a given group has been done in a preliminary stage and need not concern us here.

The principal investors in the economy are households and the government. All projects are funded in their entirety through borrowed external funds. The borrowing is done, for the purposes of our early discussion postulating full certainty, through fixed interest debentures in a capital market with a unique competitive rate of interest r. (The firms or initiators of projects can also sell variable-return securities [bonds], but we will discuss this in greater detail in Section V, after uncertainty has been introduced.) The external funding is not only a convenient analytical assumption but, in the case of a self-managed economy, a *sine qua non* of efficient operation. Another desirable characteristic of our self-managed economy— justifiable by both *a priori* analysis and actual cases of self-management—is a national or sectoral institution such as a National Labor Management Agency. In a realistic context it plays several supporting roles, but for our present purposes we will emphasize only one: its role as a financial intermediary servicing the self-managed economy or a self-managed sector. It can be thought of as a mutual fund absorbing government and private savings and acting as a purchaser—exclusive or otherwise—of the firms' (or projects') securities. These lending operations, for purposes of the early part of this discussion dealing with certainty, are all conducted at a "pure" interest rate r. Under uncertainty we will postulate that the labor-management agency borrows and lends at the rate r but also borrows and lends at an uncertain variable return with an expected return in excess of the pure rate r.

II. The Formal Criterion on Investment Decisions under Certainty

In this section we will be dealing with only one group or working collective taking an investment decision. The subject can be dealt with in several different ways, but the following appears most convenient and uses standard concepts and criteria developed for conventional investment analysis.

Given the variables defined in the preceding section, we can define a function,

$$F = F(r, y^o) = \left[\sum_{i=1}^{T} NR_i(y^o, r)(1 + r)^{-i} - c \right] \bigg/ LT, \quad (11.1)$$

which is the net present discounted value per worker and per annum of the entire present and future benefits and costs using y^o as an accounting (hypothetical) wage. NR_i represents net return in year i, including interest payments and excluding depreciation as a cost. A family of the F loci, with the market rate of interest as an independent variable, is shown in Figure 11.1 for various levels of increasing y^o, i.e., $y^o, y_1^o, \ldots$, etc. For example, for the market rate of interest r_o and the minimum acceptable income y_3^o, F is measured by the distance $0a$ in Figure 11.1.

The precise meaning of F is that for any given y^o and r, the community selects from among all the conceivable projects the one maximizing F by finding both an optimal size of the project, i.e., c, and the optimal size of the working collective, i.e., L. In this sense the F loci can be thought of as envelopes of other more partial loci.[1]

---

1. However, to avoid complications, especially for purposes of later discussion in Section V, it may be preferable to think of each project as strictly discrete, associated with fixed C and L.

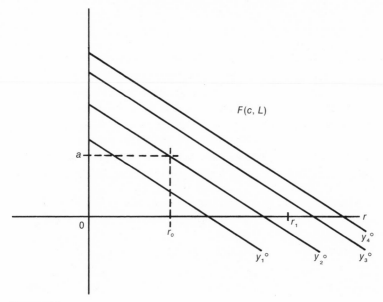

Figure 11.1

Given the assumption of a perfect capital market with a single competitive market rate r and no credit rationing, it is obvious that a project will be selected and undertaken provided that F is positive. Indeed, if F is positive, there will be some net positive residual value per worker by which the minimum acceptable income y^o can be augmented and thus the entire working collective can be made better off. More specifically we have the relation

$$F = y - y^o. \tag{11.2}$$

The project associated with a in Figure 11.1 thus would be undertaken, while that corresponding to the same $y_3{}^o$ but to r_1 would be rejected.

III. The Investment Decision and the Capital Market under Certainty

Let us now consider an entire labor-managed economy or a labor-managed sector and all the possible investment decisions for that situation. For each project we now have one function F_i, and its corresponding y_i^o. Figure 11.2 shows an illustrative set of the functions F. A significant point on the horizontal axis is the point r^*, reflecting an actual market rate of interest prevailing in a given economy or given situation. On the other hand, associated with each project is another significant point such as r_i, at which F_i just becomes zero. The rate r_i is the analogue of the internal rate of return from conventional analysis. The only change is one of interpretation, r_i being an internal rate of return on the assumption that a "shadow" wage of y_i^o was paid to the participants in the project. It is immediately apparent from Figure 11.1 that, provided the normal expectation of declining F holds, the investment criterion $F_i > 0$ is equivalent to the condition $r_i > r^*$.

Assuming now that in the entire economy or sector we have n conceivable projects, all the projects can be ranked according to declining "own rate" (we use the term to avoid the concept of "internal rate of return," which might be misleading in the context

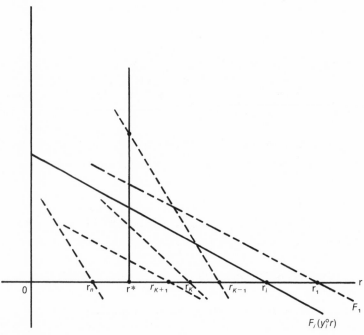

Figure 11.2

of self-management). As shown in Figure 11.2, the first $k + 1$ projects will be undertaken because the corresponding own rates are larger than r^*, and $F_i(r^*)$'s are positive, while all higher-subscript projects, including the nth project, will be rejected.[2]

The entire labor-managed economy or labor-managed sector will thus generate an aggregate demand for investment funds corresponding to the market rate of interest r^*, equal to the sum total of the initial capital costs c_i for the first $k + 1$ projects. The same construction could be performed for varying levels of r^* and corresponding demands for investment funds for all levels of market rate of interest would be obtained. Such an aggregate demand for investment funds is shown in Figure 11.3 by the uniformly declining locus marked $I(r)$. On the vertical axis we find alternative rates of market interest and on the horizontal axis the corresponding levels of aggregate investment I. When the labor-managed capital market is the entire capital market, there being no other segment of that market, under perfect market conditions, the equilibrium rate r^* will be determined at the point of market clearance. For example, as we have shown in Figure 11.3, with a total volume of available investment funds I^* we obtain a market equilibrium at point e and an equilibrium market rate of interest r^*. Also it should be noted that in this situation the I function becomes the aggregate investment function of the labor-managed economy.

Before concluding this section, a few words should be said on the subject of project interdependence. Implicit in our analysis of this section thus far is the postulate of independence of investment projects, a postulate which in the real world normally is not satisfied. If interdependence is present, then it must be recognized in constructing the various functions of F. And this may present a good deal of difficulty. One must also know existing projects which may be eliminated because of the construction of new ones, and this cannot be determined until the complete market situation is considered. I will not go any further into the problems because they are not central to our argument. However, it may be useful to note that the National Labor Management Agency introduced

---

2. If ever some F loci were locally positively sloped and permitted of multiple own rates, there would not be a unique ranking and the selection would have to be made by considering locally all the $F > 0$ in the vicinity of r^*.

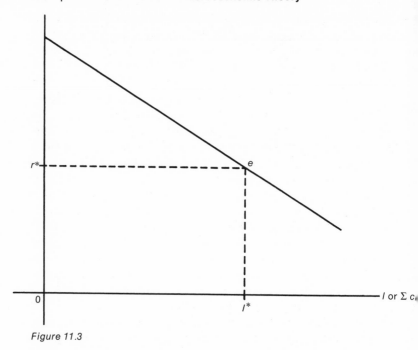

Figure 11.3

in Section I can play an extremely salutary role in helping labor-managed collectives to find out about such interdependencies of projects and to take them into consideration.

IV. The Investment Decision under Labor Management and Overall Efficiency of Resource Allocation

The key problem in this section is to decide whether an economy or an economic sector adhering to labor-management which behaves in the way described in the foregoing sections will maximize the increase in national product resulting from the investments thus undertaken. To provide the answers let us first postulate that $y_i^o = y_i^*$ for all i.

The first important thing to realize is that the increment in real national product resulting from one dollar of investment through the ith project per annum is the sum of the market rate of interest and the excess of net labor income in the new project over the income of the previous employment, per unit of capital. This excess of net income of labor enters the increment in real national products because, as is shown elsewhere for self-management equilibrium, the income per worker measures also the marginal productivity of labor. Stated in symbols we have:

$$\left(\frac{dY}{dI}\right)_i = r^* + (y_i - y_i^o)L_i c_i^{-1}, \tag{11.3}$$

and recalling relation 11.2 we have:

$$\left(\frac{dY}{dI}\right)_i = r^* + F_i L_i c_i^{-1}. \tag{11.4}$$

The investment decision, as described in the preceding section in the context of a complete capital market, leads to the selection of *all* projects which, while paying a return r^* on capital, also generate a net positive or zero F, that is, positive or zero increment in net product of labor caused by the transfer of L from the original occupation (or inactivity, with $Y_o = 0$) to the new one. Any selection of other than all of the first $k + 1$ projects would necessarily lead to a lower increment in real national product because it would imply either the selection of projects with a negative F or the omission of projects with a positive F.

Thus far we have assumed a perfect capital market. If this condition were not satisfied, and the social rate of time preference were different from the market rate r^* in Figure 11.2, or funds falling short of I^* had to be rationed at a rate r^*, then maximization of social project would call for a ranking of projects by $F_i(L_i/c_i)$ rather than by r_i. This is immediately apparent from the fact that the ranking of projects according to r_i is not the same as according to $F_i(L_i/c_i)$.

Before concluding this section let us consider the probably more general and more realistic situation where the quality and nature of work in the period preceding the investment project is not the same as that during the investment project. In other words, we are now considering the case where $y_i^* \neq y_i^o$.

As before, the investment decision now reduces to the consideration of whether $y_i - y_i^o$, i.e., F_i is positive or not. And the same formal procedure of project evaluation obtains as that explained in Section II. What concerns us here is whether with $y_i^* \neq y_i^o$ the conclusion of social optimality of the investment decision still obtains.

To find the answer, it is first useful to write the excess of the project income over the minimum acceptable income as shown below:

$$y_i - y_i^o = (y_i - y_i^*) + (y_i^* - y_i^o). \tag{11.5}$$

Since, as we have seen, under self-management labor is marginally remunerated, the first bracket on the right-hand side of relation 11.5 expresses the net gain in real (statistically measured) national product per man imputable to the new employment of labor. The second bracket, on the other hand, expresses the nonpecuniary or nonmaterial advantage (positive or negative) of the new project over the old situation. Clearly, both components are additions to national social welfare, and thus the conclusion of this section remains the same. Specifically, the investment decision discussed in this paper, assuming a perfectly competitive capital allocation, must lead to the selection of those projects which maximize the gains in social welfare. But of course it must be recalled that maximum gain in output will be the same thing as maximum gain in social welfare only in the rather unlikely situation of $y_i^* = y_i^o$. In the second alternative situation just discussed, our investment criteria will lead to maximization of social utility but not necessarily—and in fact hardly ever—to a maximization of gain in real national product. Without going into any detail, it may be pointed out that labor management as an economic system is in a far better position than a capitalist market economy in precisely this context of converging toward a true social optimum and not simply to maximization of physical output.

It should also be noted that, for our conclusions to hold, y_i^o must always reflect the initial productivity of the representative worker. For example, this may not be the case in developing countries if the participants in the project initially were unemployed or underemployed and received a subsidy not related to their work effort. Then, in order to maximize social welfare through our investment decision, it would be necessary to reckon y_i^o net of such subsidies. In the case of complete unemployment in particular, y_i^o would have to be taken as zero. Only a social institution such as the National Labor Management Agency could evaluate and implement investment projects in this manner. Relying entirely on the preferences and decision making of the working collectives who would take as their minimum acceptable income something higher than their initial social product, our investment decision would of course lead to inefficient underinvestment by unemployed and underemployed men. And, of course, this might further lead to socially undesirable postponement or slowing down of the elimination of unemployment.

Implicit in the analysis of this section is the entirely realistic notion that each working and investing collective operates within a certain framework of technical and organizational knowledge available to it, as well as its "historical" experience of previous employment conditions. All such knowledge will vary from collective to collective and engender different rent incomes, and hence different marginal value products. The solution obtained here will thus be an optimum constrained by the existing state and distribution of knowledge. Of course, with perfect knowledge by everyone of everything, an "optimum optimorum" would be obtained as all investing collectives would keep redesigning their blueprints (and presumably competing for patents and other scarce resources) until a perfect equality of all incomes were reached. An advantage of "social ownership" of all technological knowledge administered by our National Labor Management Agency is to approximate more closely such a solution.

V. The Investment Decision under Uncertainty

We now make a major step forward in our discussion. We abandon the assumption that everything in the future is perfectly well known and certain and replace it with the more realistic one that the future can be known only as an approximation and that expectations must be formed characterized by probability distributions of future outcomes.

Our first step is to introduce some additional notations, definitions and basic identities.

Additional Notations

$f \equiv$ increase in income per worker above y^o

$z \equiv$ total income per worker

$y \equiv$ labor income per worker

$x \equiv$ variable-debenture income per worker

For f, z, y, x capital letters are used to indicate average or expected values.

$V \equiv$ number of variable-income debentures
$B \equiv$ number of fixed-income debentures
$\left.\begin{array}{l} p_v \equiv \\ p_b \equiv \end{array}\right\}$ prices of debentures
$r \equiv$ return on capital in general
$r_v \equiv$ return on variable-income debenture per debenture A
$r_b \equiv$ return on fixed-income debenture per debenture B
$R \equiv$ pure riskless rate in economy
$\left.\begin{array}{l} S_z{}^2 \\ S_y{}^2 \\ S_x{}^2 \\ S_{rv}{}^2, S_{rm}{}^2, S_{rb}{}^2 \end{array}\right\}$ Expected variances
C correlation coefficient of yields

Basic Identities

$$z = x + y \tag{11.6}$$
$$z = y^o + f \tag{11.7}$$
$$S_z = S_f \tag{11.8}$$
$$c = p_v V + p_b B; \; p_v = p_b = 1 \tag{11.9}$$

Some of the variables listed are known to us already, but here they can appear either as capital letters or small letters depending on whether they express expected (average) values or values actually realized. The reader will be aided in understanding our analysis by referring to Figure 11.4, which presents a four-quadrant diagram containing all the pieces of the analysis.

As in the earlier sections of the paper the central analytical piece remains the function F given in Section II and reproduced here for convenience:

$$F = F(r, y^o). \tag{11.10}$$

F is now not an exact estimate but rather an average expected value and is shown in the second quadrant of Figure 11.4 for all possible values of r. Of particular importance is the expected value F corresponding to R which is the pure and risk-free return on capital. The important new element entering here for the first time is the expected variance S_f, which was obtained as part of the investment decision-making calculation and estimation, together with the function F, by considering expectations regarding future prices, future market conditions, future costs, and the like. It is taken to be a

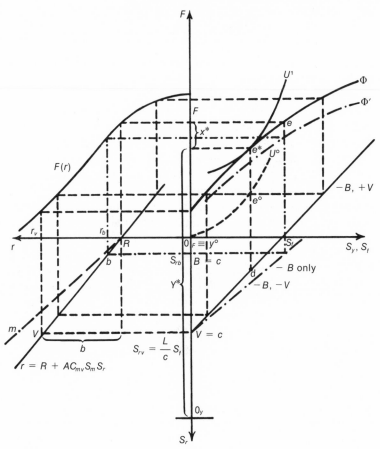

Figure 11.4

constant,

$$S_z = S_f = \text{constant}, \tag{11.11}$$

and also equals the variance of the expected total income per worker. S_f is shown on the horizontal axis in Figure 11.4, and the whole estimation procedure corresponding to our investment project corponding to the pure rate R is characterized by point e in the first quadrant.

As required by the definition of F, its origin, 0_F, coincides with the level y^o, the latter measured from its own origin 0_y. Because it can be expected that the previous employment of the working collective, determining the minimum acceptable income y^o, was not entirely risk-free, the origin in Figure 11.4 can be thought of as obtained through a procedure defining risk-free equivalent of the initial equilibrium point e^o using an indifference curve U^o shown in the first quadrant.

Point e in the first quadrant tells us what would be the expected gain in income per worker for the working collective over and above y^o provided that money could be borrowed at R, i.e., under perfectly risk-free conditions (we will assume such conditions for the moment and relax the assumption only later) and provided that the risk of variability of future incomes would be entirely borne by the working collective. More specifically, using our definitions, e in the first quadrant corresponds to the situation where the working collective uses only risk-free bonds B to finance the project. We realize that there may always be a default risk in any real situation, but we make this assumption temporarily for the sake of a clearer exposition.

The working collective, of course, might consider this situation too risky or too devoid of risk and might desire to transform it into a different risk position. This the community can do by operating in a market for variable-return securities V, offering a variable return r_v defined, with a and b two constants to be determined, as

$$r_v = R + [a(z - Z) + b]. \qquad (11.12)$$

We see that the yield of the variable-return securities is composed of a risk-free return R (we may think of it as the prime rate or a yield on government securities) and of the bracketed term, which can be thought of as the element of risk sharing. In turn the bracketed term is composed of two parts: the first lets the investor or buyer of V participate in the performance of the enterprise, and the second is a payment for the riskiness of the project. From relation 11.12 the variance of r_v, S_{rv} can easily be calculated from the variance of f (i.e., z) and the result is

$$S_{rv} = aS_f. \qquad (11.13)$$

The coefficient a in relation 11.12 will determine not only S_{rv} but also S_y, the residual variability of labor income, as is seen from relation 11.14, derived by taking expected values from relations 11.6 and

11.12 and observing that $x = r_v V/L$:

$$S_y = \left(1 - a\frac{V}{L}\right) S_f. \qquad (11.14)$$

Obviously, a can be set arbitrarily in defining the variable-income instrument V. A useful value of a which we will employ here is[3]

$$a = \frac{L}{c}. \qquad (11.15)$$

Its property is that when $V = c$, i.e., the entire funding takes the form of V, all variability of y disappears, i.e., $S_y = 0$. It is for that value of a that we have defined V and calculated S_{rv}. Recalling that S_y and S_f are measured along the horizontal axis in Figure 11.4 from 0_F to the right, the security V thus defined is characterized by point $S_{rv} = (L/c)S_f$ and $S_y = 0$ in the fourth quadrant.

Let us pause for a moment in the narrative of how the working community can divest itself of its risks and turn to the third quadrant and to what we may think of as a subsidiary subject. Using terminology and concepts from W. F. Sharpe's book on portfolio theory, we find [1], in the third quadrant what we can refer to as the investor's space. Any point in that space describes a security, or a portfolio composed of several securities, and is characterized in Figure 11.4 by an expected yield r and an expected coefficient of variability of that yield S_r. In particular we find a locus of points described by the line passing through R and m which is usually referred to as the *capital market line*. It contains, for a given capital market situation, all efficient portfolios. These portfolios are composed of two things: a number of riskless securities yielding a return R, and a number of variable-income debentures of a mutual fund, the market portfolio, characterized by point m. In the context of our labor-managed economy, a mutual fund can be thought of as issued by the National Labor Management Agency, based on securities of all the firms of the labor-managed sector, whereas the risk-free bonds are issued by the Central Bank or the Treasury.

Besides the coordinates of the third quadrant, r and S_r, each security or portfolio is also characterized by the correlation coefficient of its yield with that of the market portfolio, C_m. For given

3. Another solution would be to set a in relation 11.14 in such a way as to attain a prescribed *optimal* s_y^* with $V = c$, that is, by financing only through V.

C_m and S_m, and variable S_r, as shown by Sharpe, all securities will be located along the security market line

$$r = R + AC_mS_mS_r, \tag{11.16}$$

where A is a constant "price of risk reduction." A specific such line is represented by the locus Rv in the third quadrant, for $C_m = C_{mv}$, the correlation of the variable-return instrument of our self-managed firm, V, with the market portfolio.[4]

Let us now return to our main problem of risk modification by the labor-managed working collective. Speaking generally, quite obviously, our collective undertaking the project characterized by point e in Figure 11.4 must respect the conditions of the national capital market in trying to alter its risk and income position. Still retaining our assumption that our working collective and its investment project is perfectly risk-free if one invests into its fixed interest-bearing securities, we know already that the expected income Y and coefficient of variation of that income S_y will be those indicated by point e in the first quadrant. By contrast we know that if the entire project were to be financed through the variable-income securities V whose yield is defined by relations 11.12 and 11.15, the variability of yield to an investor would be exactly that given by point S_{rv} on the S_r axis of the third and fourth quadrants. Quite obviously the working collective will have no chance whatsoever to sell its security if it were to lead to a return less than what is given by the security market line, that is, less than the amount corresponding to point v. To sell the securities in a competitive market, one must reach point v. And this determines the necessary level of b that must be chosen in relation 11.12. The construction is shown in the third quadrant of Figure 11.4. We note that while the coefficient a can be chosen arbitrarily in determining the variable debt instrument of the firm (recall that we have chosen $a = L/c$), the parameter b will be obtained as a result depending on the nature of the capital market.[5]

---

4. C_{mv} can be thought of as evaluated by the project designers, or implicitly by the capital market itself.

5. Even without the Sharpe portfolio analysis it would be possible simply to postulate the vR locus in the third quadrant as given by the market forces. The reader who finds our excursion into Sharpe's analysis difficult or cumbersome may prefer such a "shortcut of reasoning."

Turn now to the fourth quadrant and recall that S_{rv} on the vertical axis measures from 0_F the variability of the firm's debt if $c = V$, i.e., if the entire financing takes the form of variable-income securities V, and no fixed-interest-bearing bonds B are sold. By contrast, if all financing assumes the form of B, we find ourselves in the fourth quadrant at point S_f, with $S_y = S_f$. More generally, to any debt composition V/B we can make correspond a point on the solid line $S_{rv}S_f$ in the fourth quadrant. And through the locus vR in the third quadrant we find the corresponding implicit expected yield at which the working collective actually is borrowing, given that debt composition. In particular, with $c = V$ we are at v, with $c = B$ we are at R, and with a $B = V$ split we are half-way between R and v. And thus for a given debt structure V/B we can immediately obtain through the two solid straight lines in the third and fourth quadrants, respectively, the expected yield r, the residual variation S_y, and the corresponding expected income per worker Y. Geometrically we have a construction based on the broken-line rectangles which determines an entire opportunity locus $\varnothing$. At a special point on $\varnothing$ we find e in the first quadrant which was the point of departure for our analysis.

Through the operations described here the working collective can alter its risk position by moving to any point along $\varnothing$. If we postulate a community preference map, with indifference curves such as U^o and U^1, the collective will choose point e^* in the first quadrant. As indicated by the two segments defined by point d in the fourth quadrant, the funding of the debt c will assume the form of proportions $S_{rv}d$ worth of fixed interest bonds and dS_f worth of variable-return debentures.

It will further be observed that both the security market line and the line $S_{rv}S_f$ have their extensions into the second and first quadrant, respectively, permitting the acquisition of positions along $\varnothing$ that are more risky than was the initial point e. As is indicated in the first quadrant by $-B$ and $+V$, such a change in position would involve borrowing, more than c in the fixed rate market, and simultaneously purchasing in the general capital market securities with a correlation coefficient $C_m = C_{mv}$.

What is usually referred to as self-financing, that is, purchase of its own variable-income securities by the working collective, can also be illustrated using our analysis. Suppose that the working collective, instead of borrowing through the fixed-interest instrument B, purchases variable-income debentures of its own using its own savings which were saved (embodied) previously in treasury bonds. Except for possible structural effects differentiating among members of the collective according to the degree of financing, this will be exactly the same as if initially the amount c were borrowed through the instrument B. The difference between the two situations is only one of accounting. In both cases the essential thing remains the same, namely, the outside net indebtedness of the collective increases by the amount c. Thus full self-financing is equivalent to funding entirely through B. The risks assumed by the collective remain quite considerable.

At this point we must relax the assumption that the working collective, like the treasury, can issue riskless bonds B. Normally it can be assumed, especially with new projects, that there will be a considerable risk of default on B to be borne by the investor. In terms of our diagram this means that the security B is not characterized by point R in the third quadrant, but rather by point b, with $S_{rb} > 0$ and $r_b > R$. Point b will be on the same security-market line since C_m for both V and B can be expected to be identical, both corresponding to the same project. As the reader can verify through the dashed-and-dotted construction, this will shift the $\emptyset$ locus downward to $\emptyset'$ and lead to a new optimum risk-income allocation, less desirable for the investing community. The key ingredient of the new situation is that the working community now can offer in the capital market only debt mixes represented by the range between $B = c$ and $V = c$ on the S_r axis. The line passing through $V = c$ in the fourth quadrant now pivots to a flatter position, determined by the minimum risk S_{rb} that the firm can offer through its securities B.

Our formal analysis evokes some broader issues and implications that we should note before concluding. First is the question of social optimum already dealt with under certainty in Section IV. It is immediately apparent from the first quadrant of Figure 11.4 that if the firm operating under uncertainty is constrained to borrow only through fixed-interest instruments, it could not as a general rule be socially optimal, and thus neither could the whole labor-managed economy or sector. This is seen by noting that the optimum along $\emptyset$, i.e., the point of tangency between $\emptyset$ and U, could only by the merest of accidents coincide with e. In fact, the probability of coinciding is one out of infinity. In all other cases social optimum will require movement from e, that is, trading in variable-return securities.

Our second observation also concerns social efficiency, but in a somewhat more remote sense. It is imperative that the function F in relation 11.5, with all its arguments and the calculated coefficient S_f, be made fully public not only to the members of the working collective but also to the general (investing) public, including the National Labor Management Agency. More than that, everyone must be allowed to question and probe all such data. This will guarantee optimality in many respects. It will, for example, make it impossible to "lure" the outside investors, because such dishonesty would have to be perpetrated by very few against the other members of the working collective who must base their judgment on the same parameters. Deception of the totality of investors by the totality of workers is quite hard to imagine, given the ease with which information is transmitted. This is quite different from capitalist conditions where costs, accounts, and estimates often are kept in utmost secrecy by a handful of top managers.

Our final point concerns the National Labor Management Agency. Thus far we have assumed that the agency invests along with individual households. But there may be a "social" judgment of the government that investment in risky projects, like gambling, is undesirable for individuals for a variety of reasons. In such a case the National Labor Management Agency, or independent branches of it, can remain the exclusive investors in risky debentures, and the private citizen may be asked to save only in the form of savings deposits. In that case the National Labor Management Agency actually assumes the additional function of an insurance agency.

References

1. William F. Sharpe, *Portfolio Theory and Capital Markets* (New York: McGraw-Hill, 1970).

2. J. Vanek, *The General Theory of Labor-Managed Market Economies* (Ithaca, N.Y.: Cornell University Press, 1970).

3. B. Ward, *The Socialist Economy* (New York: Random House, 1967).

12 | Sales Promotion in Labor-Managed versus Capitalist Economies*

With ALFRED STEINHERR

In a recent discussion of a study by one of the present authors [2], James Meade addressed himself to the question whether advertisement expenditures can be expected to be lower in a labor-managed than in a capitalist economy [1]. This question is of considerable interest for the comparative performance of both systems since it is widely accepted that beyond a certain level of informational communication, advertisement is a waste of social resources. Thus if it could be shown that a labor-managed economy is less prone to waste resources on advertisement this argument, among many others, of course, ought to be put on the balance of relative merits of a labor-managed economy.

In the earlier study [2] it was shown that a capitalist firm will both operate on a larger scale and spend more resources on advertisement in absolute terms. Professor Meade has rightly pointed out that the more interesting question is whether or not the capitalist firm tends to spend more in relative terms (e.g., per unit of output). However, Professor Meade thought it not possible to establish such a contention rigorously. The purpose of the present paper is to suggest such a proof.

We may rewrite the original model [2, pp. 120–123], assuming that an oligopolistic firm produces only one good, X, with one factor of production, labor L:

$$X = X(L), \text{ with } X_L > 0, X_{LL} < 0. \tag{12.1}$$

* Cornell Department of Economics Discussion Paper no. 81, September 1974. We would like to express appreciation to Connell Fanning of the Department of Economics for his constructive suggestions.

Since the output X is a differentiated product, the demand for X can be shifted through sales promotion C. Letting P represent price,

$$P = P(X, C), \tag{12.2}$$

with the following restrictions on the partial derivatives:

$$P_X < 0; \quad P_C > 0; \tag{12.2a}$$

$$P_{XX} = 0 \quad \text{(for convenience we assume a linear} \quad \text{(12.2b)} \\ \text{demand curve);}$$

$$P_{CX} = 0 \quad \text{(if anything } P_{CX} \text{ should be negative} \quad \text{(12.2c)} \\ \text{small);}$$

$$P_{CC} < 0 \quad \text{(implying a positive, but diminishing} \quad \text{(12.2d)} \\ \text{effect of sales promotion } at \ equilib\text{-} \\ rium \ levels \ of \ operation; \ \text{see also} \\ \text{footnote 1).}$$

The capitalist firm is supposed to maximize profits (π), defined as

$$\pi = P(X, C) \cdot X(L) - W_o L - C, \tag{12.3}$$

where it is assumed that the market wage rate (W_o) is fixed. The first-order conditions for an extreme value of π are (assuming that the second-order conditions are satisfied):

$$\pi_L = X_L(P_X X + P) - W_o = 0 \tag{12.4}$$
$$= F(X, C) = 0.$$

Equation 12.4 can also be expressed as:

$$\pi_L = X_L \cdot MR - W_o = 0, \tag{12.4a}$$

i.e., in equilibrium the marginal revenue product is equal to the market wage rate.

$$\pi_C = P_C X - 1 = 0 \tag{12.5}$$
$$= f(X, C) = 0.$$

The labor-managed firm, on the other hand, is thought to maximize income per laborer (y):

$$y = \frac{Y}{L} = \frac{1}{L}[P(X, C)X - C]. \tag{12.6}$$

The first-order conditions are:

$$y_L = \frac{1}{L^2}\left[X_LL \cdot (P_XX + P) - PX + C\right] = 0 \qquad (12.7)$$

$$= F^*(X, C) = 0.$$

Since $y = (PX - C)/L$ equation 12.7 can be rewritten:

$$y = X_L \cdot MR, \qquad (12.7a)$$

i.e., in equilibrium income per worker equals the marginal revenue product.

$$y_C = \frac{1}{L}(P_CX - 1) = 0 \qquad (12.8)$$

$$= f^*(X, C) = 0.^1$$

From equations 12.5 and 12.8 we see immediately that $f = f^*$. Differentiating 12.4, 12.5, and 12.7 totally and solving for the slopes in (C, L) − space we obtain:

$$\left.\frac{dC}{dL}\right|_{F=0} = -\frac{(X_{LL}MR + X_L{}^2MR_L)}{X_L \cdot MR_C} \qquad (12.9)$$

$$= -\frac{(X_{LL}(XP_X + P) + P_XX_L{}^2)}{P_CX_L} > 0$$

$$\left.\frac{dC}{dL}\right|_{F^*=0} = -\frac{(MR + X_LMR_L)}{MR_C} \qquad (12.10)$$

$$= -\frac{X_L(P_XX_LL + P_XX + P)}{1 + P_CX_LL - P_CX} \gtrless 0;$$

$$\left.\frac{dC}{dL}\right|_{f=f^*=0} = -\frac{X_LP_C}{P_{CC}X} > 0. \qquad (12.11)$$

Using these results and assuming linearity of all the loci, we can now have a look at the implied patterns. Figure 12.1 shows the three key loci F^*, F, and $f \equiv f^*$. Only the first of the three can be negatively or positively sloped; the other two must be positively sloped. F^* must be steeper than F as drawn in the diagram. This is so for

---

1. The second-order condition for equation 12.8 requires $Y_{CC} < 0$, i.e., $1/L(P_{CC}X + P_CX_C) < 0$, which in turn requires $P_{CC} < 0$.

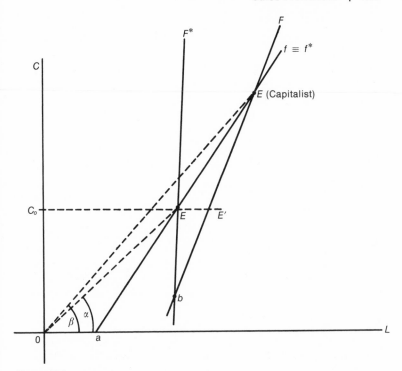

Figure 12.1

the following reasons. For a low enough promotional expenditure C the income per worker in the self-managed firm will be as low as the market wage faced by the capitalist. When that happens, as is well known, the two firms will be identical. This happens in our diagram at point b. For promotional expenditures higher than those corresponding to b, income per worker in the self-managed enterprise will exceed the market wage, the capitalist will make positive profits, and under such conditions, as is also well known, the capitalist firm must be larger than the self-managed firm. Thus, for example, for C_o, the labor-managed firm will be at its optimum at E, whereas the capitalist firm will find itself, still well under its own equilibrium position, at point E', and consequently we have the v-shaped configuration of F^* and F.

The locus $f \equiv f^*$ must in turn be flatter than both loci F. This must be so because otherwise the equilibria E and E_{cap} would be unstable ones and in fact the two firms would be at a minimum rather than at a maximum. This completes the proof of the proposition that the capitalist firm engaging in optimal advertising must be larger than and spend more on promotion than its labor-managed twin. What remains to be shown is what was contested by Professor Meade, namely, that also per unit of output the labor-managed firm will have less promotion than the capitalist firm. We will first show the even stronger result that C/L will be greater for the capitalist firm.

In terms of our diagram this implies that the slope α corresponding to $0E$ must be smaller than the slope β defined as $0E_{cap}$. Such a pattern is shown in Figure 12.1 and crucially depends, given our assumptions of linearity, on the fact that $f \equiv f^*$ has an intercept with the L axis, at a point such as a, and not with the C axis. That this must be so can be argued and can be demonstrated in the following manner. Obviously with zero employment and output there will be absolutely no scope for promotional spending. And, thus, we prove the weaker proposition to the effect that $f \equiv f^*$ cannot have an intercept with the C axis.

The stronger proposition necessary for our proof, to the effect that the intercept cannot be at the origin 0 either, can also easily be demonstrated. Recall that $f \equiv f^*$ is the locus of *optimal* levels of promotional spending corresponding to prescribed alternative levels of employment and output. To produce and sell one bottle of Coca-Cola per day or $1,000 worth of Coca-Cola per month, one certainly neither needs nor can afford an advertising campaign. Only for a rather large output will incremental advertising bring in more in terms of additional revenue than its cost.[2] And consequently points such as a in Figure 12.1 must be to the right of 0. And this completes our proof for C/L. For C/X, questioned by Professor Meade, the result is even stronger, if we recall equation 12.1. In fact, this condition guarantees a lower C/X for the labor-managed firm even if C/L is constant.

Of course, we have used here the postulate of linearity of the different loci in Figure 12.1, and it is possible to visualize in the real world nonlinear situations which would contradict our conclusion. And thus we may say that we establish here only a strong presump-

---

2. In other words, before one can benefit from promotion and advertising one must produce a sufficient level of output over which to spread the advertising cost.

tion, in any realistic context, of a greater advertising effort per worker or unit of sales under capitalist than under labor-managed conditions.

A concluding observation is in order. It is true that a lower degree of advertising and promotion per worker or per unit of output under self-management as compared to a capitalist firm is a more significant result. But the weaker result, a lesser *absolute* level of promotional activity (note that E in Figure 12.1 must be below E_{cap}), is also significant, especially today when on ecological and population grounds lesser consumption is to be preferred, *ceteris paribus*, to more consumption. Indeed, advertising and promotional activity not only lures away spending dollars from other producers without affecting global output and consumption of a given product, but it also generates demand which otherwise would not have existed at all. Since the most heavily advertised products are precisely products which are not indispensable, the effects involved can be quite significant. And thus, on grounds of both the stronger and the weaker promotional argument, the labor-managed solution can be deemed superior.

References

1. J. Meade, "The Theory of Labor-Managed Firms and of Profit Sharing," *Economic Journal*, supplement to vol. 82 (March 1972), 402–428.

2. J. Vanek, *The General Theory of Labor-Managed Market Economies* (Ithaca, N.Y.: Cornell University Press, 1970).

13 The Macroeconomic Theory and Policy of an Open Worker-Managed Economy*

I. Introduction

In terms of its contribution to the solution of important real problems, the macroeconomic theory is among the most significant branches of economic analysis. It is so important because, in a market economy, it allows policy makers to trace and identify the impact of various policies and/or spontaneous behavioral changes on the macroeconomic variables, such as the level of national product, prices, the balance of payments, the rate of interest, investment, and others.

As the historical evolution of the discipline in the context of capitalist market economies indicates, the subject of macroeconomics is by no means a simple one. Throughout the nineteenth century and through the Great Depression and the so-called "Keynesian revolution" it has been dealt with by Western economists (perhaps in the scientific tradition of the nineteenth century) in a partial equilibrium manner, that is, as a series of exercises establishing causal links within pairs or other subsets of variables, but never in the context of the aggregative structure of the economy. Only after World War II, in the post-Keynesian and Patinkin tradition, were complete general equilibrium *macroeconomic* models explored. To this day some theoretical questions in this field remain unanswered and, especially in the area of monetary economics, constitute the principal preoccupation of Western experts. A good deal of econometric work in capitalist countries is designed to substantiate these simultaneous theories through empirical observation.

Our macroeconomic understanding of the labor-managed market economy of the Yugoslav type is quite inadequate, at least as far as

* Cornell Department of Economics Working Paper no. 28, April 1972; this paper was published in *Ekonomska Analiza*, no. 3/4 (Summer 1972).

the present writer is able to judge. First of all, this economic system is fundamentally different from the Western market economies, and thus any direct transposition and application of Western macro-economic analysis to the case of Yugoslavia would be quite incorrect. Second, and more practically, the experience of a self-management economy in Yugoslavia has been only two decades, a period con-siderably shorter than that offered to the observers of capitalist systems.

To my best knowledge (conditioned and limited by my difficulty in reading the Yugoslav languages) two attempts have been made at a *simultaneous* theoretical analysis of the labor-managed economy, one by Benjamin Ward [4] and the other by myself [2]. Ward's analysis suffers from three major defects which make it quite in-operative. First, and probably least of all, he uses too simple a theory of the money market, that is, the quantity theory of money. Second, he takes too seriously his earlier result of a backward-bending supply curve of real national product in the short run. Third, and by far most important, the equilibrium on which he bases his analysis of change (and by implication of policy) is an unstable one, so that his results are just the opposite of what they truly should be.[1]

For the purposes of the present analysis my own earlier work also is not fully adequate, and this in fact is the main inspiration for writing this article. First, in my book I was interested in producing a careful and detailed exposition of the macroeconomic structure without paying much attention to its practical applicability. Second, I have produced an analysis as general as possible with respect to the signs and values of key parameters, without considering possible simplifications arising from a closer knowledge of behavior of self-managed bodies. Third, being primarily interested in the logical structure of the theory, I have not included the foreign-trade sector of the economy, an omission which would be most unwarranted if one wants to deal with a country like Yugoslavia.

Given these considerations, the plan of work in this paper will be as follows. First in the next section I will reproduce briefly the formal simultaneous model as developed in my *General Theory of Labor-Managed Market Economies*. The only new thing here will be

---

1. For the interested reader, all this is carefully explained in Section 17.5 of my *General Theory* [2].

the introduction of the foreign-trade sector, that is, of the foreign-exchange market. In Section III, I will derive from the complete formal model a somewhat simpler one which, almost without loss of generality, lends itself to simple diagrammatic use. In Section IV, I put to work the simplified model of Section III and derive a set of comparative-static results bearing on problems of short-run economic policy and of autonomous disturbances. Finally, in Section V I draw the conclusions of the study. The Appendix is devoted to a mathematical presentation of the reduced (simplified) model,[2] and the study of its comparative-static and dynamic properties.

II. The Complete Formal Theory

The fundamental notion on which our formal theory of determination of macroeconomic variables is based is that all these variables are mutually dependent, influencing each other and simultaneously finding an equilibrium value—if an equilibrium exists. More specifically, this interdependence is the result of the fact that the various macroeconomic variables are determined through the operation of various markets, the supply and demand sides of these markets themselves being influenced by all the variables. Thus, for example, the price level will be determined in the market for (real) goods and services through the interaction of supply and demand of such goods and services, each in turn depending not only on price but also on the level of national product, the exchange rate, the rate of interest, and the like.

There are altogether five markets in our simultaneous macroeconomic theory: markets for goods (and services), money, bonds (i.e., financial capital), foreign exchange, and a quasi-market for labor. We use here the term quasi-labor market because in a self-management economy (i.e., of associations of free producers) we cannot have a market for labor in the traditional sense of the word.

As I explain in greater detail in my earlier study [2, Part II], the equilibrium condition in the goods market can be stated in functional form as

$$\bar{Y} = Y(\bar{Y}, p, r, i), \tag{13.1}$$

where we use a bar on top to express supply and a variable without a bar to express demand, and where Y, p, r, and i stand respectively for

2. Note that the mathematics of the general model is given in my earlier study.

real output, the general price level, the rate of exchange, and the rate of interest. The right-hand side of the equation is a behavioral function, indicating that the demand for domestic goods depends on real national income (because the higher such income, the more goods will be demanded); on the price level (because if prices vary, international competition will change, *ceteris paribus*); on the rate of exchange (because that rate will determine the balance of payments, which in turn contributes to the demand for domestic goods); and on the rate of interest (because it influences the investment and consumption demand of domestic firms and households).

The equilibrium in the market for money, M, can similarly be written as

$$\bar{M}_o = M(\bar{Y}, p, i), \tag{13.2}$$

where the subscript o is used to indicate that the supply of money is a parameter, determined through the country's monetary policy.[3] The behavioral demand for money simply states the obvious fact that demand will vary with the general price level and level of real income: the argument is perhaps less obvious but it becomes clear if we realize that depending on the level of the interest rate, people will be willing to hold more or less money balances (rather than bonds or other assets).

To describe the market for financial capital, we assume that all domestic debt is held in the form of bonds of indefinite maturity, B, and the equilibrium in the market is determined by the equality of supply and demand, i.e.,

$$\bar{B}(i, p, \bar{Y}, r) = B(i, p, \bar{Y}, r). \tag{13.3}$$

Note that here the supply side is also a behavioral function. The reader will easily find for himself the rationale of the various arguments of the two functions.

The market for foreign exchange we consider for simplicity as depending on visible and invisible trade only (and not on an autonomous capital account). For the moment, we take the rate of exchange as a variable price determined in that market. Using m_{12}

---

3. It could also be postulated that $\bar{M}_o$ is a variable determined by the state of the balance of payments through inflows or outflows of international reserves. But because in the real world we seldom find this to be the case, we can disregard this possibility.

and m_{21} to stand for physical exports and imports respectively, we obtain an equilibrim condition, stated in terms of domestic currency and assuming foreign prices to be constant at unity:

$$pm_{12}(p, r) = rm_{21}(p, r, \bar{Y}, i), \qquad (13.4)$$

where the left-hand side represents the supply of foreign exchange and the right-hand side the demand for that exchange. It is again easy to comprehend the arguments of the export and import functions.

Finally, we have the quasi-labor market condition postulating that in the short run, with capital stock, K_o, and the number of firms essentially given, an equilibrium employment L will be reached when the marginal productivity of labor $\partial \bar{Y}(L)/\partial L$ is equal to the income earned by each worker, i.e.,

$$\partial \bar{Y}/\partial L = (p\bar{Y} - p_k K_o)/L, \qquad (13.5)$$

where p_k is a constant price of use of capital. Note that relation 13.5 is one in variables $\bar{Y}$, L, and p.

Last of all, we introduce the short-run production function linking labor input to output, for a given capital stock K_o, i.e.,

$$x = x(K_o, L). \qquad (13.6)$$

We thus have six equations in our five variables, $\bar{Y}$, L, r, p, and i. All that we can say thus far is that these equations may be consistent with a simultaneous equilibrium set of values of our five variables. Much more has been said about this type of general equilibrium system in my earlier book, and we will examine in greater detail a realistic reduced form of the system in the rest of this paper.

III. The Operational Model

With six equations and five unknowns, obviously, our model appears overdetermined, and moreover is too complex to be operational. Fortunately, it is possible to clarify and simplify it and reduce it to manageable dimensions by performing a set of steps, based in part on the mathematical properties of the model, in part on the observation of some real values of parameters.

The first step is based on the application of what is referred to as Walras's law. This law, not difficult to comprehend, tells us that in a complete system of general equilibrium including all relevant equations, if for some set of values of the variables (five in our case) all equations but one are in equilibrium (i.e., are fulfilled), then the remaining one must *ipso facto* be also in equilibrium. Consequently, any one of our equations (restrictions) can be taken as redundant, and thus we obtain a system in five independent equations and five variables, consistent with a general equilibrium solution. For our purposes, following the majority of writers, we will drop the bond or financial capital market equation (13.3).

In the next simplifying step we make the realistic observation that foreign exchange rates in general, including that of Yugoslavia, are fixed. Consequently, we can consider r as a constant, r_o (hereafter for simplicity referred to as r), and transform relation 13.4 into an identity defining the balance of payments on current account:

$$B_{din} = p_1 m_{12} - r p_2 m_{21}. \tag{13.7}$$

We are thus left with only four independent equations in only four unknowns. The next step is a very simple one. We merely introduce the production function (13.6), into the remaining equations (13.1, 13.2, and 13.5), and thus are left with three independent equations in three unknowns, L, p, and i. The additional advantage of this operation is that by eliminating our one defining equation (defining the production process) we are left with three equations which are all market-equilibrium equations.

The final reduction, which will lead us to a system of only two endogenous variables, is somewhat more complex, and deserves more attention. To state the essence of the step even before explaining it, we claim that in a pure *short-run* macroeconomic representation of the labor-managed economy, the levels of employment and output can largely be taken as constants L_o and X_o, fundamentally determined by long-range processes of growth and not subjects to short-run forces. But we should now go to work and explain this contention.

First let us re-emphasize the notion of a *pure* representation. By this I mean the absence from the model of institutional or custom-based rigidities, especially those of prices and wages. If such rigidities exist, my statement above and our last simplifying reduction become invalid. But of course, the model can then be adjusted to account for them.

In the pure representation, with perfect competition and no rigidly prescribed wages, prices should vary freely up and down with changing aggregate demand. The reaction of self-managed firms and industries, contrary to Professor Ward's contention [3], should by and large be nil in the short run. The first and most obvious reason for this is that over short periods, with increasing prices, it would be absurd for the working collective to fire some of its members in order to increase the remaining workers' incomes, very likely by an insignificant amount, over the increase already gained from higher prices. But even without such an expression of solidarity, the supply of goods will be highly inelastic or zero-elastic for reasons of technology. In Figure 13.1, the value-of-national-product function (given in our relation (13.6) as considered by Ward is illustrated by the broken contour. But a much more realistic short-run relationship, with installed plant and equipment, will be either contour a or contour b, reflecting situations of divisible and indivisible processes respectively.

With an equilibrium solution—i.e., maximum income per worker—at point e, in the cases a and b a change in prices will only

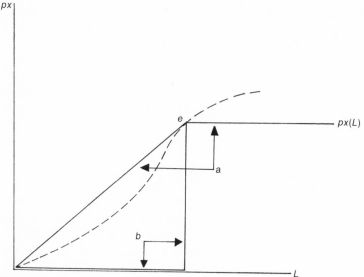

Figure 13.1

produce an upward shift of either of the two solid contours, the equilibrium clearly remaining at the corner-point e, with unchanged employment and output.

It may be of significance to note that the fact that the "social" or "solidary" behavior of the collective does not reduce its size in the face of changing prices is not at all contradictory to the assumption of maximizing income per worker. But, unlike Professor Ward, we must remember that the income of all is to be maximized, not only that of those remaining in the enterprise after a "Wardian" price adjustment.

I believe, then, that we have ample justification for our claim of a zero or virtually zero-elastic supply function of national product. We can thus put $\bar{Y} = \bar{Y}_o$ and $L = L_o$, and disregard equation 13.5.

We should note at this stage of our argument, and we will elaborate on this point later in Section V, that the short-run equilibrium levels of income and employment *need* not be at full employment of resources. Only a long-run process of adjustment, involving proper capital pricing and freedom of entry (i.e., forming of new enterprises) and a well-functioning capital market can produce such conditions.

We are now left with two endogenous variables i and p, the equilibrium conditions in the goods and money market (equations 13.1 and 13.2), the balance of payments (13.7), and three constants (in the short run) Y_o, L_o, and r. It may be useful to restate the two market-equilibrium relations in a new form:

$$\bar{Y}_o \overset{e}{=} Y[i, p; \bar{Y}_o r] \equiv m_{11}[i, p; \bar{Y}_o, r] + m_{12}[p, r] \quad (13.1a)$$

and

$$\bar{M}_o \overset{e}{=} M[i, p; \bar{Y}_o]. \quad (13.2a)$$

where e is used to indicate an equilibrium condition, and m_{11} and m_{12} reflect domestic and foreign demand, respectively, for domestic products. Of course, both m's are composed of consumption and investment demand.

Both new relations are functions of two variables, i and p, and can be decribed graphically as contours (or collections of points) in the i–p plane, fulfilling the respective equilibrium combinations. This is shown in the first quadrant (with respect to point O) in Figure 13.2. The locus corresponding to equilibrium in the real goods market is negatively sloped because, in order to keep demand for goods in equilibrium, i.e., equal to a constant supply, with declining interest

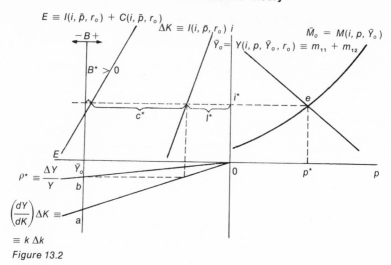

Figure 13.2

rates (which *per se* increase demand) it is necessary to increase prices (which reduces demand through both the terms of trade effect and the so-called real balance effect). On the other hand, the money-equilibrium equation will be upward-sloping, because to keep demand for money constant with increasing interest rates, one must absorb the thus created transaction balances through higher prices.

Of course, the general equilibrium solution is found when both markets are in equilbrium, that is, at point e in Figure 13.2, corresponding to equilibrium values of the two variables, i^* and p^*.

The diagram permits us to identify other key magnitudes of macroeconomic analysis. First of all, measured to the left of point 0 we have point Y_o reflecting the constant real national product of the economy in the short run. In the second quadrant thus defined, measured to the left of the i axis, we now have two well-known expenditure functions, the real investment function I and the real investment plus consumption function $I + C$, corresponding to i, and the price levels $\tilde{p}$ (more exactly we might write this as $p[i]$ as defined by the $\bar{Y} = Y$ function of the first quadrant). Both contours are downward-sloping, basically indicating an increased real demand for both investment and consumption with declining interest rates. It must be recalled that both expenditure functions contain demand for both domestic and foreign goods. As shown in the diagram, corresponding to e, we can also read the equilibrium levels of consumption and investment, C^* and I^*.

Recalling that total national expenditure E equals $C + I$, and that the balance of payments on current account B is the difference between national expenditure and national product, we can immediately read the balance of payments as a horizontal distance between the $E = I + C$ contour and a vertical line (axis) originating at $\overline{Y}_o$ in Figure 13.2. In this way we also find the equilibrium solution B^*, a positive (surplus) balance of payments because for i^* and p^* national expenditure falls short of national product.

Finally, another useful piece of information—a first step in the direction of a dynamic analysis—is contained in the third quadrant with respect to 0. The slope of the line $0a$ measured from the axis $0\overline{Y}_o$ expresses the incremental capital-output ratio of the economy. Because I^* is the current increase in capital stock, the vertical coordinate of point b, constructed in the way shown in the diagram, indicates the corresponding increase in income in the next period, assuming that the new installed capacity is utilized in production. But because the distance $0\overline{Y}_o$ is the current real national product, the slope of the line $0b$ shows the rate of growth of the economy.

Of course, next year the point $\overline{Y}_o$ would have to shift to the left by the amount given by point b, and all the functions would have to be adjusted throughout the model; but this would go beyond the scope of this paper. Rather, we shall now turn to the problem of how alterations in the short-run macroeconomic structure affect the key macroeconomic solutions.

IV. On Short-Run Economic Policy

We are now reaching a crucial point in our exposition. We can use the equilibrium structure developed in the foregoing sections to determine some important policy and other conclusions. We will do so here verbally, referring to our diagram, and in the Appendix mathematically.

In Figure 13.3 we have reproduced the diagram of Figure 13.2, but now considering various policy-induced or autonomous changes. The first and most simple is the effect of a policy of monetary expansion, or, what is equivalent, an autonomous reduction in demand for money. Such a change induces the equilibrium money-market locus ($\overline{M} = M$) to shift to the right and down, and, as is

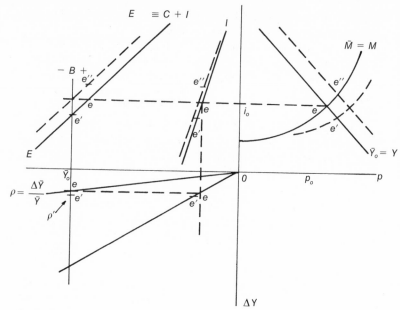

Figure 13.3

shown in the first quadrant, this will displace the equilibrium point from e to e'. The result is that the rate of interest will decline and prices will increase. Accordingly, in the second quadrant, moving along the E-contour (which has not shifted because there was no disturbance in the expenditure structure), we reach point e' at a worsened balance on current account, and a higher expenditure, primarily investment expenditure. The new investment level is also shown by e'. There is an unambiguous expansion in investment, and, as shown by e' and the construction in the third quadrant, this will unambiguously increase the rate of expansion, ρ, of the economy. Of course, in a realistic context, such an acceleration will occur with some time lag, through a faster shifting outward of the more or less vertical *short-run* supply function of a constant national product.

The second policy—also second in analytical complexity—is a government-induced expansion in expenditure through budgetary expansion. It is equivalent to an autonomous increase in spending by households or investors. In the first quadrant this will shift the

$\overline{Y} = Y$ line to right and produce a new equilibrium at e'' with both higher prices and higher interest rates. In the second quadrant both the E and I lines will move to the left, and a new equilibrium will be established at e''. The balance of payments now can improve or worsen depending on the comparative importance of the shift on the one hand and of the movement along the E locus to a point of a higher interest rate on the other. The more likely expectation perhaps is a balance-of-payments deterioration; this becomes a certainty if, together with budgetary expansion, the authorities keep (peg) the rate of interest at its initial line i_o through monetary and credit expansion.[4]

The effect on investment and the national rate of growth is again ambiguous because of two offsetting effects of shift and slope. As shown by e'' on I, the volume of investment need not increase. However, if the expanded government spending is directed exclusively to investment, or if together with budgetary expansion the monetary authorities peg the rate of interest, investment and the rate of growth of the economy are bound to increase.

We turn now to a policy of devaluation and import tariff increase, which, when it comes to the balance-of-payments effects, may need some more extensive elaboration. But let us first turn to the effects of these (external) policies on the rate of interest and the domestic price level. Because both devaluation and higher import duty will put additional pressure on demand for goods Y (because through these policies domestic goods become cheaper to buy than foreign goods), we have in the first quadrant a shift of the $\overline{Y} = Y$ locus to point e'', similar to that produced by budgetary expansion. And consequently, prices as well as interest rates will go up, again with unchanged real product (and national income) in the short run. But what will happen to real expenditure and the balance of payments? One would normally expect that the balance of payments would improve from devaluation or a higher tariff barrier. But this need not be the case by any means, and this may bring into question a policy of devaluation by a country like Yugoslavia, especially if the dinar appears undervalued on just about any purchasing-power calculation.

---

4. Note that we speak here of the balance of payments in real terms, and that an additional correction of the estimates would have to be performed to obtain results in terms of domestic or foreign currency.

The key argument here is that both devaluation and tariff policy will worsen the terms of trade for the domestic consumer or investor, and this will make him poorer in real terms. But poorer people usually increase the proportion of their income (whether more or less than 100 per cent) spent. In other words, *ceteris paribus*, either of our two policies is bound to move the E-line in the second quadrant to the left. And thus the real balance will deteriorate on that account. It is only the movement along the E-line upward with higher interest rates that can offset this deterioration. The conclusion is that the total effect is ambiguous and probably small. The effects on investment and the rate of growth are also ambiguous because of two offsetting impacts on I. However, if a tariff policy is so designed as to prevent imports of nonessentials and favor investment goods, both the rate of growth and investment are bound to increase.

V. Overall Conclusions of the Theoretical Analysis and Some Further Considerations Bearing on Economic Policy in Yugoslavia

We can first summarize our conclusions in the form of a table. Table 13.1 shows the direction of effects of alternative policies as they emerged from our analysis of the labor-managed economy. In the rows we read the results for endogenous variables affected while the columns correspond to alternative policy instruments.

Table 13.1.

Change in	Policy instrument		
	Monetary and credit expansion	Budgetary expansion	Devaluation or tariff increase
Price	> 0	> 0	> 0
Interest rate	< 0	> 0	> 0
Real balance of payments on current account	< 0	$\lessgtr 0^a$	small $\gtrless 0$
Rate of growth and investment	> 0	$\gtrless 0$	$\gtrless 0$
Real product and national income in short run	$\cong 0$	$\cong 0$	$\cong 0$

^{a} A double inequality indicates a considerably more likely outcome.

The first thing that must be emphasized for a market economy based on self-management of the Yugoslav type is that the standard tools of short-run economic policy cannot be used in the same way and for the same purposes as they are in Western market economies. Perhaps the most important is that real income and employment will not react rapidly to monetary, budgetary, or exchange policies. Only rates of growth will change, often with some time lag, as a result of properly designed policies or policy mixes.

The implication of this is that if there is unemployment or under-employment, stable and lasting long-run strategies must be adopted to cope with the problem, including abundant supply of long-run investment funds, not on abnormally easy terms (to guarantee proper factor proportions of projects), and possibly an active promotion of entry of new firms, to absorb the unemployed.

At the same time, the comparative short-run inertia of real product (the short-run vertical supply curve) has the great advantage of virtually eliminating the danger of short-run recessions of the type we have in Western economies. Only rates of growth—through the mechanism shown in the foregoing sections—are likely to vary if investment rates fluctuate widely.

Monetary policy in a pure labor-management economy should primarily be used to cope with price and inflation problems. These problems can be quite serious precisely because of the very low supply elasticity of national product. In situations where downward price rigidities prevail, as seems to be the case in Yugoslavia, such policies may have to be assisted by price controls. Income controls should be avoided at all cost, as they tend to destroy some of the very essence and advantage of self-management.[5]

Another key conclusion of our analysis is that devaluations—and even increased tariff barriers—are unlikely to help the balance of payment significantly. In fact, the exchange rate should be readjusted from time to time according to some more or less precise purchasing-power-parity formula, and should otherwise be viewed as a long-range variable, directly linked to the rate of growth and economic expansion.

---

5. The argument that without wage controls and with price controls investment would be adversely affected is utterly out of place; such conditions must be produced as to do away with the direct interdependence of labor incomes and investment on the level of individual firms.

Budgetary deficit spending is a useful tool for directing resources in the direction desired by the government, but is likely to be quite detrimental to the balance of payments and will be inflationary unless counteracted by monetary restriction.

For many reasons, some of which we may not yet be able to understand, there may be a marked asymmetry in real situations between price movements up and down, the latter being subject to considerable resistance. If such is the case, vigorous counterinflationary pressures may carry too high a cost in terms of rates of growth, and even employment, and it will then be preferable to accept some "reasonable" rate of inflation as the price for rapid development of the country. It will only then be imperative to recognize this fully and consistently as a fact of economic life and adjust various variables to that fact. In particular, all interest rates and other debt-service magnitudes must be reckoned in real (not nominal) terms, nonlabor incomes—especially pensions and retirement funds—must be put on a price-related escalator, and a similar escalator must be devised for the foreign-exchange rate.

Before concluding, let us try as far as we can to look at the reality of the Yugoslav economy in the light of our macroeconomic theory. Of course, such a confrontation of facts and theory must be taken, for the moment at least, as a crude first attempt leading to what we may call a set of plausible hypotheses rather than definitive results.

Perhaps the first thing to look at is our postulate of a low or zero short-run elasticity of supply. The behavior of Yugoslav prices and volumes of national (and also industrial) product do not contradict that hypothesis. There is no immediate short-run link between price variations and variations in volume (even though Professor Horvat has established a *negative* one for the period preceding 1967 [1, p. 232], but this may be more of a result of price controls than of purely economic forces). Rather it appears that prices vary in different ways with changing real output at different times, as a result of shifts in a vertical supply curve—conditioned by the level of investment determined in preceding periods (as our ρ in Figure 13.2)—and the current state of credit, monetary expansion, and demand for goods and services.

It would appear that a very important factor of cyclical variations in the rate of expansion of the national economy is a self-perpetuating shifting of the investment function—to the left and to the right in Figures 13.2 and 13.3—which accelerates or decelerates the rate of expansion of productive capacity and of national product some three to four years later. Such accelerations, in turn, with relatively more steady expansion of personal incomes, regenerate an investment boom which leads to an accelerated expansion in the next cycle, and so on.

The entire expansion-inflation pattern is considerably complicated and blurred by price controls of variable intensity which, when relaxed after a period of considerable money expansion (as around the year 1965), lead to delayed price expansions. A similar complicating effect can be imputed to currency devaluations. On the whole, in the intermediate and long run, however, a crude quantity theory certainly does hold, the rates of growth of prices and real output roughly adding up to the rate of expansion of the stock of money.

Both the problem of rate of growth instability and less than full employment, as suggested by our analysis, must be dealt with through a conscious and well-informed long-range effort: the first primarily through proper and effective capital pricing and facilitation of entry of new firms (or diversification of existing ones) and the second through a stabilization of the long-range expansion of investment. In the latter context not the only method, but probably the most natural one, would be to let firms pay an appropriate debt-service charge on *all* capital, and earmark such funds exclusively for accumulation. Besides the economic advantages of such an arrangement, one would also have the assurance that all "income of capital" goes for national enlarged reproduction, and not into anyone's pocket for consumption.

This method of funding the national investment effort would also make it possible to control prices (a highly desirable tool of control of monopolistic tendencies) without in any manner taking determination and distribution of labor incomes out of the hands of the work collectives.

We can now have a brief look at the foreign-trade sector. Contrary to our expectation, statistically there was no deterioration in Yugoslavia's terms of trade following the devaluation from 7.50 to 12.50 in the mid 1960's; rather the terms improved somewhat. But a closer examination of facts puts this result in doubt. First, an extremely important service export sector—tourism—is not included in the index, and there, very likely, the terms of trade deteriorated. Second, the dinar index of imports increased by only 26 per cent between 1963 and 1970. This would imply that dollar prices of Yugoslav imports declined by some 35 per cent, and even more if the period were expanded through the end of 1971. There would be a similar but somewhat milder decline in dollar export prices. While the latter is a real possibility following devaluation, the 35 per cent decline of a meaningfully constructed dollar price index of world exports to Yugoslavia is virtually an impossibility. And if the real decline was significantly less, then the terms of trade would have deteriorated.

Whether such a deterioration took place or not, the main conclusion of our paper is vindicated: At best, devaluation in Yugoslavia has a very short-run effect on the balance of payments; but all things considered, such a policy is not one leading to any good or bad lasting effects on the balance of payments.

This conclusion has a further significant implication. If the balanced payments effect of devaluation is small or nil, then the Yugoslav policy makers should become much more keenly conscious of possible terms-of-trade effects. Deteriorations in or a permanent low level of terms of trade may have a serious immiserization effect on the Yugoslav worker. As someone accustomed to think in terms of dollar values, living in Yugoslavia I have a distinct feeling of a strong undervaluation of the dinar, and if there is any continuity between internal and export prices, then the Yugoslaves are bartering their products and services too cheaply with the rest of the world. It may well be that the quest for "convertibility"—whatever that may be good for in a country which above all needs high employment and a high rate of growth—imposes too much of a burden on the working man of Yugoslavia.

Mathematical Appendix

Differentiating relations 13.1, 13.2, and 13.7 with respect to the three policy parameters (instruments) we obtain in matrix form

$$
\begin{bmatrix}
A_1 & -m_{11}{}^i & 0 \\
-M_p & -M_i & 0 \\
A_3 & -m_{21}{}^i & -1
\end{bmatrix}
\begin{bmatrix}
dp \\
di \\
dB
\end{bmatrix}
= dr
\begin{bmatrix}
A_1 \\
0 \\
A_3
\end{bmatrix},
d\bar{M}
\begin{bmatrix}
0 \\
-1 \\
0
\end{bmatrix},
dG
\begin{bmatrix}
a \\
0 \\
1-a
\end{bmatrix}
$$

where the coefficients of determinant D must be negative for dynamic stability (according to the Routhean conditions) and where A_1 and

A_3 respectively express the increase in demand for domestic goods (i.e., for Y) and the improvement or deterioration in the balance of payments resulting from a change in the terms of trade. The term A_1 normally can be expected to be positive, terms of trade being defined as r/p, and the term A_3 negative. Subscripts or superscripts of endogenous variables stand for partial differentiation. The nine key multipliers, obtained through Cramer's rule, and underlying Table 13.1, are

$$
\begin{array}{cccc}
 & dr & d\bar{M} & dG \\[2ex]
dp: & \dfrac{1}{D}A_1 M_i & \dfrac{1}{D}m_{11}{}^i & \dfrac{1}{D}M_i a \\[2ex]
di: & -\dfrac{1}{D}M_p A_1 & \dfrac{1}{D}A_1 & -\dfrac{1}{D}M_p a \\[2ex]
dB: & \dfrac{1}{D}(A_1 D_{13} + A_3 D_{33}) & \dfrac{1}{D}D_{23} & \dfrac{1}{D}(aD_{13} + (1-a)D_{33})
\end{array}
$$

where the terms D_{ij} stand for cofactors of the ij'th elements of the cooefficients matrix.

References

1. B. Horvat, *Business Cycles in Yugoslavia*, tr. Helen M. Kramer (White Plains, N.Y.: International Arts and Sciences Press, 1971).

2. J. Vanek, *The General Theory of Labor-Managed Market Economics* (Ithaca, N.Y.: Cornell University Press, 1970).

3. B. Ward, "The Firm in Illyria: Market Syndicalism," *American Economic Review*, 48 (Sept. 1958), 566–589.

4. _____, *The Socialist Economy* (New York: Random House, 1967).

14 | Labor-Managed Firms and Imperfect Competition*

**With ANDREW PIENKOS
and ALFRED STEINHERR**

In 1974, J. E. Meade [7] analyzed the behavior of the labor-managed (LM) firm under conditions of imperfect competition and reconfirmed the results previously obtained by Vanek [13] and Ward [14]. The three well-known conclusions emerging from such neoclassical analysis are that (1) an elasticity-preserving increase in demand will cause a decline in the output of the labor-managed firm, (2) the labor-managed firm will employ less labor with a given stock of capital and hence produce less, and (3) a reduction in financial charges on fixed financial debts of the firm tends to reduce the optimal level of employment in the firm.

Meade interprets these results as implying a misallocation of resources. According to Meade, only two types of policies could counter this—facilitating entry of new firms or reserving decisions about hiring and firing workers to some outside authority. Moreover, as long as increasing returns to scale persist in a given firm, state subsidies would become necessary to induce this firm to expand production up to the point where average earnings are equal to those in other firms. Meade, therefore, concludes: "Fully independent labor-managed co-operatives are thus appropriate only in those industries in which there is room for many small scale enterprises of an efficient scale and in which entry for new competing concerns is easy" [7, p. 824].

In Section I of this paper we show that Meade's conclusions are derived from a very restricted and partly incorrect review of the theory of labor-managed firms, and that his policy conclusions do

* Cornell Department of Economics Discussion Paper no. 97, July 1975. The authors express their gratitude to Erwin Blackstone, Cornell University, for his helpful comments on an earlier draft of this paper.

not necessarily follow from the theoretical analysis. In Section II we generalize Vanek's analysis [13, chap. 16] and develop a general equilibrium theory of optimal control of a labor-managed monopoly. Finally, in Section III we suggest some extensions of the restricted approach Meade has chosen by considering the consequences of the institutional form implied by labor-management for the behavior of firms, market structure, and performance of the economy. A general framework for analysis of labor-managed firms would be based on the following scheme:

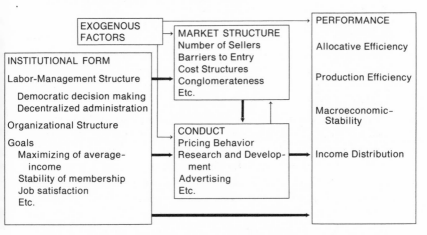

Meade deals only with the direct link between one aspect of institutional form—the goal of maximizing income per worker—and one aspect of performance—allocative efficiency.[1] The restricted nature of such a focus is immediately evident from the above scheme.

I. Critique of Meade

Meade characterizes imperfect markets by a downward-sloping demand curve for the product of the firm. Since no assumptions are made with respect to other firms' reactions, this describes the case of a monopolist. Although no references are made, LM monopolies are analyzed by Vanek [13, chap. 6, sections 2 and 3] and Ward

---

1. Note that Vanek [13] uses this simplified objective function only in parts I and II of his book, but devotes part III to the discussion of a more general and realistic objective function.

[14]. In addition, Vanek deals with oligopolistic market structures [13, chap. 6, sections 4, 5, and 6]. It may, therefore, be useful to complement Meade's survey with a brief description of the main results pertaining to oligopolistic market structure under labor-management.

Under various assumptions about oligopolistic competition, Vanek has shown that for a given number of firms any realized outcome tends to be more stable than in a capitalist economy. Since efficient size is attained at smaller levels of output, entry should be easier and market structure more competitive. The criticism that such firms will be producing at less than minimum cost under increasing returns to scale over the relevant range of production should not be put too strongly; the more firms there are, the more elastic will be the demand curve facing each one. Each will produce a greater output, possibly as great or greater than the output of a smaller number of capitalist firms which face more inelastic demand curves. Since the market structure under labor-management should result in more competitive pricing, it is no longer certain that imperfect competition under labor-management results in a more serious misallocation of resources than is the case with capitalist firms. At any rate, in view of the empirical work on price distortions by Harberger [4] and Schwartzman [12], the welfare loss from resource misallocation under monopolistic behavior appears not too significant (dead weight loss is less than .1 per cent of GNP). This is especially true when the loss is compared with the costs associated with unemployment, x-inefficiency, and the like. Nonetheless, to confront Meade's argument that restrictive output by labor-managed firms results in resource misallocation, let us assume that the welfare losses are significant enough to cause concern.

Several considerations work in favor of labor-management. More often than not, capitalist oligopolies are at the same time oligopsonies in factor markets; for labor-managed oligopolies the magnitude of resulting distortions is reduced owing to their smaller scale of operation. And as can easily be shown for a pure monopsony (selling at a constant price), labor will not be exploited (that is, will not receive less than its marginal product) as is the case in a capitalist oligopsony, especially in the absence of countervailing power. Furthermore, oligopolies do not arise only out of greater technological efficiency. With constant returns to scale and positive profits, firms are motivated to expand output until either profits are wiped out or the market structure is no longer competitive. By contrast, with the same assumption, the short-run equilibrium of the labor-managed firm is also its long-run equilibrium, and market structure is preserved.[2] Note that the labor-managed firm in equilibrium always produces at lowest average cost; this is true for the capitalist firm only if profits are zero.

The analytic part of Meade's paper is limited to the short run with fixed capital and variable labor inputs. On the other hand, when turning to policy considerations he is concerned with the case of increasing returns to scale. We will address this inconsistency and deal with both of these cases in turn.

A number of points can be made in reference to the short run. First, it is by no means certain that a positive subsidy will bring about the desired increase in output. As Vanek has shown [13, pp. 331–332], when capital is fixed a lump-sum tax and *not* a subsidy is required to increase output. Second, as shown by Vanek [13, p. 332], for the one variable factor case (demonstrated in the next section for the more general case of variable labor and capital inputs), there exists a policy combination achieving a Pareto-optimal solution. This optimal policy consists of combining price ceilings in order to expand the output of the monopolistic sector with a lump-sum tax to equalize marginal returns to factors in both the competitive and the monopolistic sectors. Finally, it should be noted that the suggested and, to be sure, unattractive policy of having employment fixed by an outside authority is clearly inappropriate, since it would imply a general equilibrium solution off the contract curve. Moreover, if returns to scale are increasing to such an extent that least-cost production would only be assured by a monopoly, then policy intervention is needed for both labor-managed and capitalist firms. Indeed, even the firm producing a larger output at a lower price faces two problems: consumers pay a price above marginal costs and the allocation of resources is suboptimal. Thus the difference in policy intervention required for the labor-managed as compared with the capitalist firm is one of degree only.

2. This is proved by Vanek [13, p. 32].

Given such policies as those mentioned above, one can view the entry of new firms more positively. Not only do labor-managed oligopolistic firms tend to be smaller and less aggressive in their market conduct, as mentioned earlier, but price ceilings would have the effect of increasing market stability even further. They imply that limit pricing, for example, would turn out to be relatively unprofitable owing to the impossibility of raising prices above the ceiling level once the potential newcomer was fended off. At any rate, labor-managed firms are less likely to be concerned about entry, and perhaps are less inclined to retaliate upon entry.

II. Optimal Control of a Labor-Managed Monopoly

We now consider explicitly the case of increasing returns to scale, involving at least two variable inputs. It can be shown that a lump-sum tax induces increased production by the labor-managed firm, the rationale being that in this way the fixed tax will be reduced per unit of output. Let the labor-managed firm maximize income per laborer, y, defined as:

$$y = \frac{V - rK - T}{L}, \tag{14.1}$$

where V = total revenue = $P \cdot Q$

$Q = Q(L, K)$;

$Q = K^{\alpha}L^{\beta}$ is a Cobb-Douglas production function; if $\alpha + \beta > 1$ then returns to scale are increasing;

L = labor input;

K = capital input;

$P = P(Q)$ is the demand function of the firm with $P'_Q < 0$;

r = rent on capital;

T = lump-sum tax.

To maximize y with respect to K and L the following first-order conditions need to be satisfied:

$$y_L = V_L - y = 0 \tag{14.2}$$

$$y_K = V_K - r = 0 \tag{14.3}$$

where subscripts indicate partial differentiation. To evaluate the impact of a change in T on the equilibrium level of L and K (denoted by L^*, K^*) one takes the total differentials of relations 14.2 and 14.3

to obtain:

$$\begin{bmatrix} a_{11} & a_{12} \\ a_{21} & a_{22} \end{bmatrix} \begin{pmatrix} dL^* \\ dK^* \end{pmatrix} = \begin{pmatrix} -\dfrac{1}{L} \\ 0 \end{pmatrix} dT, \qquad (14.4)$$

in which, as is easy to derive:

$$a_{11} = \beta(3\beta - 1)P'_Q K^{2\alpha}L^{2(\beta-1)} + \beta(\beta - 1)PK^{\alpha}L^{\beta-2} < 0, \qquad (14.5)$$

if $\frac{1}{3} < \beta < 1$;

$$a_{12} = a_{21} = \alpha\beta PK^{\alpha-1}L^{\beta-1}(3\varepsilon + 1) > 0 \qquad (14.6)$$

if $|\varepsilon| < \frac{1}{3}$, where $\varepsilon = P_Q \dfrac{Q}{P} < 0$;

$$a_{22} = \alpha(3\alpha - 1)P_Q K^{2(\alpha-1)}L^{\beta} + \alpha(\alpha - 1)PK^{\alpha-2}L^{\beta} < 0 \qquad (14.7)$$

if $\frac{1}{3} < \alpha < 1$.

The assumptions on α and β are easily satisfied, as is the one on ε. Should $|\varepsilon|$ be larger than $\frac{1}{3}$, then a_{12} and a_{21} are small relative to a_{11} and a_{22} and the sign of the determinant would remain unchanged. Given the signs of the a_{ij}'s the determinant Δ of the matrix $A = [a_{ij}]$ is positive. One then obtains:

$$\frac{dL^*}{dT} = \frac{-1/L \cdot a_{22}}{\Delta} > 0 \qquad (14.8)$$

$$\frac{dK^*}{dT} = \frac{1/L \cdot a_{21}}{\Delta} > 0. \qquad (14.9)$$

Thus, in response to a higher lump-sum tax the optimal amounts of both labor and capital inputs increase, and so must production.

It can also be easily shown that with decreasing costs a lower price ceiling always leads to increases in output. Consider Figure 14.1. If price ceiling P_a is effective then output will be at least Q_1 since if any lower output level is profitable at price P_a, then Q_1 must be more profitable with decreasing costs. The same being true for P_b and Q_2, our assertion is thus established. For each price ceiling and corresponding output level there exists an isoquant (see Figure 14.2). With the output level and price determined and capital cost

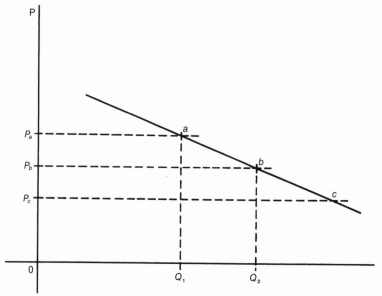

Figure 14.1

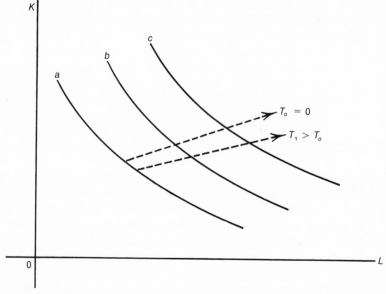

Figure 14.2

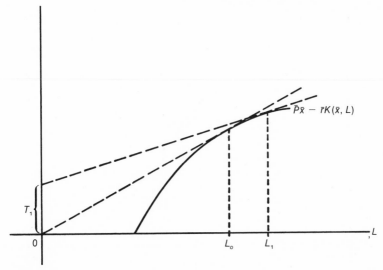

Figure 14.3

given exogenously, the only remaining magnitude to be determined is the capital-labor ratio. This is found by maximizing income per worker $y = [\bar{P}\bar{x} - \bar{r}K(\bar{x}, L) - T]/L$ (where a bar denotes a variable held constant). In Figure 14.3 maximum y is equal to the slope of the line tangent to curve $\bar{P}\bar{x} - \bar{r}K(\bar{x}, L)$ and intersecting the vertical axis at a height determined by the lump-sum tax. From the K/L ratio one can easily determine the marginal rate of factor substitution from the isoquants in Figure 14.2.

Note that an increase in the lump-sum tax from 0 to T_1 moves the tangency point to the right in Figure 14.3, indicating a substitution of labor for capital and hence a movement down the isoquant in Figure 14.2. We therefore have two expansion paths in Figure 14.2, generated by gradually declining price ceilings and two alternative lump-sum taxes, T_o and T_1, with $T_o < T_1$. We now have all the analytical elements necessary for a general equilibrium analysis of optimal control of a monopolistic market under labor-management. Assuming a simple bifurcation of the economy into a competitive and a monopolistic sector, we are faced with the transformation curve of Figure 14.4 and the Edgeworth-Bowley box of Figure 14.5. Suppose the initial equilibrium is indicated by points a

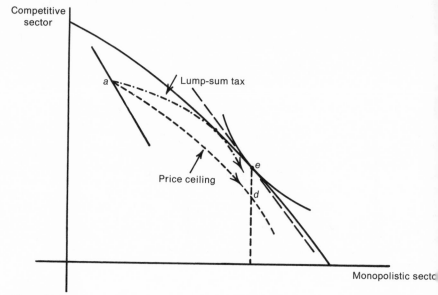

Figure 14.4

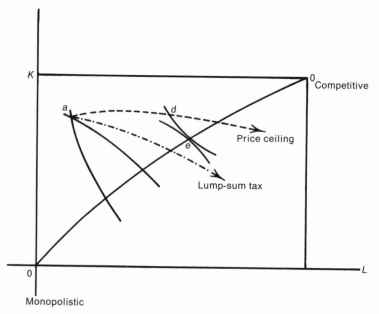

Figure 14.5

in both figures, corresponding to monopoly price P_a in Figure 14.1. Point a is off the contract curve since marginal value products are not equal in both sectors and income per worker is presumably much higher in the monopolistic sector. The corresponding production point is obviously inside the transformation curve.

Now suppose that either price ceilings or lump-sum taxes are imposed. From the previous analysis we know that output of the monopolistic sector must expand, drawing resources from the competitive sector. Supply will expand more, the lower the price ceiling or the higher the lump-sum tax. This is depicted in Figure 14.4 and 14.5 by the dashed (ceiling) and dashed-and-dotted (tax) lines.

Clearly, to achieve a Pareto-optimal solution one cannot rely on one policy instrument alone but rather a combination of both. One such combination would consist of letting the price ceiling be such as to push the monopolistic sector's production level to d, given by the tangency of the community welfare function and the transformation curve. Now impose a lump-sum tax moving point d down the isoquant in Figure 14.5 and up vertically in Figure 14.4. This means that labor will be transferred from the competitive sector to the monopolistic sector and vice versa for capital. Production in the monopolistic sector thus remains constant, while production in the competitive sector increases. At the final equilibrium e the marginal rates of transformation must be equal, and, since by virtue of the capital market r is the same for both sectors, the marginal value products of labor are also equalized. From this it follows that average incomes are equalized in both sectors.

Meade's claim that only external controls of labor employment could be used to deal with a labor-managed monopoly is clearly unwarranted. A more desirable, effective, and efficient policy exists. In terms of the Meade-Tinbergen instrument-target approach, this can be illustrated by looking at the box diagram of Figure 14.5 as a two-dimensional target space; to go from point a to point c two independent policy instruments are necessary. Meade's single tool of employment control cannot suffice.

III. Broader Considerations

It was argued in Section II that Meade analyzed only one characteristic of the labor-managed firm, relating it to only one performance criterion. Now some broader considerations are indicated.

Like others before him, Meade shows that the labor-managed firm reacts to an elasticity-preserving increase in demand by reducing its output. However, this result holds only when it is assumed that labor is the sole variable input and joint production is ruled out. But more important: Is it really meaningful to derive general conclusions from a model which assumes that labor-management changes only the simplified objective function to be maximized? Clearly, workers' management will affect the goals and the internal organization of the firm in still other, more significant ways, with repercussions on the structure of motivation, information, and the like. Two illustrations of the reservations one should have about Meade's results are offered.

First, the Marshallian short run probably misrepresents the short run under labor-management. Both Robinson [10] and Vanek [13, p. 287] as well as empirical evidence suggest that the employment level in self-managed firms is practically invariant in the short run and is certainly likely to vary a great deal less than in capitalist firms. Workers will be more reluctant to lay off their fellow workers than an entrepreneur would be, and any such decision would be taken collectively, so there is a risk of laying oneself off. Two important consequences are that the negatively-sloped supply curve disappears and that the business cycle will be more stable, with workers accepting a lower average income instead of laying off part of the work force. Thus, a further aspect of performance, macroeconomic stability, can be linked directly to institutional form, in addition to being indirectly fostered by the more competitive market structure likely labor-management.[3] Real output and employment cycles are therefore smoother under self-management than in a capitalist economy.[4]

Second, the Marshallian short run also implies a strict relationship between employment of labor and product supply. In fact, labor input can be varied not only by changing membership in a self-

3. Scherer [11] has empirically found investment to be most stable in competitive sectors. Note also a nice property of a negatively-sloped supply curve: in a demand recession employment in existing self-managed firms would increase.

4. Moreover, "if there is a lack of effective demand and unemployment in the capitalist world, the very forces which produce the situation also serve as a barrier to new entry and corresponding increases in employment. On the other hand, the forces which lead to unemployment in the labor-Managed world are also the forces which stimulate the entry of new firms and the employment in such firms" [13, p. 362].

managed firm, but also by changing the duration, quality, and intensity of effort of the existing membership. Since the institutional form under labor-management provides for a more flexible effort-leisure trade-off it is no longer clear whether short-run supply curves of labor-managed firms are less elastic than those of capitalist firms.

This point leads us to the matter of production efficiency. As Leibenstein [5] has shown, x-efficiency is likely to be more important than allocative efficiency. The institutional form under labor-management can be expected to result in less organizational slack, increased two-way information flows, and a lower cost of control and decision making.[5] Empirical research also indicates that participation provides increased worker satisfaction and individual motivation and also leads to higher qualitative as well as quantitative work performance [1], [2], [9].

As a result of these institutional and motivational changes the labor-managed firm requires fewer supervisory and coordinating functions. Hierarchical control will be partly replaced by motivation and peer group pressure. In hierarchical organizations management can collect intrafirm information and can carry out efficiency control only at increasing costs, whereas in a self-managed firm vertical and horizontal information flows are stimulated and control may be replaced by motivation. Hence the expanding self-managed firm experiences less cost increase due to such managerial diseconomies of scale. These considerations suggest, then, contrary to Meade's results, that the optimal scale of a labor-managed firm may in certain circumstances even exceed that of a comparable capitalist firm. Indeed, Boulding [3, p. 8] has argued: "There is a great deal of evidence that almost all organizational structures tend to produce false images in the decision maker, and that the larger and more authoritarian the organization, the better the chance that its top decision makers will be operating in purely imaginary worlds. This perhaps is the most fundamental reason for supposing that there are

---

5. "In principle every worker is a potential channel of communication, but when control is from the top down, there is little or no incentive to the worker to realize this potential. . . . Labor-managed firms would give the worker incentive to realize this potential . . . the resource in question is entrepreneurship, as conceived by Leibenstein . . . 'collective entrepreneurship' is a powerful means of conserving entrepreneurship, a resource which other systems waste" [6, p. 386].

ultimately diminishing returns to scale."[6]   Hence one should be skeptical of Meade's belief that labor-managed firms must be smaller than their capitalist counterparts.

Our discussion of the theory and the related policy issues of self-managed monopolies and oligopolies indicates that Meade's conclusion regarding the viability of such firms is ill-founded. The proper control policy can yield optimal or near-optimal solutions for imperfectly competitive labor-managed firms. Moreover, a broader and more relevant view of the issue is necessary to assess the efficiency of labor-managed firms.

References

1. C. J. Bellas, *Industrial Democracy and the Worker-Owned Firm* (New York: Praeger, 1972).

2. K. V. Berman, *Worker-Owned Plywood Companies* (Pullman, Wash.; Washington State University Press, 1967).

3. K. E. Boulding, "The Economics of Knowledge and the Knowledge of Economics," *American Economic Review*, 56 (May 1966).

4. A. C. Harberger, "Monopoly and Resource Allocation," *American Economic Review*, 44 (May 1954).

5. H. Leibenstein, "Allocative Efficiency vs x-Efficiency," *American Economic Review*, 56 (Sept. 1966).

6. R. A. McCain, "Critical Note on Illyrian Economics," *Kyklos*, 26 (1973).

7. J. E. Meade, "Labour-Managed Firms in Conditions of Imperfect Competition," *Economic Journal*, 84 (Dec. 1974).

8. *Proceedings of the First International Conference on Participation and Self-Management* (Zagreb, 1972).

9. *Proceedings of the First National Conference on Worker Self-Management* Jan. 12–13, 1974, M.I.T. Cambridge Mass.

10. J. Robinson, "The Soviet Collective Farm as a Producer Cooperative: Comment," *American Economic Review*, 57 (March 1967).

11. F. M. Scherer, "Market Structure and the Stability of Investment," *American Economic Review*, 59 (May 1969).

6. Emphasis added.

12. D. Schwartzman, "The Burden of Monopoly," *Journal of Political Economy*, 67 (Aug. 1959).

13. J. Vanek, *The General Theory of Labor-Managed Market Economies*, (Ithaca, N.Y.: Cornell University Press, 1970).

14. B. Ward, "The Firm in Illyria: Market Syndicalism," *American Economic Review*, 48 (Sept. 1958).

PART VI | **SELF-MANAGEMENT IN THE THEORY OF HISTORY**

15 | Toward a General Equilibrium Theory of Social Transformation and History*

In a recent study of mine, *The Participatory Economy* [2], I attempted to construct a broad theory of evolution of socioeconomic systems based on the notion that certain equilibrium conditions of such systems can be identified and that their movement through time—that is, their evolution—can be explained in terms of certain relationships between the actual (observable) state and the equilibrium state. During a colloquium a few years ago, discussion with some of my colleagues led me to conclude that the theory of evolution of systems could be made a good deal more correct, explicit, and descriptive of what actually happens in the real world. In what follows I summarize my thinking on such a possible generalization of the theory.

I. The Variables or Dimensions

The six variables, or dimensions, of my earlier analysis can be retained; they are (1) outer and (2) inner political self-determination, (3) outer and (4) inner economic self-determination, and (5) allocational and (6) distributional economic efficiency.[1] We may refer to each of these dimensions as variable Z_i, i running from 1 to 6. The Z variables are measured from some more or less arbitrary origin, on which I will elaborate presently, and only their absolute value is

* Cornell Department of Economics Discussion Paper no. 56, July 1973. I should like to thank Tom Bayard, Douglas F. Dowd, Peter Miovic, Chandler Morse, Dennis Mueller, and Alfred Steinherr, of the Cornell Department of Economics, for their invaluable help in the preparation of this paper.
1. By "outer" self-determination I mean the absence of external interference with the rights of a nation, enterprise, or other social group. "Inner" self-determination, by contrast, refers to the democratic exercise of decision making and other fundamental rights within the group in question.

significant. All the Z's thus can be thought of as nonnegative numbers.

Although in my *Participatory Economy* I distinguished between two levels or aspects of each of the six variables Z, namely the equilibrium level (which can be thought of as the origin of our scales) and the actual level of achievement (such as the actual degree of outer political self-determination), I feel now that it is necessary to think in terms of four significant levels of each variable. As before each variable can assume only positive values, measuring the absolute distance from the origin (i.e., from zero). The first level is denoted by Z_i and may be understood as some function of time. It is the *actual level* of achievement or fulfillment of the ith condition. The second magnitude, denoted by $\bar{Z}_i$, also a function of time, is to be understood as what we may call the *generally recognized* optimum level. Its magnitude is less than or at most equal to Z_i. By "generally recognized" I assume through a process of majority voting, or some other objective evaluation of consensus as determined by the researcher. The third variant, to be denoted $\tilde{Z}_i$, corresponds to what can best be described as the *known optimum*, that is, known by at least one man irrespective of the general consensus regarding that level or that situation. Again $\tilde{Z}_i$ can at most attain the level of $\bar{Z}_i$ in the case where the two are equal. Finally, the fourth characteristic level of the ith variable is the origin itself, denoted by Z_i^*. It really is not an operational concept because it can never be known with certainty; but philosophically it can be thought of as the absolute, or ideal, state for each particular dimension.

To illustrate the four characteristic levels with an example, let us say that $i = 2$, referring to inner political self-determination for the United States. Z_i then reflects the actual state, while $\bar{Z}_i$ represents the general consensus that simple majority voting is the best possible instrument of political self-determination. In this case Z_2 and $\bar{Z}_2$ are equal (or more or less equal) because the general consensus actually corresponds to the real practice. On the other hand, the level $\tilde{Z}_2$ can be thought of as some system of optimal point—voting or consensus formation through dialogue just developed (or discovered). Finally, Z_2^* is some ideal state of perfect inner political self-determination, never to be known. It is entirely nonoperational and can be taken simply as an abstract philosophical concept, or it may be neglected, or rejected entirely.

II. The Operational Links

Of greater importance than the absolute ideal level of Z_i is what we will refer to as the "operational link" between the four variables. The link between Z_i^* and $\tilde{Z}_i$ is invention or discovery, that is, transposition of social or technological forms from the realm of the unknown into the realm of the known. The transition from $\tilde{Z}_i$ is performed through the operational link of learning and/or education. Finally, the operational link from $\bar{Z}_i$ to Z_i is through implementation.

With four rather than two significant levels of variables, the concept of equilibrium becomes more complicated, and in fact a large number of "partial" equilibria can be conceptualized.[2] It is possible to think of at least three types of equilibria (or quasi equilibria, or simply states, depending on one's point of view). The first can be referred to as the real, the second as the potential, and the third as the absolute state of equilibrium of social transformation. The first is characterized by the equality of Z_i and $\tilde{Z}_i$ for all i's. It of course also implies the equality of each magnitude with $\bar{Z}_i$. The simple common sense of the real state of equilibrium is that when all the required equalities are fulfilled, given what is known to men, there will be no further forces for change in the social situation (i.e., all the operational links will be exhausted or at zero level).

The potential equilibrium, on the other hand, implies equality for all i of $\tilde{Z}$ and $\bar{Z}$ alone and implies that the general consensus process has been accomplished in all dimensions through learning and education, and implementation is the only thing that separates the situation from a real equilibrium. Finally, we can think of an absolute equilibrium where the actual state coincides with the absolute ideal Z^* for all six variables. Again it is only an abstract philosophical concept, but it is of the utmost importance for reasons which will become apparent.

III. Dynamics and Transformation Theory

Of greater importance than the equilibrium states is the dynamics of the system and the corresponding disequilibrium motion—i.e., the

---

2. We retain here the simple term equilibrium, but we should keep in mind that really these partial equilibrium states belong to an overall state of general disequilibrium.

theory of social transformation itself. This theory could be formulated in several different ways, any one of which would not be clearly superior to the others. Thus what follows in this section ought to be taken only as a suggestion, open to improvement, clarification, and generalization. In later sections some more general and I hope, realistic dynamic hypotheses will be examined.

My basic proposition is that the three observable levels of Z_i—Z, $\bar{Z}$, and $\tilde{Z}$—change in time at rates (to be denoted by $\dot{Z}$) depending on the divergences between the variables and their respective next qualitatively superior states, with factors of proportionality which can be thought of as the speed of adjustment. Thus, for example, the rate of change of the actual state of inner economic self-determination, $\dot{Z}_4$, is equal to the product of a coefficient A_4 times $(Z_4 - \bar{Z}_4)$. The expression in parentheses measures the deviation between the actual state and the accepted or recognized optimum and can also, in terminology proposed by Chandler Morse, be thought of as a measure of the "strain" of this part of the situation. The term A, on the other hand, is the speed of adjustment at which Z_4 reacts to the deviation or the strain just identified. In its most general form, A can be thought of as a function of the deviations of all six variables in their levels Z and $\bar{Z}$ from their level $\tilde{Z}$. The deviations from Z^*, which are unknown, of course, cannot have any dynamic impact for the very reason that they are unknown.[3] In many instances not all the possible deviations will appear as arguments of the function A.

In a similar manner rates of change of variables $\bar{Z}_4$ and $\tilde{Z}_4$ will depend on their deviation from $\tilde{Z}_4$ and Z_4^*, respectively, and on the speeds of adjustment B_4 and C_4; and similarly for the other five variables. Of course, the explanation of the rate of change in the known optimum, $\tilde{Z}_4$, depends in part on an unknown magnitude Z^* and thus again can be thought of as a philosophical rather than an operational law of behavior. This dynamic force, for all six variables, will always constitute an element of uncertainty and unpredictability in the social universe studied. The speeds of adjustment, A, B, and C, now can be understood as directly associated with what we have earlier referred to as the operational links, that is with (1) implementation, (2) learning and education, and (3) invention,

---

3. For example, in 1800 atomic technology, then unknown, could not have influenced the movement away from economic self-determination.

respectively. The coefficients A, B, C will often be negative, but they need not be so, and can assume positive or negative correlations with their arguments.

Again, an example should be used to further clarify the dynamics of the system of social transformation. Consider the variable Z_4, that is, economic self-determination (or labor management, or industrial democracy), and consider it in the context of Soviet Russia. Obviously it is a known state from both the Yugoslav experience and theoretical work, including Marxist prognostics, but it is not applied at all in Soviet Russia. In other words, the difference between Z_4 and $\tilde{Z}_4$ is quite considerable. On the other hand, the difference between Z_4 and $\bar{Z}_4$ is very small because in Russia the general consensus is that the state of a complete absence of economic self-determination is a desirable one. In consequence the change in Z_4, that is $\dot{Z}_4$, is negligible. Again, there is a considerable difference between $\bar{Z}_4$ and $\tilde{Z}_4$, which implies a considerable strain and hence a considerable force of adjustment. Of course the speed of adjustment itself, B_4, is very small. Functionally, B_4 (or its small value) is a result of the high degree of nonfulfillment of inner political self-determination: a result of the fact that the oligarchy or the ruling central committee of the party is afraid to institute labor-management because of potential loss of political power. In fact, we find these arguments quite explicitly used by Stalin and Lenin in 1919 and 1920. The leaders of the party today are trying to slow down or completely arrest the learning process, and even if the learning process were to succeed, they would still have tools to slow down the process of implementation after the general consensus had been attained. In other words, A_4 itself is strongly dependent on the absence of political self-determination in Soviet Russia, i.e., on a large value of Z_2 minus $\tilde{Z}_2$.[4] At the same time, with an inverse sign, B_4 also depends on the degree of nonfulfillment of the condition of economic efficiency, that is, the difference between Z_5 and $\tilde{Z}_5$. This difference is important but not significant enough to change the rulers' attitude toward economic self-determination . However, with time and the increasing inefficiency of resource allocation because

---

4. In addition to a lack of political democracy, the lack of freedom of expression and communication—also determining the state of political self-determination—diminishes both speeds A_i and B_i, for all i.

of centralization and the disappearance of extensive economic resources and growth, the strain in variable Z_5 may be expected to become so important as to increase both B_4 and A_4 significantly. Moreover, if we interpret the Cold War and the threat of intervention as a possible expression of the absence of outer political self-determination, then even in the case of Soviet Russia we may say both speeds of adjustment A_4 and B_4 are affected by the nonzero value of Z_1 minus $\tilde{Z}_1$. If this value declines with the cessation of the Vietnam war, in turn, A_4 and B_4 may be expected to increase.

Let me also observe that the forces of action and reaction, or the conflict between the ruling group and the underdog, in part reflected by the strains in some of the six dimensions, can also be subsumed under the speeds of adjustment A and B, and even the speed of adjustment corresponding to inventive activity, C.

The formal aspects of our theory of evolution of systems are summarized in Table 15.1. The four rows of the table correspond to the alternative four states of the six variables or dimensions (for that matter, the table is perfectly general and could refer to an

Table 15.1.

Variable dimension condition (1)	Variable definition (2)	Operational link (3)	Equilibrium			Dynamics (7)
			Real (4)	Potential (5)	Absolute (6)	
$Z_i(t)$ $(\geqq \tilde{Z}_i)$	Actual state	↑ Implementation	$Z_i = \tilde{Z}_i$ $[= \bar{Z}_i]$	$\bar{Z}_i = \tilde{Z}_i$	$Z_i = Z_i^*$	$\dot{Z}_i = A_i(Z_i - \tilde{Z}_i)$ with $A_i = A_i(Z_1, \ldots, Z_6; \bar{Z}_1, \ldots, \bar{Z}_6; \tilde{Z}_1, \ldots, \tilde{Z}_6)$
$\tilde{Z}_i(t)$ $(\geqq \bar{Z}_i)$	Generally recognized optimum	↑ Learning and education		FOR ALL i's		$\dot{\tilde{Z}}_i = B_i(\bar{Z}_i - \tilde{Z}_i)$ with $B_i = B_i(Z_1, \ldots, Z_6; \bar{Z}_1, \ldots, \bar{Z}_6; \tilde{Z}_1, \ldots, \tilde{Z}_6)$
$\bar{Z}_i(t)$ $(\geqq Z^*)$	Known optimum	↑ Invention				$\dot{\bar{Z}}_i = C_i(\bar{Z}_i - Z_i^*)$ with $C_i = C_i(Z_1, \ldots, Z_6; \bar{Z}_1, \ldots, \bar{Z}_6; \tilde{Z}_1, \ldots, \tilde{Z}_6)$
Z_i^*	Absolute ideal (unknown)					$\dot{Z}^* = 0$

arbitrary number of dimensions). The columns are largely self-explanatory. Column 1 identifies the variable or dimension, column 2 describes the state of the variable, and column 3 identifies what we have referred to in the text as the operational link. Columns 4 through 6 identify the various equilibrium or disequilibrium conditions. Finally, in column 7, the dynamic laws of motion, as developed in the text, are summarized.[5]

IV. Some Reflections on the Marxist Theory of History

Of course, any of our six dimensions could be further subdivided into other more subtle variables, just as a more aggregate index can be subdivided into less aggregate ones. At least one subdivision appears to me to be of considerable interest: our dimension 5, which we have called the allocational efficiency. By it we understand the efficiency of allocation of all productive resources in satisfying all economic needs of individuals and society. Logically this efficiency of resource allocation can be associated with two broad categories of phenomena. One can be referred to as technological efficiency, concerning how well resources are utilized in the technological process of production. The other we may refer to as structural efficiency, having to do with how productive resources, and for that matter goods produced, are allocated among alternative uses. It may be interesting here to point out that it is the technological dimension that plays a primordial role in the Marxian theory of sociopolitical evolution. On the other hand, Marx hardly mentions structural efficiency of allocation of productive resources, and this

5. It should be noted that there are some similarities between the basic dynamic forces in this model of social change and Hegelian dialectics. However, our explanation of history is both more specific and more general. Differences between $\bar{Z}_i$ and Z_i, $\tilde{Z}_i$ and $\bar{Z}_i$, and finally Z_i^* and $\tilde{Z}_i$ keep the system in motion. Since $\bar{Z}_i$ stands for the socially agreed upon desirable state for variable i, and $\tilde{Z}_i$ for the optimum value of variable i known to human intellect, it is the intellectual activity of man which keeps $\tilde{Z}_i - Z_i$ apart and provides, on that level, the necessary stress-inducing changes in Z_i. Intellectual discovery continuously moves $\tilde{Z}_i$ toward Z_i^*, which could be thought of as Platonic "forms." The interpretation is, however, more general than Hegel's insofar as: (1) $\bar{Z}_i$ is determined through personal and social interactions; (2) Z_i is, in part at least, determined by the material infrastructure; and (3) social change interacts on three different levels, i.e., the Z_i's, $\bar{Z}_i$'s, and $\tilde{Z}_i$'s, and through six dimensions, $i = 1, \ldots, 6$. Our theory is also more specific, and therefore more operational, than Hegel's insofar as it spells out precisely the main determinants of social change and the causes of acceleration and retardation of history.

area has constituted a significant point of contention between Marxist and non-Marxist economists and social scientists.

It may be convenient to think of the structural aspects of the allocational dimension as allocational efficiency narrowly defined, that is, our variable Z_5, and create a new dimension and variable, Z_7, for the strictly technological variable. All the earlier discussion for the first six variables now pertains to the new variable. Thus there is an absolute and unknown state Z_7^* which is being continuously approached by inventive activity, which in turn determines the $\tilde{Z}_7$. And in turn the accepted and implemented states of the variable are reached from $\tilde{Z}_7$ through educational and implementation operational links, respectively.

It may again be interesting to note that Marx's fundamental theory of technological and material conditions influencing the other variables or dimensions now becomes a partial aspect of our broader theory. Specifically, Z_7, or its deviation from Z_7^*, is a factor of the adjustment in all or most of the other dimensions. However, our theory as stated is weaker than Marx's in the important respect that the technological dimension affects only the speeds of adjustment A, B, and C of the other variables and does not directly determine their absolute levels. And in my personal opinion this makes a good deal of sense: Man will always strive for liberation from economic domination and from political domination and from distributional injustice (those are our dimensions 1 through 4 and 6), whatever the conditions of technology, but our variable Z_7 can significantly affect the speed of adjustment of Z_4, that is, inner (in the firm) economic self-determination, as a result of the technological developments underlying the industrial revolution. By contrast, the automation phase of technological progress experienced most recently very definitely increases the speeds of adjustment of Z_4 and perhaps also of Z_2.

In turn, several of the variables 1 through 6 have a definite impact on the speeds of adjustment of Z. As an example, the newly created dimension Z, allocational efficiency narrowly defined and referring solely to the structural aspect, has a definite impact on all or at least some of the three speeds of adjustment of the seventh dimension. With a high degree of centralization of the Soviet system and corresponding unsatisfactory level of Z_5 (under the new definition, allocational efficiency), $\tilde{Z}_7$ is likely to move very slowly. In turn, on the international level the learning process and thus $\bar{Z}$ and corresponding implementation can progress very fast, that is, A_7 and B_7 can be quite high in absolute value, through exchange of information and imitation.

V. An Alternative Dynamic Hypothesis Involving Cooperative Forces

The dynamic hypotheses proposed in Section III may be too serious an oversimplification of the phenomena which they are intended to describe. In the real world, normally, systems and sociopolitical states are propelled by forces of the type described earlier, but often they are opposed by conservative or reactionary forces attempting to preserve the status quo. At times even these status-quo-oriented forces can be strong enough to prevail over the forces of progress toward equilibrium.

To introduce these conservative forces into our analysis in a more formal manner, let us first postulate the following. While the positive or direct forces described in Section III are absolute in the sense that they emanate from certain distances (or strains) from an ideal equilibrium state (even if unknown) at a given point in time, the forces of reaction or the conservative forces depend in some broad sense, to be explored presently, on what we may term social memory; that is, on states of some or all of our variables experienced in some preceding period.

For example, a society for which a given $\bar{Z}$, that is, the generally accepted state, remains unchanged over a long period of time is unlikely to experience any strong reactionary forces for that dimension. On the other hand, if the variable $\bar{Z}$ is rapidly changing from generation to generation, it is very likely that the society will experience for that dimension a considerable force resisting implementation, that is, adjustment in the actual states within that dimension.

More formally, the conservative forces will depend in some way on the rate of change or the first time-difference of our variables. In equation form we can write, using our preceding notations:

$$\dot{Z}_i = (dZ_i/dt) = A_i(Z_i - \bar{Z}_i) + A_i'(Z_i - Z_i^{-1}) \tag{15.1}$$
$$(i = 1, \ldots, 7),$$

where A_i is the direct speed of adjustment function of the various strains, and A'_i is the force of reaction reflecting what we may call the memory of the system. Both A_i and A'_i are functions of all the possible strains. While this hypothesis and formulation may appear more complex than that of Section III it results in a significant simplification of the earlier version. We can now postulate that A_i is always negative while A'_i is always positive. (We recall, of course, that the origin of the system is at zero and progress means movement of positive values toward that origin, that is, movement at a negative rate.)

We have stated our equation reflecting the new hypothesis only for the actual state of the variable Z. But it would be perfectly reasonable—even if perhaps less necessary—to postulate analogous equations for the other observable states $\bar{Z}$ and $\tilde{Z}$. Especially with respect to $\bar{Z}$ a reactionary force can be easily thought of. For example, many totalitarian states, and even states which call themselves democratic, will often use propaganda and other devices such as distorted education to forestall adoption of a given social state superior to the status quo. But we should return to the actual state Z where the reactionary forces are most relevant. Indeed, it is the resistance to the change in things as they are, rather than to changes in *Weltanschauung*, that is most violent in a period of rapid sociopolitical change.

In relation 15.1 we have used in the second term of the right-hand side a simple first-time difference between the current state and the state in the previous period. As a unit of measurement of time here we may conveniently think of something like a generation, perhaps twenty-five years or so. The time difference is that of the actual variable Z rather than of the accepted state $\bar{Z}$, and this calls for some explanation. It is implicit in this formulation (as contrasted with the formulation where the first-time difference was in the accepted state $\bar{Z}$) that the forces of resistance must emanate from something that has been experienced over a period of time rather than from a state of mind which might not have been experienced in actual practice. This implies, and to a degree conforms with, a Parsonian theory of development and adaptation of values to what is actually experienced over time by society [1]. For example, in the United States, capitalism and the implied state of capital domination after several generations has been adopted by the majority as a positive value. And it is the realization of experience of this value that provides, in a figurative sense, the fuel for an extremely powerful force of reaction to a movement toward a more democratic organization in the place of work.

Beyond saying that A' must be positive and that it is a function of the various possible strains, that is, differences between the various levels of the variable Z, we cannot, at least at this stage, make any further specifications. That the strains are actually determining factors of that coefficient A' must be obvious. For example, the state of income and world distribution expressed in our system by the variable Z_6 will strongly influence how powerful the forces of reaction to change actually will be. Indeed, for a minority opposed to progress, money has always been the best substitute for votes. But perhaps even a more significant argument than Z_6 is Z_1, the state of outer political self-determination. With a considerable state of disequilibrium in that dimension—as that which arose after August 1968 in Czechoslovakia—the size of A' can turn the whole right-hand side of equation 15.1 from negative to positive and frustrate the entire process of equilibrium adjustment.

Postscript

The logical next step in our analysis would be to start studying the specific forms of the functions A, B, C, and A'. For example, certain nonlinearities, critical masses, and explosive (revolutionary) adaptations can be expected. I covered some of this ground in a rudimentary form in the later chapters of my *Participatory Economy*. Any further steps must wait for a more formal and careful empirical investigation.

References

1. T. Parsons, *The Social System* (Glencoe, Ill.: Free Press, 1951).

2. J. Vanek, *The Participatory Economy: An Evolutionary Hypothesis and a Strategy for Development* (Ithaca, N.Y.: Cornell University Press, 1971).

Index

Library of Congress Cataloging in Publication Data
(For library cataloging purposes only)

Vanek, Jaroslav.
   The labor-managed economy.

   Includes bibliographies and index.
   1. Employees' representation in management—Addresses, essays, lectures. 2. Employees' representation in management—Yugoslavia—Addresses, essays, lectures. 3. Industrial management—Addresses, essays, lectures. I. Title.
HD5650.V3315   658.31′52′09497   76-16682
ISBN 0-8014-0955-1

DATE DUE

NOV 20 79			
NOV 8			
DEC 1			